THE WINDOW
AND THE GARDEN:

THE MODERNIST FICTIONS
OF RAMÓN PÉREZ DE AYALA

John Macklin

THE WINDOW
AND THE GARDEN:

THE MODERNIST FICTIONS
OF RAMÓN PÉREZ DE AYALA

Society of Spanish and Spanish-American Studies

The Society of Spanish and Spanish-American Studies promotes bibliographical, critical and pedagogical research in Spanish and Spanish-American studies by publishing works of particular merit in these areas. On occasion, the Society also publishes creative works. SSSAS is a non-profit educational organization sponsored by the University of Colorado, Boulder. It is located in the Department of Spanish and Portuguese, University of Colorado, Campus Box 278, Boulder, Colorado 80309-0278, U.S.A.

International Standard Book Number (ISBN): 0-89295-053-6

Library of Congress Catalog Card Number: 87-62378

Printed in the United States of America

Impreso en los Estados Unidos de América

This text was prepared on the Xerox Star word processing system by Sandy Adler, Foreign Language Word Processing Specialist for the College of Arts and Sciences, University of Colorado, Boulder.

For

HANNAH

CONTENTS

PREFACE

The impetus behind the present monograph is a series of questions which have arisen in my mind about the nature of narrative fiction through working on the modern Spanish novel in general and on the work of Ramón Pérez de Ayala in particular. These questions relate essentially to the vexed question of the relationship between "real" experience and the fictive text which seemed to be implied within the very substance of the novels being dealt with and yet which never appeared to be a cause of concern to critics working exclusively in the field of Hispanic literature. Looking back over my various writings on Spanish fiction, it is clear to me that I have touched on many of the issues raised in this book — the nature of realist writing, the relationship of art to life, our need for imaginative and fictive constructs, and so on — but without the benefit of that wider frame of reference and theoretical and methodological support provided by the work of, among others, David Lodge, Malcolm Bradbury, Jonathan Culler, Gabriel Josipovici, Linda Hutcheon, Frank Kermode, all of whom helped to elucidate problems which the fiction of Ramón Pérez de Ayala in particular seemed to pose. Moreover, my own misgivings about the version of Spanish literary history that had been bequeathed by earlier critics in the quaint and rather awkward notion of the Generation of 1898, and about the methodological fallacies it seemed to entail, were given a more positive and illuminating orientation by the discovery of the advances made in other areas by continental and Anglo-American critics. Above all, critical work on the concept of Modernism seemed to provide a more satisfying foundation for an understanding of Pérez de Ayala's fiction. A study of that fiction in the light of Modernist aesthetics not only provides the perspective from which Pérez de Ayala's full significance and originality can be appreciated, but also begins to undermine the Hispanic critical orthodoxy of the Generation of 1898 and demonstrate that there was a Modernist novel in Spain showing marked affinities with the fiction being written elsewhere in Europe at the beginning of the twentieth century.

The essence of that novel is what I have tried to capture in the title of this book, inspired by that section of José Ortega y Gasset's *La deshumanización del arte* (1925) which considers two kinds of approach to artistic reality in terms of looking at a garden through the pane of a window. One can see either the garden or the window, but not both. The art which sees only the garden is, arguably, Realism; that which sees the colours of the garden reflected back onto the window is Modernism. Another image which well describes this difference is to be found in H.G. Wells' *Experiment in Autobiography* (1934) where he considers how the assumptions of the nineteenth-century novel no longer seem appropriate for the twentieth century:

"Its standards were established within that apparently permanent frame, and the criticism of it began to be irritated and perplexed when, through a new instability, the splintering frame began to get into the picture." This image of the splintering frame, more graphic than Ortega's, applies to the great wave of Modernist experiment which altered the relations between novel and world, which held the frame to be part of the picture too.

Some parts of this book draw upon material used in some of my previous writings on Pérez de Ayala. In particular, it develops out of the approach suggested in "Pérez de Ayala y la novela modernista europea," (*Cuadernos Hispanoamericanos* 367-368 [(1981)]: 21-36 [reproduced in *La novela lírica* II, ed. Darío Villanueva (Madrid: Taurus, 1983)], but I am indebted also to the *Bulletin of Hispanic Studies, Hispanic Review, Insula, Neophilologus, Anales de la literatura española contemporánea* for permission to use material originally published in these journals, and to the Editors of the Critical Guides to Spanish Texts series, Professors John Varey and Alan Deyermond, as well as to Mr. Frank Cutler, for allowing me to incorporate into the present book, particularly in Chapter IV, parts of my study on *Tigre Juan* and *El curandero de su honra*. Finally, my greatest debt of gratitude is due to Karen Tipper, secretary of the Department of Hispanic Studies in the University of Hull, for her patience, helpfulness and constant encouragement, as well as for the great skill with which she transformed pages of nearly indecipherable handwriting into an impeccable typescript.

J.J.M
University of Hull, May 1986

INTRODUCTION

The prolific and highly persuasive Hispanic critic Donald L. Shaw ended his important book, *The Generation of 1898 in Spain*, with the words, ". . . the Generation of 1898 has been unjustifiably neglected by critics and historians of European literature as a whole. But the appearance of these writers as a united group when elsewhere only isolated figures were beginning to formulate a view of the human condition similar to theirs underlines emphatically that, however, underdeveloped Spain was in other ways at the turn of the century, she was in the forefront of modern cultural development."[1] Whether or not this neglect is justified, there is little doubt that it exists. A year after the publication of Shaw's book, a significant volume entitled *Modernism 1890-1930* and edited by Malcolm Bradbury and James MacFarlane, appeared in the Pelican Guides to European Literature series.[2] Spain is barely mentioned in the text and is virtually limited to brief biographies of Juan Ramón Jiménez, Federico García Lorca (whose name is sprinkled here and there in the text) and Miguel de Unamuno, and a reference to Echegaray's sharing of the Nobel Prize in 1904! Clearly this situation is due in part to a generalised ignorance of Spanish literature compounded by the absence of good translations (a disadvantage not suffered by Cervantes or the writers of the Latin-American "boom"), but if the writers mentioned are as significant as Shaw claims, then their lack of prominence might well be due to the way in which their significance is perceived by the Hispanic critics who champion them. Whatever the ideological attractions of the Spanishness of the myth of a Generation of 1898 in Franco's Spain, the literary significance of the writing of the period can only be diminished by linking it firmly to the historical circumstances of the land in which it was conceived. On one level, of course, the philosophical import of these writers — the emphasis on alienation, anguish and nihilism — does identify them unmistakably with the later wave of existentialist writing in France and elsewhere after the war. But this is only one version of the evolution of modern fiction and not by any means the most suggestive one in the light of more recent developments in both literature and criticism. What makes of Modernism a literature both of challenge and of crisis is its preoccupation with the processes of the imagination itself, with the medium in which fiction (which is what we are concerned with) is constructed, and with the role of art not in reflecting a metaphysical crisis but in shaping reality itself. That dominant strand of Modernism is present in the work of all the writers in early twentieth-century Spain and without reference to it the novels of Pérez de Ayala in particular could not be accorded their rightful place in the history of man's imaginative response to the world which he both inhabits and creates for himself.

When we look at the critical evaluations of the prose fiction of Ramón Pérez de Ayala, we are confronted with an almost universal sense of unease. Even his most fervent admirers feel obliged to apologise in some measure for the apparent peculiarity of his work and proclaim that appreciation of him is some special kind of acquired taste. Andrés Amorós places him "al margen de la gran tradición española," and states that "Pérez de Ayala no podrá nunca ser un escritor popular ... exige un lector inteligente."[3] Although he never develops his ideas, however, Amorós does place Ayala alongside other experimental practitioners of the novel (Joyce, Proust, Kafka, Musil, Robbe-Grillet, Cortázar) and sees in him a kind of precursor of Luis Martín-Santos. It is true that Pérez de Ayala's fiction makes more sense when viewed retrospectively from the fiction of our time than when considered in the light of the novelists who preceded him. The judgement of Rafael Cansinos-Assens is typical: "Para llamar novelista a Pérez de Ayala es menester modificar un poco el apelativo que con tan plena medida se les aplica a un Galdós, un Blasco Ibáñez o un Baroja."[4] Quite apart from the fact that the critic persists in seeing Baroja as a late Realist, it is clear that his view of the novel is permeated by an allegiance to a particular kind of Realist fiction. However, Cansinos-Assens' evaluation has the merit of pointing up the radicality of Pérez de Ayala's work which, although sensed by contemporary critics, was dismissed through not being understood. Indeed, critics writing at a much later date have been similarly unappreciative, criticizing Ayala for his intellectualism and his novels for their lack of realism. Emiliano Díez-Echarri and José María Roca Franquesa, in a history of Spanish literature published just two years before Ayala's death, complained that:

> La sólida formación humanística, que en otros géneros, el ensayo y el periodismo, contribuyen a realzar las calidades de escritor, perjudican su novela. Pérez de Ayala cae inevitablemente en el error de hacer hablar a sus personajes, a muchos de sus personajes, en un estilo que no les corresponde .. Ayala se coloca muchas veces fuera de lo real .. Sus relatos llevan demasiado lastre intelectualista para que se las pueda considerar auténticas novelas.[5]

Criticism has of course come a long way since then, not least in its acceptance of the problematic nature of a concept such as reality. At the same time, while Realism and reality are quite distinct in one sense, in another they are indissolubly linked. Realism in the novel is wedded to a particular form of social seeing, and the language of Realism effaces itself apparently behind that reality which it purports to represent. The most radical alteration in our view of fiction has been in our awareness of the fallacy — or perhaps more accurately the circularity — of such a position. An eloquent expression of this change is the description given by Stephen Heath:

> If the term "realistic" is examined and the question formulated as to what is "realistic," it will be seen that the answer cannot lie in any absolute conception of "Reality" (of "the Reality"), but, on the contrary, in the recognition of the representation of reality, which a particular society proposes and assumes as "Reality." "Reality," that is, needs to be understood not as an absolute and immutable given but as a production within which representation will depend on (and, dialectically, contribute to) what the French Marxist theoretician Louis Althusser has described as "practical ideology," a complex formation of montages of notions, representations, images and modes of action, gestures, attitudes, the whole ensemble functioning as practical norms which govern the concrete stance of men in relation to the objects and problems of their social and individualistic existence, in short the lived relation of men to their world.[6]

If this is so, then a writer like Pérez de Ayala who deviates from the norms of nineteenth-century (or any other kind of) Realism is engaged in a radical probing of what it means to create fictions that lie alongside or help to make sense of reality. The abandoning of a facile commitment to verisimilitude represents a step forward in an understanding of the nature of fiction. Such radicality resides not in content but in form, a stripping away of the illusions nurtured by traditional Realism. The main illusion of Realism was founded on creating a perfect equivalence between conventional views of reality and conventional assumptions about the processes of narrative literature. David Lodge provides a minimalist definition of realism in literature: "the representation of experience in a manner which approximates closely to descriptions of similar experiences in non-literary texts of the same culture."[7] Realist writing has therefore been modelled on various kinds of historical writing, writing which locates individual experience in the wider context of a complex reality only partly apprehended. But the manner of the writing — objective, past tense, causally connected — confirms a belief in the existence of that greater and potentially knowable reality. Moreover, the reality that mattered — and this surely confirms Heath's point — was above all social: moral questions were explored in terms of the relationship between personal and collective values, and these were considered to be of significance to both the writer and the reader. The perfect match of book and world was complemented by an identity of concern between author and audience. The breakdown of this comfortable situation coincides with the Modernist revolution. In a crude way, Rufino Blanco Fombona reacts to this changed situation by protesting against Pérez de Ayala's lack of realism in characterisation.

Of his characters "aun los más humildes," he writes, "suelen dis-
currir como doctores de Salamanca,"[8] clearly uneasy about Ayala's
radical departure from the conventional expectation that characters
should be fully delineated individuals, plausible models of the kind of
people one might meet in the real world. Here again, Pérez de
Ayala's novels are evaluated by reference to the implied norm of
traditional Realism. Whatever the simplicity of such a response, it is
not entirely surprising, for Ayala's radicality is in a sense covert. His
experimentalism is contained within a mimetic framework, and critics
have frequently mistaken the framework for the substance, considering deviations from verisimilitude to be artistic errors. In fact, what we
find is a process of significant foregrounding — the deviant elements
of the text are signalled by being set against a background of familiar
or "automatised" elements, in this case, the conventions of Realist
writing. Ayala's novels absorb and work with the prevailing literary
tradition.

    This, of course, implies that Pérez de Ayala is a thinking novelist,
and critics who have refrained from categorising him as some kind of
Realist writer tend to present him as an intellectual novelist and his
works, in the words of Curtis Millner, "as nothing more than an
attempt to exemplify, through character and situation, certain ideas
Ayala had about life."[9] Thus Donald Shaw uses Pérez de Ayala's
novels as a means of charting his spiritual biography, aligning him
with the writers he categorises as the Generation of 1898. For Shaw,
Ayala works his way through metaphysical despair to achieve a kind
of serenity built upon a purely private set of values [10] An approach
not unlike Shaw's, but relying less on quasi-biographical data, is
that of Julio Matas, who is concerned with the normative nature of
Pérez de Ayala's fiction.[11] The tendency to see Pérez de Ayala as
an intellectual writer is of course consecrated in the title of Andrés
Amorós' fundamental study *La novela intelectual de Ramón Pérez de
Ayala*[12], and it is a common denominator of nearly all approaches to
his work. In particular, it is seen as having repercussions for the
creation of character. For F.C. Sáinz de Robles, Pérez de Ayala's
characters are "personajes símbolos, personajes paradigmáticos, de
quienes se sirve el novelista, amañadamente, para la oratoria de su
filosofía o de su estética."[13] Max Aub claims that Ayala writes "un
tipo de novela — la de su segunda época — para personas que se
interesan por problemas estéticos y aun históricos, donde
generalmente brilla el ingenio del autor, dejando los protagonistas en
la penumbra."[14] Max Aub is, of course, hostile to the kind of novel
Ayala writes, but even a devotee like Andrés Amorós, defending his
preference for the earlier autobiographical cycle of novels over the
later ones, claims that once he has overcome his philosophical crisis
(echoes of Shaw), any subsequent novel could only be "un producto
cultural más," as if a novel could be anything other than a cultural
product. The time has surely arrived for a questioning of the received

4

picture of Pérez de Ayala as intellectual, or failed realist. Indeed, despite Aub's vague allusion, there is little in the way of historical reference in Pérez de Ayala's fiction, and this is surely significant. Modernist fiction, of which Ayala was Spain's most intelligent exponent, is a reaction in various guises against nineteenth-century Realism, and it is true to say that it was deeply influenced by symbolist poetry and poetics, in particular the belief that history and society do not give a sense of reality. The symbolist poet and, in a modified way, the Modernist novelist, believes that the human imagination actively constructs the world and does not simply reflect it. This is in essence a complete reversal of the Realist premise and involves a shift in emphasis away from physical reality to mental reality. Inherent in such a shift is an awareness of an increasing instability in the relationship between mind and reality, for reality becomes personal and individual and therefore subject to constantly shifting perceptions. The instrument by which the world is constructed is language itself, and symbolist poetics becomes increasingly concerned with the creative function of language, with the invention of linguistic fictions. Not surprisingly, a shift away from Realist representation involved a concentration upon the artist himself. The novel of experience (*Bildungsroman*) leads naturally to the *Künstlererroman* with its emphasis upon the growth of the artist. This is followed by a switch from the writer to the act of writing. Such a pattern can be easily discerned in the fiction of Ramón Pérez de Ayala in, say, the development from *La pata de la raposa* (the progress of the artist)[15] to *Belarmino y Apolonio*, the complete narcissistic text. Such a preoccupation, of course, antedates the novel proper with its insistence on truth-to-life. Gabriel Josipovici observes that the tradition which precedes the novel (Lucian, Erasmus, Rabelais, Swift, Sterne) was

> less interested in the presentation of character and society and more concerned with the problems of discourse itself: what happens to words when they get into novels. What distortions inevitably occur when I put my life into a book? These questions do not seem to exist for the traditional novel, which complacently takes its own values for granted and draws a veil over the time and effort required for the creation of art. But they are the very questions we have come to associate with modern art.[16]

Central to any consideration of Modernist fiction is the complex relationship between literature and life, and this is theoretically problematical in that narrative has, of all the genres, come closest to the direct representation of ordinary experience and indeed has been most easily understood in a social context. One aspect of Ayala's shunning of history is his concern with what is most typically and essentially human, free from the restrictions of a historical time or a social space. This manifests itself in a preference for myth over history in an endeavour to weaken the nexus between the universal human situation and the specific, historically-defined situation in which the general is particularised. It manifests itself too in a rejection of any approach to reality based on a concern with the empirically verifiable in favour of an artistic or aesthetic approach which strives to grasp, perhaps intuitively, the underlying and invisible patterns or forms of reality. In the domain of the novel there will exist always a dynamic tension between form and contingency, pattern and experience. This tension is particularly acute in the Modernist novel, where the aesthetic impulse is frequently arrested by a residual mimeticism. Some critics have described this as a kind of debate between the fictive and the real, between Poetry and History, and while according primacy to the former still subject it to the intense questioning that pervades all aspects of the Modernist enterprise:

> The grand thrust of the modern novel toward its fulfillment as art — its stress upon the power of form and technique, on the drama of the artist's consciousness, on the musicalities of composition, on the disposition of thematic and spatial aesthetic blocks, which stitch a novel together from inside, appeal not to the reader's sense of history but his sense of aesthetic harmony — has always been part of an intense questioning of art, and a sense of the existence of a difficult divergence between art and reality. Awareness of the discontinuity and ephemerality of modern reality, of the evanescence of character, the disorderly sequence of time, invades the Modernist novel.[17]

This is one way of conceiving Modernist fiction, but a more positive conception will need to take into account man's need to create fictions in the first place and then openly to acknowledge their fictive character. Realism, in its perfect match of book and world, derived its authority from its verisimilitude but, as Frank Kermode observes, Realism itself is a kind of aberration, for much modern writing, in repudiating it, links up with earlier modes:

> much writing we think of as peculiarly modern is in part a rediscovery of the oracular ... One motive of this modernism was the desire to break with a tradition of writing supposed to have been based on a mistaken or dishonest desire to eliminate the oracular by simple plausibility in the registration of the real world, and by connivance with vulgar notions of cause and closure — to make false sense by means of a false realism.[18]

Even in the Realist novel, however, we are both persuaded by the fact that the story provides the reassurance that reality has a meaningful order and simultaneously aware that the story falsifies experience by adhering to the conventions by which narrative is produced. The art of the Realist novel is to disguise the conventions in the pattern of life itself, to make compatible fictional and extra-fictional reality. A Modernist like Pérez de Ayala creates a work in which everything holds together as a kind of analogy for a universal, if unperceived, order. Imaginatively constructed pictures seem to respond to a fundamental need for order in human experience, and to that extent they perform a function similar to other systems of ordering in any culture — scientific, sociological, religious — the difference being that they are not verifiable or at least that they are not subject to a demand for verification. What is usually demanded of them, however, is coherence, and Modernists therefore strove for methods that could create forms which would satisfy a desire for inclusiveness, a desire to hold all of experience together in an aesthetically meaningful way. These methods could not be the traditional ones: history is converted into myth, successiveness into simultaneity, character into states of consciousness. In all cases, the internal relations of the work itself took precedence over any need for fidelity to ordinary experience. It is in this light that we can understand some of Pérez de Ayala's more assertive claims for the power and potentiality of art: "el arte es una realidad más verdadera que la realidad tópica" (III:415), where art appears to be afforded a privileged access to truth, or "La imaginación . . . es la forma plástica de la inteligencia y del sentimento. Tiene su mecánica, sus leyes, su realidad, realidad más alta que la misma realidad externa," as expressed by a character in *Troteras y danzaderas* (I:704-5) asserting the distinctiveness and superiority of art over life. Art and life must of necessity diverge, but they are not unrelated:

> Toda obra de arte genuino es un trozo de realidad verdadera, en donde están resumidas totalmente, y como en epítome, dos altas realidades: Vida y Arte. Toda obra de arte genuino es condensación de realidades múltiples, forma somera y adamantina donde se compendian formas innumerables. (III: 42)

This desire for comprehensiveness, for totality, is highly characteristic of literary Modernism and is fundamental to Pérez de Ayala: "Una novela es una obra de totalidad."[19] In other words, literary fictions exist as a kind of religion, and the sacramental nature of the art of the Romantics and Modernists coincides with the decline in confidence, firstly in the authority of a divinity, and later in the validity of scientific positivism. Moreover, the imagination that creates art is an inalienable element in man's freedom — from the tyranny of time, fact, reality. It is a faculty which is both revered and mistrusted — the imagination provides forms which console and satisfy, but only as long as we assent to it, as long as we consecrate only artistic truth. It is hardly surprising that a consequence of art's elevation has also

7

been its relegation to triviality, game, marginality. In other words, the premise that art offers a privileged insight into reality leads to the view that art creates its own reality, which is only a step away from maintaining that art has nothing to do with reality at all, but is just an activity all of its own. From the point of view of the novel, this can logically lead only to the creation of a pure fiction, with no referent in the external world. The answer to this is that imagination is inimical to reason, that its processes for making sense are radically different. It is an acknowledgement of the difficulties inherent in the relationship of language to knowing and the acceptance of uncertainty as an inescapable element of the human situation. One dimension of Modernist fiction is its overt dramatization of this fact and the foregrounding of the imaginative act in the imaginative work. Linda Hutcheon asserts that

> the making of fictive worlds and the constructive, creative functioning of language itself are now self-consciously shared by author and reader. The latter is no longer asked merely to recognise that fictional objects are "life-like": he is asked to participate in the creation of worlds and of meaning through language ... he is caught in that paradoxical position of being forced by the text to acknowledge the fictionality of the world he too is creating, yet his very participation involves him intellectually, creatively and perhaps even affectively in a human act that is very real, that is, in fact, a kind of metaphor of his daily effort to "make sense" of experience.[20]

Faced with the chaos of experience, man has an urge to order it, to create significant patterns, to establish relations, to construct artistically coherent worlds, but this desire is quite naturally compromised by a skepticism that this aesthetic ordering of experience is problematical and by a feeling that it is false to experience. The essential difference between Realism and Modernism is that the latter openly acknowledges its fictionality, exposes its own ambivalent status as an artifact. As such it invites a literary reading.

What makes this so interesting from the point of view of the novel is the fact that it appears to conflict with the very nature of narrative, dealing as it does in history, time and character. The Modernist writer's view of such categories is of course radical, treating them not as objective realities but only as variable modes of thought, and his intellectual mentors are, among others, Freud, Jung, Bergson, William James, Marx, Darwin, Spengler, Dostoievsky. Narrative comes to be disposed in aesthetic patterns rather than in obedience to the logic of the story, the progress of history, the consistency of character. Such a development cannot be effected without imposing considerable strain on the concept of novel which has been a mode of exploration of the socially knowable, facilitated by its clear lack of generic character which leaves it open to political, moral and social enquiry. The language of fiction approximates to non-literary discourse. Modernist fiction highlights formal literary elements — reality is distorted through language, the logic of the work is generated by metaphor or symbol — in order to show its differential relation to other kinds of discourse. It destroys the innocence of the Realist view, and a Modernist novel presents itself not as reality, but as text. Such a view naturally invites a different kind of reader and, of course, critic. Formalist criticism is the natural response to Modernist literature: it deals not with content and interpretation but with the ways in which literary texts work, with uncovering the laws, structures and devices which make them literary works, capable of being apprehended as such. This conception is well captured in the words of Jonathan Culler: "To engage in the study of literature is not to produce yet another interpretation of *King Lear* but to advance one's understanding of the conventions and operations of an institution, a mode of discourse."[21] A concern with the author's message is replaced by a concern with the organization of language within the text. David Lodge puts it this way: "Everything is form, from the individual phrase or sentence, up to the structure of a plot, or plot-type ... Wherever we cut into the literary text, and in whatever direction, we expose not 'content,' but a systematic structure of signs in which content is made comprehensible."[22] In a sense this is an extreme of Formalist or Structuralist criticism and necessarily omits a large amount of what is interesting in novels in terms of their vital significance. The relationship of form to content is a complex one, but it is the most basic relationship in any literary work and is most acutely experienced in the novel. It would appear that the ultimate radicality will reside in the creation of totally pure fictions. Pérez de Ayala certainly projects his work in this direction, but the tension remains, as this statement of residual dedication to content demonstrates: "si [la obra] carece de contenido, que es por donde el arte se inserta en la naturaleza humana, o su contenido repugna a la naturaleza humana, esta obra, aun cuando algunos profesionales la tengan en estima, a causa de la habilidad o novedad de su factura, no es una obra de arte" (III: 225-26). This notion of content is nowhere defined, however, and it seems clear that it is not meant to refer to realistic imitation, but simply to warn against an art made up entirely of figures without meaning. In fact, some of the initial impetus for Modernist writing came from a sense of the inadequacy of Realist representation as much as anything else. Thus a writer like Pérez de Ayala does not abandon the realist dimension entirely. On the contrary, his fiction, like much Modernist writing, exhibits an inherent duality, a combination of two theoretically opposed principles, the mimetic and the poetic, into a new artistic synthesis. For Ayala this is a kind of intensification of reality. "Presentemos la realidad tal cual es, si bien con luz más viva, luz que mana de la síntesis artística" (III:29), and this concept of artistic synthesis also involves a reliance not only upon experience but upon other books. A recognition of all this is necessary for an understanding and evaluation of the achievement of Pérez de Ayala as a writer and indeed of Modernism as a literary phenomenon. A reader will have to have some sense of a novel as a thing in the world as well as an autonomous artifact, and it is in the indeterminate terrain between fiction and history, each hostile to and dependent upon the other, that the tactics and tensions of the Modernist novel are most sharply perceived.

NOTES

[1]Donald L. Shaw, *The Generation of 1898 in Spain* (London: Benn, 1975) 213. Pérez de Ayala himself, in his Prologue to *Troteras y danzaderas* (Buenos Aires: Losada, 1942), comments on this same phenomenon: "la literatura europea de postguerra se asemeja, y más aún se identifica, en el interior de cada país, con el movimiento que en España se ha convenido en caracterizar como generación del 98" (9).

[2]Malcolm Bradbury and James MacFarlane, *Modernism 1890-1930* (Harmondsworth: Penguin, 1976).

[3]Andrés Amorós, *La novela intelectual de Ramón Pérez de Ayala* (Madrid: Gredos, 1972) 398-99.

[4]Rafael Cansinos-Assens, *La nueva literatura: La evolución de la novela* (Madrid: Paez, 1927) IV:105.

[5]Emiliano Díez-Echarri and José María Roca Franquesa, *Historia general de la literatura española e hispanoamericana* (Madrid: Aguilar, 1960) 1382.

[6]Stephen Heath, *The Nouveau Roman: A Study in the Practice of Writing* (London: Paul Elek, 1972) 20.

[7]David Lodge, *The Modes of Modern Writing. Metaphor, Metonymy, and the Typology of Modern Literature* (London: Edward Arnold, 1977) 25.

[8]Rufino Blanco Fombona, *Motivos y letras de España* (Madrid: Renacimiento, 1930) 145.

[9]Curtis Millner, "Ontological Inversion in the Novels of Ramón Pérez de Ayala," *Mester* 5.2 (1975):109. This, it should be pointed out, is not Millner's view but a tendency he detects in other critics.

[10]D.L. Shaw, "On the Ideology of Pérez de Ayala," *Modern Language Quarterly* XXII (1961):158-66, and his later *The Generation of 1898 in Spain* (see Note 1).

[11]Julio Matas, *Contra el honor: Las novelas normativas de Ramón Pérez de Ayala* (Madrid: Ediciones y Seminarios, 1974).

[12]See Note 3.

[13]F.C. Sáinz de Robles, *La promoción de "El Cuento Semanal"* (Madrid: Espasa-Calpe, 1975) 144.

[14]Max Aub, "Discurso de la novela española contemporánea," *Jornadas* 50 (1945):69.

[15]See Donald L. Fabian, "The Progress of the Artist: A Major Theme in the Early Novels of Pérez de Ayala," *Hispanic Review* XXVI (1958):108-16.

[16]Gabriel Josipovici, *The Lessons of Modernism* (London: Macmillan, 1977) 97.

[17]Bradbury and MacFarlane, *Modernism* 410-11.

[18]Frank Kermode, *The Genesis of Secrecy* (London: Harvard University Press, 1979) 15.

[19]*Pequeños ensayos* (Madrid: Biblioteca Nueva, 1963) 166.

[20]Linda Hutcheon, *Narcissistic Narrative. The Metafictional Paradox* (London and New York: Methuen, 1984) 30.

[21]Jonathan Culler, *The Pursuit of Signs. Semiotics. Literature. Deconstruction* (London: Routledge and Kegan Paul, 1981) 5.

[22]*Metaphor and Metonymy* x.

11

CHAPTER ONE
CONTINUITIES AND DISCONTINUITIES:
THE EMERGENCE OF THE MODERNIST NOVEL IN SPAIN

Literary historians who have interested themselves in early twentieth-century Spanish fiction have, on the whole, been concerned to bring out the peculiarly Spanish qualities of that fiction, or at least the very Spanish circumstances which helped to shape it. In contrast, critics who have dealt with the phenomenon known as Modernism have been unanimous in highlighting as one of its defining features its international character. As a prelude to a detailed analysis of the Modernist features of the fiction of Ramón Pérez de Ayala, I wish in this chapter to construct a model of Modernism appropriate to modern Spanish fiction which will underline its formal affinities with fiction produced elsewhere in Europe and at the same time show how some of these features are already latent in the Spanish fictional tradition. The outline I give here, conceived as a basis for charting a typography of twentieth-century Spanish narrative, will of necessity be tentative, and not everyone will agree with its emphases. It should, however, demonstrate that the novel in Spain is not divorced from developments elsewhere, that its achievements are as much aesthetic as ideological, and that it made a full contribution to that movement away from Realism in pursuit of both a deeper reality and a greater art which has made Modernism the quintessence of the artistic potential of our age.

Modernism, as distinct from *modernismo*, is not a term commonly used in Hispanic criticism, where the changes that took place in the novel in the wake of Realism are more usually considered and explained in the ideological context of the Generation of 1898. The purely Hispanic connotations of this term are, in my view, prejudicial to a true appreciation of the writers to whom it is applied. Even more prejudicial, however, is the rigid distinction which has become established between Generation of 1898 and *modernismo*, largely through the solid and detailed work of Guillermo Díaz-Plaja which has in turn been followed by commentators like Donald L. Shaw.[1] Despite Díaz-Plaja's arguments, it seems highly unlikely that literary history would lend itself to the neat division suggested by two opposing groups. Any cultural situation is highly complex, and impulses from many directions coalesce to create a fluid rather than a static situation. We can see that this is the case if we look at the actual literary activities of the writers themselves and the concrete manifestations of those activities: literary magazines. For example, even at the level of the binary opposition advanced by Díaz-Plaja, the 98 magazine *Alma Española* can be seen to contain some very *modernista* pronouncements. Indeed, the term itself, *modernista*, was in common use among the writers themselves as a means of defining their reaction to what had gone before. In general, Hispanic critics have considered formal change in narrative almost exclusively in terms of either the impact of public events or the spiritual evolution of individual writers. It could even be said that they have been more concerned with the writers than with the writing. It is not my aim here to rehearse and then refute the general arguments put forward, but broadly speaking they imply a view of literature either as the expression of some *Volksgeist* or national spirit or as the expression of an individual philosophical quest.[2] Literary change was seen as a response to external circumstances but rarely have Hispanic critics considered the novel's potential for formal change residing within the conventions of narrative itself. Form, for them, has almost always been a consequence of intended content. My lack of sympathy with this approach, if not explicitly formulated, will be implicit in the method I propose to adopt. It is for this reason that this study of Modernism in Spain, as exemplified in the fiction of Ramón Pérez de Ayala, begins with a consideration of some of the most important formal strategies of Realist fiction. To do this is to accept the Saussurean distinction between causes which are external to a phenomenon and those which are intrinsic to it and therefore to endorse the notion of "literature as system."[3] I shall therefore not engage in a series of causal explanations of the emergence of Modernist fiction on the basis of temporal development (although one cannot deny chronology altogether) but will endeavor to show how Modernist fiction foregrounds its own tactics and techniques against those of its Realist predecessor. Indeed, the Modernist novel can be seen for what it is only in terms of its differential relation with Realism. A second problem which arises from the traditional division is that much time and energy is devoted by criticism to the establishment of an appropriate membership for each group — this particularly applies to the 98 — and attention is thereby deflected away from the intrinsic literary qualities of the works themselves towards the beliefs and feelings of their authors. An unfortunate consequence of this is that a concept such as the Generation of 1898 is extended to embrace different genres so that like is not compared with like: imaginative works are related to ideological treatises and interpreted as such. Ideas voiced by, say, characters in a novel are often accepted as straightforward statements of belief by their creators without having regard to the modifying context of the literary work. Relations forged in this way can only be sustained on a very broad level of generalisation and bring us no closer to understanding how the conventions deployed in narrative texts enable them to produce meaning. Most of the more significant criticism written in recent years has focussed on this question and not surprisingly has interested itself in Modernist works, where the reader's expectations of a coherent meaning are often frustrated. Literary modernism, in a sense, generated a whole new critical discourse centred on the concept of text. Moreover,

Díaz-Plaja's binary model has produced an opposition between prose and poetry, the Generation of 1898 having prevailed as the designation of the novel of the period, with all the connotations it evokes, while *modernismo*, which would have been instantly recognizable as denoting an affinity with an international cultural phenomenon, has been restricted in its meaning and applied almost exclusively to a certain kind of poetry. There are those who would applaud this restriction in meaning and object to the elasticity of the term Modernism, but in a sense it is its very breadth which is appealing. Naturally, any concept of Modernism applied to Spanish fiction must be applied flexibly and taken broadly to mean a set of assumptions (which we will ultimately define) based on a radical vision of the artist and a sense of crisis in the relationship between art and reality. This seems inevitably to entail in some measure a historicist perspective.

Standing as we do less than twenty years away from the dawn of a new millenium, it is tempting to glance retrospectively over our century, over the age that we call modern, and assert with conviction that our view of the human condition has changed more in these years than ever before. Whether we see this as a cataclysmic break with the past, a rupture of sensibility, or as the culmination of a process with its roots deep in the nineteenth century, there is a universal acceptance of a radical reappraisal affecting all spheres of human life and culture, and this acceptance has itself shaped man's view of the modern situation. Indeed, even if the antecedents of the modern movement can be traced back to earlier times, it is difficult not to see the modern mood as in large measure antagonistic to that of its immediate predecessor. A good illustration is *The Education of Henry Adams* (1907) by Henry Brook Adams, in which the hero finds his education inadequate to the needs of twentieth-century man, living now in a multiverse rather than a universe. In this work we read: "The child born in 1900 would be born into a new world which would not be a unity but a multiple. Adams tried to imagine it and an education that would fit it. He found himself in a land where no one had ever penetrated before, where order was an accidental relation obnoxious to nature."[4] Broadly, a simple opposition suggests itself: the nineteenth century was on the whole characterised by confidence in human progress, in the eventual triumph of scientific optimism and rational thought, in the possibility of apprehending reality and communicating it through language. The watchwords of the twentieth century, on the other hand, are nihilism, alienation and despair. The Modernist world is an absurdist world in which God is dead, social hierarchies are not respected, moral values are seen to be relative, human personality is assailed by dark forces, unknown and unknowable, language is divorced from reality, the forms of art are dislocated beyond immediate recognition. Stability and certainty have yielded to insecurity and chaos. A rift has been driven between past past and present. We can therefore interpret Modernism and its formal experimentation as a response to this changed situation, but it is also a flight from it into the creation of an alternative reality. In both senses, Modernism is a literature of crisis.

It can be argued, and with some justification, that to classify a work of literature as Modernist is not to make a critical statement about it and will certainly bring us no further along the road to under-standing. But, as David Lodge has explained so lucidly, no literary work exists in isolation. It draws its meaning from the fact that it is both like and unlike other works of literature.[5] Indeed, this principle of similarity and dissimilarity is one that is often consciously exploited by Modernist writers. Innovation is born out of a reaction to or an extension of what has gone before. It is precisely for this reason that it is particularly illuminating to consider the Modernist novel in rela-tion to its predecessor, the Realist novel. The Modernist novel fre-quently subverts the most basic premises of Realist practice, so that it is common in literary criticism to see the two modes in sharp con-trast to one another. In Spain at least, however, there are in the Real-ist novel the seeds of the Modernist novel, and the Modernist ten-dency to portray the Realist novel as something old-fashioned and rigid in its approach to reality is something of a simplification. In dealing with Realism and Modernism, it is important not to take up exclusivist positions. There are those who would say that Realism is the novel, that it survives until the present day albeit in a form modi-fied to take account of changed circumstances, and that Modernism in the novel is an aesthetic aberration. In turn, there are those who maintain that Modernism is the only true art of our time and indeed use Modernism as a term of praise and Realism as a term of abuse. Many Modernist critics write as though Realism were something monolithic, when in fact there are many kinds of Realist writers, some of whom, especially in the later stages of their work, question the scientific assumptions on which their work is said to be based. What some Modernists portray as Realism is in fact a caricature of it. In fact, the charge that Modernist writers and critics underestimate (perhaps wilfully) the complexity of the relationship between the Realist novel and reality has become as much a commonplace of modern criticism as the original Modernist repudiation of Realist aes-thetics. This intellectual exchange is proof alone, if any is needed, that the central battleground in the debate between the ancients and the moderns, if they may be so called, is precisely the question of the nature of reality and the nature of fictional representation. Of course, the tradition of the Realist novel was so strong that the Modernist novel emerged only slowly and it did not in any sense replace its predecessor. The realist novel in modified form continues to survive to the present day. It could, in fact, be argued that the novel as a genre is somehow inherently mimetic or, at least, that realism is inseparable from it, and that the novelists of the early cen-tury, in striving to capture and render reality more intensely, gradually went beyond Realism, so that progressively the center of attention is diverted away from external reality towards individual perception of reality, towards consciousness, with the consequence that the novelist comes to rely increasingly on non-representational techniques. The novel itself becomes inevitably more complex as it seeks to render a reality that is in itself problematical. This complexity in turn becomes in itself an object of exploration, so that ultimately there is a divergence in the theory and practice of fiction. On the one hand, there stands the view that the novel should imitate life, that it should be representative or mimetic, and on the other stands the view that sophistication of technique inevitably turns the novel inward towards exploring its own internal organization and generating its own artistic logic. Such a novel is justified not by fidelity to any model of external reality but by virtue of its own inner coherence, its aesthetic integrity. Behind both views lies the question: what is the relationship between the fictional world and the so-called real world? The answers given in either case are very different, and the particular usefulness of Realism and Modernism as literary-historical terms is that they enable us to see the two modes in relational terms. In this respect David Lodge's account of the literature of the modern period is highly suggestive. He sees the modern period as being characterized by alternating phases of dominance of modernist and anti-modernist writing and this process as having a cause within the system of literature itself: "Literary innovation is achieved by reacting against and contrasting with the received orthodoxy."[6] Signs communicate, using Saussure's terms, by virtue of the differences between them. Modernism, as I have implied, is profoundly Saussurean in spirit, and it is therefore not inappropriate to consider it in terms of its differentiation from Realism. For our purposes the work of Benito Pérez Galdós offers a perfect illustration of the emergence, evolution and exhaustion of Realist fiction in Spain.

Realism made a relatively late appearance in Spain, and explanations of this are most commonly sought in the economic and political backwardness of the country itself. The fundamental traditionalism of Spanish society and its inherent resistance to change, so the argument runs, produced a reaction to Realism akin to that produced by Romanticism earlier in the century. This resistance, and the opposition to it, forms part of the conflict of the "dos Españas," between liberals and reactionaries, which Galdós' early novels are said to reflect. Progressives as well as traditionalists wrote biased and partisan novels so that whereas the first important Realist novels were produced elsewhere in the 1850's and 1860's: *Madame Bovary* (1857), *Salammbô* (1862), *Fathers and Children* (1862), *War and Peace* (1863-9), *Sentimental Education* (1869), in Spain they do not appear until the 1880's and are strongly influenced by the theories of Naturalism.[7] Indeed, Galdós uses the terms "realismo" and "naturalismo" without making any distinction between them. In the 1880's

16

Galdós published his great novels of contemporary life, initiated in 1881 by *La desheredada*, which marks a shift away from the ideologically-conceived novels of the previous decade, of which *Doña Perfecta* (1876) is a prime example. It is not too harsh a judgement to say that in *Doña Perfecta* we are offered an over-simplified view of reality distorted by the need to see things in terms of issues and problems which require solutions. On the surface, the characters seem to fall into categories of good and bad, liberal and reactionary, and, even if the novel is an attack on misguided religiosity rather than on Catholicism as such, its tone is markedly polemical. The problem with this novel is the brief last chapter which imposes on us an interpretation based on the forces of good against the forces of evil, whereas in fact Galdós' approach is rather more ambiguous. Such ambiguity, of course, is of a moral kind, and is taken to refer to the complexities of human behavior. In this sense, the emergent Realist novel was judged to be more "true to life" than, say, popular "heroes and villains" fiction. In other words, its success was not in some way intrinsic to itself but assessed on its fidelity to a generally accepted model of reality which it was purported to reflect. *Doña Perfecta* does not, it must be said in fairness, present a totally simplistic view of moral behavior. If the provinces are shown to be brutal and backward, Madrid comes over as corrupt, clumsy and inefficient. Pepe Rey is far from perfect: he is tactless and mildly aggressive. The behavior of doña Perfecta herself can partly be justified in terms of her upbringing, her grudge against Madrid and her growing suspicion that Pepe is not her nephew. There is therefore already an awareness of the complexity of moral conduct, of the shifting relations between principle and personal need, which makes the work a plausible enough account of the lives of real people. Yet the really interesting thing about the novel, which anticipates the later Galdós, is the way in which the characters assume a fixed emotional stance which distorts their perception of reality. Inocencio nurtures the myth of Orbajosa as a rural Arcadia contaminated by progress; Pepe has all kinds of prejudices about the place; he himself is judged and prejudged. So even this early novel, for all its weaknesses, is an early exploration of the theme of the contrast between reality and appearance which is central to Galdós' vision of Madrid society in his mature novels. High principles conceal personal motives: Inocencio in particular is skilled in the art of causistry, an attenuated form of lying. Reality is falsified through egoism. We can see how this theme assumes central importance in a later novel, *Tormento*, published in 1884.

Galdós' treatment of the theme of the falsification of reality in *Tormento* is related to his critique of that kind of sentimental and popular literature which satisfies people's needs for stereotypes with simplified images with which they can identify. Thus *Tormento* opens with a satirical presentation in dramatic form of the romantic approach to the writing of novels, which manifests itself in Spain as the *novela por entregas* or *folletín*, in which the poor are good and exploited and the rich are evil and exploiters. Ido del Sagrario, the writer of this kind of novel, is in fact writing a novel about the same characters as Galdós is writing about, and Ido's simplified view of reality contrasts with Galdós' more complex view of that same reality.[8] At the same time, Galdós' own approach is self-consciously literary: the title of his novel is more appropriate to popular than Realist fiction; suspense is built around the slow revelation of Amparo's secret; Chapter 34 ends with her swallowing "poison," and the reader has to wait until the next chapter to discover that she has not in fact died; and there are in addition other obviously literary elements such as the idea of the poor orphan being wooed by the rich *indiano*, of her lover sacrificing himself to her happiness, which is itself achieved only after the suicide attempt. These elements stand in self-conscious contrast to the more "realistic" elements. Amparo is indeed an orphan, but she is no virgin: she has been seduced by a bohemian priest. The ending is decidedly unromantic: she ends up as Agustín's mistress, not his wife. The real significance of the foregrounding of the narrative against the background of popular fiction is that it provides an analogy for a process which nearly all the characters undergo: they see reality in a simplified way. Rosalía deceives herself about her social position and about her own motives. Her materialism is made to contrast with the social non-conformism of Agustín, who appears as the very antithesis of Madrid society which is based on the pursuit of material wealth, knowing the right people and maintaining a façade of respectability. This naturally inclines the reader in his favor, but Agustín, no less than the other characters, sees reality in terms of simplified patterns. His hopes of finding peace and order in Spain are an illusion, a misreading of the true nature of things, a falsification of reality, and it is, moreover, precisely this view of Spain which leads him to seek a wife in Amparo, not the real Amparo, but his own idealised image of her — an image incidentally, not very different from the stereotype portrayed in Ido's romantic novel. In fact, Amparo is far from virtuous, and her social ambition leads her to treat her former lover, Pedro Polo, with extreme cruelty: she wants him to go as far away as possible lest her terrible secret be revealed, but she convinces herself that all would be for his own good. Her conscience and self-interest are made to coincide. Polo is the real victim of the novel. He is undoubtedly an unattractive individual, immature and unable to organize his own life properly, but of all the characters in the novel he is the one who most clearly sees the falseness of his own life based on an erroneous choice of the priesthood as a career. His true self is stifled in a conventional social role, and it is this authentic self which he wishes to recover. Other characters fail to grasp this. Amparo does not see his real problem and Padre Nones thinks only of regenerating him, bringing him back to the fold. This conventional solution — and the novel is replete with conventional solutions — will destroy all his latent potentialities as an individual.

I have given only a very brief sketch of a novel which is very extensively worked out in terms of technique, but enough, I hope, to show how Galdós' analogical imagination combines different areas of experience to reveal how each, seen in terms of the other, is subject to a constant process of simplification and distortion. The real links in the novel are provided not by a chain of cause and effect or linear narrative but by a steady build-up of complementary patterns. These patterns impart to the text its "literariness;" they are the means by which, to use the terminology of the Prague School, the *fabula* becomes *sujet*. Already we can be made aware of a divergence between the text's apparent mimetic urge, its validity as a reflection of empirical reality, and the fact that it is a coherent construct in itself. In other words, the text is not so much the result of a desire to copy reality, but rather reality has provided the motivation for the creation of a self-sustaining artifact. The laws which govern the making of *Tormento* are those of art, not of the world. Galdós' objective, however, despite the parallel with Ido's novel, has not generally been seen by critics to be of a literary or philosophical nature, but has its basis in social observation. The use of analogies, in other words, is intended to assist us in making value judgements on the character's social behaviour.[9] Nevertheless, the underlying theme of self-deception raises the inevitable question: can man's view of reality be anything other than subjective? Galdós, at this stage, never doubts the existence of something that can be called truth, but before looking at this question in detail, I wish to illustrate some other aspects of Realism by referring to Galdós' masterpiece, *Fortunata y Jacinta* (1886-87).

The whole question of Realism is a very complex one, especially when considered from a philosophical rather than from a strictly literary point of view. Indeed, the question: "What is reality?" and the answers given to it partly account for the movement from Realist to Modernist representation, and it is my aim in this chapter to isolate features in the practice of the Realists in order to show how the Modernists extend, invert or deviate from them. Basically, the Realist novel is social in character, and the Realist writer creates a fictional world which is an acceptable model of the real world and of the conditions, laws and circumstances which are commonly held to prevail in the real world. Galdós, writing in 1870 in his "Observaciones sobre la novela contemporánea en España," puts this at its most basic: "Imagen de la vida es la novela ..."[10] On the basis of its inherent mimeticism, David Lodge construes Realist fiction as being essentially metonymic (as opposed to Modernist fiction, which tends towards the metaphoric): "The narrative text necessarily selects certain details and suppresses or deletes others. The selected details are thus foregrounded by being selected and their recurrence and interrelation with each other in the narrative become aesthetically significant."[11] The most basic critical response to this kind of fiction is to resupply the deleted material. In its worst form, it amounts to paraphrase; at best, it is thematic or perhaps sociological in inclination. Realism to this extent depends upon a cultural consensus, both in the sense of the assumption of an accepted view of reality and of the expected conventions of fictional narrative. The Realist novel purports to be based on direct observation of the society it depicts, and considerable attention is devoted to the exact and detailed description of people and places in order to convey a sense of the density and solidity of the material world. The language of Realism approximates that of historical or factual writing of various kinds — biography, history, journalism. Realism concentrates on the everyday experience of the real, tracing out in meticulous detail the small and seemingly trivial events which make up the texture of the lives of ordinary people. Characters are seen in the context of their environment and change in relation to it. Emile Zola's remark is characteristic: "Les milieux proprement dits, milieux de lieu et milieux de société, déterminent la classe du personnage ..."[12] Often the relationship between the individual and his environment is conflictive, and a persistent Realist theme is that life is not as it is presented in a good deal of romantic literature. Again the literary and the real merge: the individual's perception of reality is shaped by literature as much as it is confirmed by it.

Fortunata y Jacinta is a love story and a study of class distinctions. Though it begins as the chronicle of two upper middle class families, the Santa Cruz and the Arnáiz, united by the marriage of their children, Juanito and Jacinta, the novel broadens out to bring in the proletariat in the person of Fortunata, Juanito's mistress, and the petty bourgeoisie in the person of her husband, Maxi Rubín. Clearly, social relations are crucial in this kind of fiction, and *Fortunata y Jacinta*, in its sensitivity to social gradations, combines an analysis of class conflict with a study of personality as it explores the collision of individual impulse and aspiration with social restraint and convention. The novel is firmly set in the period 1868 to 1876, thereby conforming to the general Realist practice that the novel have a contemporary or near-contemporary setting and accepting the assumption that human life is most truthfully presented in terms of the individual's milieu, his social and historical circumstances. In fact, events are traced as far back as 1796, when the Santa Cruz business was established. This orderly sequence of time is something which the Realist takes for granted, and it implies a belief in causality which is the underlying principle of plot. In fact, the aesthetic wholeness of the work may be said to depend upon it: the determinist model justifies the imposition of a pattern upon the novel. Artistic coherence and causation go hand in hand, and the novel thereby gives an impression of logical development and orderly progression. The final outcome can be seen to be the consequence of certain "historical" antecedents which led up to it, and thus there can be observed some loosely interpreted notion of progress. Even if the outcome is tragic, its actual causes are still capable of being traced, explained and understood. The precise dating of *Fortunata y Jacinta*, then, contributes to a view of human social evolution with its victories and its casualities. It also serves to add authenticity to the chronicle of family life and to bring out the particularity of the historical period, a period in which the middle classes had come to dominate virtually all spheres of Spanish society. The nature of this class is perhaps most clearly revealed in the character of Juanito Santa Cruz, who conforms to the Realist notion of the type, embodying social forces at a given period. In fact, history is used as a means of characterisation in that a parallel is drawn between Juanito Santa Cruz and Spanish public life. A similar technique can be observed in the characterization of Galdós' famous moneylender, Torquemada. The opening chapters of *Torquemada en la hoguera* (1889) draw parallels between Torquemada's life and important historical events in the nineteenth century. The sale of Church lands and the rapid expansion of industry offered opportunities for the speculator and moneylender, so that the 1850's and 1860's were a period of consolidation and unprecedented prestige for the bourgeoisie. Torquemada emerges as a type, the self-made man, representative of the nineteenth-century capitalist. Clearly, the values which are important in the Realist novel are social and collective values, and the standards of conduct and norms of behavior which apply are a matter of consensus between the author and his readers. In this sense, we may speak of the objective nature of the Realist novel.

Objectivity, though, is not a simple concept. Insofar as the writer does not openly voice his opinions in the novel he may, broadly speaking, be deemed to be objective. Yet the very selection of the material and its presentation in the narrative implies certain value judgements, and few of us would want to read a novel which did not in some way invite us to share the writer's way of looking at the world. Any novel is a structure of persuasion, the creation of an individual subjectivity. This is the central paradox of Realism and in its resolution (or dissolution) resides the prime achievement of Realist aesthetics. In *Fortunata y Jacinta*, Galdós uses the device of a personal narrator who acts as the reader's guide into the world of the novel and, since this narrator is part of the society he describes, the device enhances the illusion of the real in the work. This narrator, moreover, shares the values of the society he is portraying but deftly, as the novel progresses, Galdós undermines the authority of his narrator by counterpointing his complacent view of reality to the author's own more skeptical vision. In addition, the objectivity of the narratorial voice gradually gives way to more or less total omni-science. This is important for the overall vision of the work to emerge, but it is also important in the sense that the Realist writer strives to offer as broad a panorama of society as possible, and just as Realist novels, despite their titles, rarely deal exclusively with single individuals, as this would limit unacceptably the range of experience portrayed, so does the Realist need to transcend the restrictions of a fixed narrator. Galdós accepts that any one definition of reality is limited and strives therefore to present a pluralistic view of the world. In terms of narrative technique, this conviction manifests itself in a mixed approach, ranging from an almost complete identifi-cation between narrator and character to the documentary approach of the social historian. This latter approach is adopted in Part I of *Fortunata y Jacinta,* and its effect is to keep the reader detached from this world, which is presented extensively rather than intensively. The death of Fortunata, on the other hand, is approached very differently. There the narrator gives precedence to the consciousness of the character and makes his own presence less obtrusive. At the same time, however, by giving the flow of impressions of a character he is going beyond the limits of what he could reasonably, objectively know, and yet if he were to restrict himself to a purely outside view he would fail to render adequately the "feel" of experience, which is by its nature subjective. Such contradictions are hedged around any consideration of objectivity in Realist fiction and it is doubtful whether many Realists considered the question in these terms. Most of them, seemingly unconsciously, created an apparently impersonal illusion of reality to convey the impression that what was being narrated existed independently of the mind that created it. The devices by which the novel is constructed are kept distinctly out of sight. The reader was to accept the world of the novel as objectively valid.

We have seen how in *Tormento* the characters' perception of the world was affected by their emotional attitude to it, and this is an idea which is continued in *Fortunata y Jacinta,* where the theme of roman-tic illusion is worked out through a pattern of analogies. The core of the novel centres on the clash between aspiration and reality as the struggle to attain an ideal is thwarted by circumstances. This gives rise to a constant process of adjustment, particularly in the cases of Fortunata and Maxi Rubín. Maxi, in fact, anticipates the anguished protagonists of twentieth-century fiction: an abnormal personality overwhelmed by his sense of inferiority, induced by a physical unattractiveness and constant ill-health, who compensates by day-dreaming and living in an imaginary world. Such subterfuges keep painful reality at bay. Progressively, his experience of reality is so fragmented that he can no longer perceive it correctly. He is finally broken by the conflicting and irreconcilable demands of self and environment. The conflicts are felt, too, by Fortunata, a woman of the lower class grappling on a moral and psychological plane with the

22

problems posed by her association with the middle class. Unlike Maxi, Fortunata is partly able to adapt, eluding the simple determinist pattern. Through these characters Galdós explores a more positive version of determinism: individual and environment shape and modify each other as individuals develop morally and psychologically through conflict. So there is some progress, however slow and faltering. But Galdós' optimism is qualified. Fortunata has some success, but around her are ranged a host of minor tragedies, and it is this sense of the diversity of human experience rather than any notion of causality and historical linearity which creates the novel's sense of reality. Although I have only touched upon a few of the novel's many aspects, there is here enough, I think, to dispel any simplified notions of what constitutes Realism sometimes advanced by Modernist theoreticians. Modernism is a movement away from Realism, yes, but this movement should not blind us to the very real achievements and great sophistication of the major Realist works. I now wish to take this point just a little further by reference to two more novels by Galdós, *El amigo Manso* (1882) and *Misericordia* (1897).

I have argued thus far that a recurrent theme in Galdós' novels, one which has repercussions for any discussion of Realism, is the way in which romantic attitudes distort the characters' view of themselves and of the world around them. In *El amigo Manso* the main protagonist is, in fact, a rationalist who deeply distrusts the power of the imagination, and the interesting thing about this novel is that Manso's powers of reason deceive him in his perception of reality. His powers of reason lead him to generalise rather than to come to terms with the particular. Galdós' exploration of the theme of self-deception, then, embraces reason as well as emotion, and he suggests that our view of reality is something we construct as we experience; it is not something fixed or static. This in itself is a major insight of the novel, but no less interesting for a consideration of Realism and Modernism is the manner in which Galdós both begins and ends his novel. The opening of the novel, which is a first-person narration by Manso himself, is "Yo no existo": Manso asserts that his existence is merely fictional. The ending is equally non-realistic: Manso has died and contemplates the action of the novel, which continues without him, from an otherworldly vantage point. This dislocation of Realism is something of a shock for the reader, and it is not easy to know how to react to it. Galdós in one sense shatters the Realist illusion by foregrounding Marco's fictional existence against an otherwise highly mimetic narrative. The implication is perhaps that all the detail, substantiality, "realness" of the physical world is not the essential reality. Moreover, this conclusion is reached by showing the so-called rational interpretation of reality to be potentially very misleading. There is, in other words, in *El amigo Manso* a questioning of the idea of a stable, ordered reality in which every effect has its logical cause, a questioning of the generalising capacity of the human mind which constantly seeks reassuring patterns in experience.

The final text by Galdós which I wish to consider is *Misericordia*, published, as it happens, in 1897, the year of Galdós' speech to the Real Academia Española in which he implies that it is no longer possible to write novels in the Realist mold. Here we have a clear example of a Realist challenging the premises of Realism. *Misericordia* deliberately plays with the planes of reality and fiction and explores the capacity of the human imagination to create reality. Rather like *El amigo Manso*, however, *Misericordia* exhibits much of the detail and density we expect from a Realist novel, or more accurately a Naturalist novel. In the early chapters we sense the influence of Darwinian theories, especially of the survival of the fittest. Man's animal characteristics predominate as he selfishly strives to preserve himself at the expense of others. It is clearly implied that man is conditioned by his environment, determined by circumstances he cannot control and from which he cannot escape. Physical and economic laws work against him, but already Galdós alludes to the shifting nature of reality: there is a blend of realism and idealism in the descriptions of characters and places. The first words of the novel, "Dos caras," allude to the double-faced quality of reality, and ultimately the novel transcends Naturalism to reveal aspects of human experience beyond and above the immediate and the tangible. *Misericordia* is very much concerned with illusion and paradox: little is what it seems to be. In his 1897 lecture, Galdós alluded to the example of Cervantes. This is not the place to dwell on such a complex issue, but it must certainly be significant that in Spain novelists who were concerned with exploring the problematical nature of reality had a native tradition to draw on, a tradition which, through the example of Don Quijote, was well accustomed to probing the relative nature of fiction and of reality itself.

One way in which we can illustrate Galdós' departure from Realist practice is by looking briefly at the handling of time in the novel. In this context Gérard Genette's categorisation of time into order, duration, and frequency is helpful.[13] The second category — duration — is concerned with the duration of events in the *fabula* and the time taken to narrate them in the *sujet,* which need not be the same. It is a truism that Realists construe time as linear (although the order in which events are narrated need not be chronological), and *Misericordia* does indeed exhibit that slow pace we associate with the Naturalist novel, where detail is painstakingly and carefully provided. The novel covers two days in the first twenty chapters, then the pace quickens as five days are covered up to Chapter 29. Thereafter, however, exact chronology is abandoned. The novel's illusion of reality is no longer dependent upon chronological accuracy. For one thing, don Romualdo appears in a way designed to undermine our conventional expectations about reality. We are now more concerned with psychological time as Benina is liberated through the power of imagination. The imagination, called on one occasion "esta divina facultad," is a source of strength, a means of overcoming what society accepts as real, "la facultad preciosa de desprenderse de la realidad." One way of interpreting this is to see it in psychological terms: all of the characters show signs of mental disorder, and these neuroses or psychoses can be functional in that they keep a painful reality at bay, or at least enable characters to adjust to it. While some of the characters, for example Obdulia and Ponte, may seem to be both disturbed and pathetic, others, especially Almudena and Benina, seem to escape the weight of Naturalism. The narrator frequently alludes to the shifting nature of reality, "esta vaga fluctuación entre lo real y lo imaginativo," and observes how uncertain we often are about the true nature of things: "¿quién va a saber lo que es verdad y lo que es mentira?" *Misericordia* finds several means of bridging the gap between imagination and reality. Firstly, the narrator stresses the truth of what he is recounting—a very Cervantine device—and this truth contrasts with Benina's lie that she is working for don Romualdo. But in stressing the truth of his narrative, the narrator clearly suggests that he is not just inventing don Romualdo: he is not responsible for the unusual occurrence. So a kind of game is being played with the concepts of falsehood and truth. Romualdo is both a real and an invented figure: the lie or invention becomes part of everyday reality. Eventually he appears, so that invented reality is seen to have been a prefiguration of concrete reality. We find, therefore, that in the novel reality and imagination are at first seen to be in confrontation, then they are fused into one, and finally imagination creates reality. We can interpret don Romualdo as a kind of narrative game: Benina usurps the novelist's role by creating the character who provides the denouement of the novel. Or we can take a more psychological view: reality is not fixed, the human mind creates reality. There is a basic shift in emphasis here from physical to mental reality in which the human imagination constructs the world and does not simply reflect it. Thus the making of narratives is a natural human activity, the exercise of the imagination is a kind of freedom, offering liberation from the tyranny of the empirically real. Whatever the case, *Misericordia* clearly rejects any unilateral, materialistic or deterministic conception of reality. This is no longer the world of the classic nineteenth-century novel, and it is no exaggeration to say that as far as Spain is concerned, 1897 represents the coming of the Modernist novel.

Summarising thus far, we can say that the Realist novel in Spain is social in inspiration, drawing its raw material from contemporary society and depicting that society as fully as possible. Exact and detailed description of character and milieu is considered important, and the action of the novel takes place in a near-contemporary setting. Individuals are seen as representative, and the values explored are collective ones. Characters are studied in relation to their environment. On a technical level, Realist novels are influenced by a causal concept of history and a linear concept of time. Narrative progresses to an end. The Realist author strives to be objective and accepts that reality is stable and that language is capable of interpreting and communicating it accurately. However, the determinist pattern is not universally adhered to. In Galdós there is a growing awareness of man's spiritual and psychological complexity, of the diversity and plurality of reality, and of the reality-creating capacity of the human mind. These notions, though, are still controlled within a largely mimetic framework, and it is not until the early twentieth century that these concerns are intensified and developed to the point of crisis that characterises the truly Modernist novel.

It is generally agreed that a significant change took place in the nature of Spanish fiction early this century, as it did in the fiction written in European countries generally, and this change is most usually explained in terms of social, political, economic or cultural changes which affected fiction while remaining, as it were, external to it. In fact, if one examines the history of the development of art forms there appears to be, with gradations, an oscillation between two poles. Wilhelm Worringer, for example, discusses the alternation between naturalistic and non-naturalistic styles in the plastic arts, the former including the classical age of Greek art, the Italian Renaissance, the art of Western Europe until the nineteenth century, and the latter, most primitive art, Egyptian monumental sculpture, Byzantine art, Romanesque sculpture, the dominant art styles of the twentieth century. Worringer concludes that naturalism and non-naturalism are created to satisfy different spiritual needs, naturalism corresponding to stable, balanced cultures and non-naturalism to cultures undergoing processes of insecurity or instability.[14] This kind of explanation, suggestive by virtue of its very neatness and simplicity, omits entirely to take into account the possibility of the impetus for change residing within art itself. In the case of prose fiction, the experiments of the moderns are striking essentially because of the way in which they contrast sharply with the existing tradition. In Spain, later in the century, the Post-Civil War novel reveals a whole new generation of social realists whose impact depends on their outright rejection of the "aestheticism" of the Modernists.[15] Thus it can be argued that literature changes in a way which can be said to be generated by literature itself: formal change is characterized by an emphasis of difference from the prevailing mode. In other words, innovation is only meaningful in terms of the background of convention against which the innovatory elements are foregrounded.

Such a view of literary innovation and change is profoundly appealing in the context of Modernism in particular because it seems to be entirely consistent with the dominant philosophy of the movement, which has been convincingly shown to have strong affinities with the spirit of Saussurean linguistics, or at least to have anticipated it by breaking the link between word and object and stressing instead the relations between words themselves.[16] This is to say that Modernism rejects the notion of art as imitation and replaces it with the idea of art as autonomous activity. It is the relationships within the work itself, and within the body of literature, which are important, rather than the relationship between literature and "external reality." More importantly, Saussure's view that signs communicate by virtue of the differences between them and not because of any relationship between sign and object reinforces the outline of literary history sketched above, in which the notion of inherent formal change is paramount. The individual novel then stands in the same relation to the body of literature as *parole* does to *langue* in Saussure's original formulation. Literature is a system (*langue*) of which the text (*parole*) is a partial realisation.

The first feature that we can detect as the novel moves into the twentieth century is an abandonment of the social or public perspective that was associated with Realism. It might be more accurate to say that the Realist novel achieves a constant interplay between public and private perspectives through the adroit manipulation of a combination of narratorial omniscience and limited perspective. This more private or personal perspective marks the beginning of the increasing self-consciousness or introversion of the new narrative mode, and it marks too, as a consequence, the breaking of the traditional molds of fiction, for if the experience to be portrayed is avowedly subjective, then form itself will become more and more a matter of individual style. Novels written in this way will be markedly original and of course strikingly problematical. However, it must be emphasized that this originality is recognizable only in terms of the conventions from which the work deviates and therefore needs as its implied referent. The year 1902 would seem to confirm this generalisation, for in that year were published four novels by young writers, each of which by virtue of its form alone signalled its essential difference from the prevailing fictional mode. Pio Baroja's *Camino de perfección*, Miguel de Unamuno's *Amor y pedagogía*, Ramón del Valle-Inclán's *Sonata de otoño*, and José Martínez Ruiz's (Azorín's) *La voluntad*. This last novel could be said to epitomise the new approach to the representation of reality in fiction. One of the most striking features of *La voluntad* is the manner in which the chronology of the narrative is broken up to undermine the sense of linear progression which gave the Realist novel its formal unity. Human experience, Azorín suggests, is not necessarily understood in terms of causal explanation and temporal development, which are the habitual orders of understanding. In an attempt to break the traditional mode of thought, Azorín replaces linearity and succession with fragmentation and discontinuity, in his own words "fragmentos, sensacio-nes separadas." Azorín's rejection of plot in this respect is crucial, and his conviction that "no debe haber fábula ... la vida no tiene fábula, es diversa, multiforme, ondulante, contradictoria"[17] anticip-ates Víctor Goti's assertion in *Niebla* (1913) that the *nivola* "no tiene argumento."[18] Even Baroja imagines that a novel is possible "sin argumento."[19] Azorín, in creating a collage of disparate elements — description, dialogue, scraps from newspapers, anecdotes and so on — confounds our sense of logical development and linear sequence and thereby suggests both the difficulties and potential varieties of the modes of knowing. Moreover, he conveys something of the chaos of experience before it has been rationally ordered. However, given the mind's resistance to disorder, works like *La voluntad* may be said to involve the reader in the act of creation in that he is forced to create an order out of the apparent chaos of the work, which is itself controlled inevitably by being contained within the fictional form, and make sense of a world which at first may seem totally inaccessible. The novel becomes a kind of laboratory where philosophical ideas and novelistic theory are worked out in conjunc-tion, and some novelists, aware that language cannot be trusted to give an adequate account of the world, and aware too that narration involves the imposition of a plot upon the world, turn away from the confrontation with reality to explore only the worlds created by the imagination. Thus the movement away from Realism takes different forms: towards the refined, elaborate literary world of a writer like Ramón Pérez de Ayala, where the rules of art take precedence over all else, towards the *nivola* of Unamuno, where the peculiarity of the writer's philosophical preoccupations lies parallel to the peculiarity of narrative form, towards the apparently late-Realist novels of Baroja, where all is seemingly directly towards the effacement of art in pur-suit of the immediacy of experience.

Modernism, then, represents the coming of a new age character-ised by an extreme self-consciousness and a tendency towards anti-representational art which strives to overcome the real and create a new order of art. But, of course, like Realism, Modernism is no monolith and can be construed only as a set of works exhibiting certain family likenesses. Some of the following features at least will, however, be characteristic of any Modernist novel. The familiar forms of the external world are taken and distorted in accordance with the author's vision. This in part is what was meant by Ortega y Gasset's compelling description of the "deshumanización del arte," and a corollary of it is that the reader is no longer expected to respond to the text in purely human terms (i.e., in terms of involvement, say, with the characters as though they were real individuals) but rather to respond to it as an aesthetic object in its own right.[20] Any simple identification between art and life is rejected, any single view of real-ity is shown to be deficient. Modernism is a literature of crisis, and this crisis is felt most acutely in the novel which had established itself as the genre which had engaged most directly with reality. The early moderns, in a sense, were true to this aim, in that their quarrel with the Realists was initially on the grounds that Realism was not sufficiently real. Unamuno describes "el llamado realismo" as a "cosa puramente externa, aparencial, cortical y anecdótica."[21] Furthermore, if time is no longer considered as a sequence nor history as a process of causal evolution, the novel can no longer limit itself to narrating events. It constructs an alternative order of relations, based on metaphor or form, justifying itself as a total self-sustaining image rather than as a reflection of some other reality beyond itself.

Such a version of Modernism may not seem immediately apparent when one comes to consider some of the earliest experimental novels of this century in Spain. Baroja's *Camino de perfección,* for example, is relatively straightforward in terms of narrative technique, and its structure is broadly linear and sequential. The only obvious narrative experiment is the change of narrative voice between first and third-person narrator, which indicates an insecurity or uncertainty on the author's part as to how he should mediate his material and, more importantly, betrays a concern with perspective in that there is an implicit acknowledgement that the way in which reality is perceived modifies that reality. One character in the novel, Nicolás Polentinos, asserts that "la vida no es más que una ilusión. Cada uno ve el mundo a su manera," and the protagonist himself, Fernando Ossorio, insists that "el mundo de afuera no existe; tiene la realidad que yo le quiero dar."[22] This questioning of the truth of the external world is something very characteristic of Modernism and is a central preoccupation of Baroja's *El árbol de la ciencia*. The discussion of this problem in the central section of the novel, entitled "Inquisiciones," is an excellent illustration of the insecurity of the Modernist writer. Although apparently identified with the protagonist, Andrés, the author, in this part of the novel, undergoes a process of interior duplication (analogous but not identical to that of José Martínez Ruiz and Antonio Azorín in *La voluntad*) by means of which the author expresses his inner conflict through the contrasting opinions of Andrés and his interlocutor, Iturrioz. Here each point of view is subjected to its opposite, just as in the novel the events of the narrative appear to conflict with the philosophy which is progressively built up within it. *El árbol de la ciencia*, in its undermining of its own apparent philosophical perspective, is characteristic of the insecurity and ambivalence of literary Modernism. But more significantly, there are serious implications for the novelistic representation of reality, for traditional mimesis, in Andrés' recognition that there is no all-embracing explanation of the universe and that there is no reality outside individual consciousness: "el mundo no tiene realidad; es que ese espacio y ese tiempo y ese principio de causalidad no existen fuera de nosotros tal como nosotros los vemos, que pueden ser distintos, que pueden no existir."[23] What is real is simply what we experience. Intelligence, or reason, cannot apprehend this reality but merely try to explain it in terms of its own, that is, reason's, characteristics. It is precisely this sense of insecurity about the true nature of reality which generates the most radical experimentation with the forms of fiction. Traditionally the novel has tended towards the real, and the novelist has traditionally taken for granted that to narrate is to represent a reality which exists prior to and independent of the act of narration. This is not to say that for the Realist there were no problems in writing — of presentation, selection, and so on — for of course there were, but the point is that writing was not considered to be problematical in itself. Expression followed from observation, and the work produced was in some measure faithful to the reality it copied. Realism is, as we have seen, much more than simply a copy, but in so far as language stands for reality it was considered to be unproblematically at the service of the Realist project, transparent and essentially an instrument which was taken for granted, as distinct from explored, in the narrative itself. This, in fact, is the most characteristic attitude to language in fiction and it persists well beyond the nineteenth century and indeed well beyond Modernism. From a formal point of view, the Realist novel's acceptance of a common phenomenal world that may be reliably transcribed more or less as history is embodied in the persistent use of third-person, past-tense narratives which appear to imply some kind of wider context, some reality greater than that contained within the confines of the consciousness of any one individual. Thus one of the principal ways in which the Modernist novel differs from its Realist predecessor is precisely through the increased attention it affords to consciousness, both in the sense of the creative consciousness of the novelist himself and in the more general sense of the workings of the mind. Naturally this cannot be divorced from Modernism's formal experimentation, for both imply a situation of crisis between the artist and the world and also between the work and the world. Hence Modernist novels frequently convey a sense of loss and alienation, and it is this aspect of *Camino de perfección*, for example, which sets it out as an early Modernist work. If, in the nineteenth century, novelists were primarily interested in conscious social behavior, for twentieth-century novelists consciousness is something complex, intense and mysterious. They recognise that man is driven by obscure forces and inhabits a world which lacks the overall meaning formerly provided by religion. It could even be said that the energy once devoted to achieving salvation in former times now finds a new outlet in the restless search for self-knowledge. It is a fundamental paradox of Modernist art that it asserts, on the one hand, that existence is quite senseless and yet, on the other, it never abandons the search for order and meaning amidst the apparent chaos of the modern situation. For many Modernists, it is art alone which provides that order. Art is one way of reintegrating the disparate elements of a lost unitary reality; the coherence of art provides the order and meaning which are absent in everyday experience. Such a role for art is sought by Fernando Ossorio, the protagonist of *Camino de perfección*, who is presented as a complex and hypersensitive personality whose disorientation and detachment from reality are initially explained in terms of the importance of childhood experiences on his adult psyche: lack of parental affection, ideological conflict, sexual repression, religious education, alienation from prevailing conventions, experience of death. Ossorio emerges as a man without identity, a mere succession of *personae*, in whose case the normal relationship between the self and the world breaks down to be replaced by fragmentation and disjuncture. Nothing could be further from the nineteenth-century concept of the symbiotic relation between the self and the world in which each sustained the other. The novel, modelled on the archetypal pattern of the journey, takes the form of a quest for identity, a process involving a movement from alienation to integration. The extent of that final integration is never made fully clear, however, and *Camino de perfección* shares that characteristic of failing to conclude with very many Modernist novels, of which Unamuno's *Niebla* is perhaps the most striking Spanish example.

Niebla recalls Galdós' *El amigo Manso* in that it focusses on the fictionality of the protagonist in a way that undermines the realistic expectations of the conventional reader. It has always been held that Unamuno's aim in doing this, and the motive behind his other novelistic tricks, is to use the novel as a vehicle for exploring his own very individualistic and agonic philosophy of existence. At its most basic, the relationship of the fictional character to the author provides an analogue of man's relationship to God and a framework for discovering the sources of identity and exploring the age-old question of free will versus determinism. Most criticism, even when it is concerned with form, has tended to read the novel in search of a statement of the author's beliefs on these great issues. It would, of course, be absurd to claim that these questions have no relevance whatsoever to *Niebla*, but the point is surely that experimentation with fictional form implies a concern above all with fictional form. Moreover, a novel differs formally from a philosophical essay and will itself affect the ideology by creating its own meanings. In other words, it gives a literary form to ideas expressed elsewhere but without that form, and thus inevitably links, in this case, existential questions with fictional questions. It is this concern which marks out *Niebla* as a significant Modernist work.

What this means in effect is that Unamuno's *nivola*, as he chose to call it, abandons the Realist convention of disguising as far as possible the devices that have gone into the novel's production, in

31

other words, of making the medium as transparent as possible. *Niebla* openly problematises all narrative conventions — time, plot, character, beginning and ending, point of view, and so on — to indicate precisely the dissonance between narrative form and brute reality. In Realism there is purported to be a perfect match between the fictional forms and the received forms of reality in the society which Realism reflects and at which it is directed. It is the innocence of such a view that *Niebla* aims to destroy. In the process the boundaries of fiction are altered, but as well as attempting to release the potentialities of fiction, *Niebla* paradoxically reveals its inherent limitations. Realism is its inevitable point of reference, and any reader of the Prologue, once he has realised that Víctor Goti is a fictional character within the very novel itself, is struck by the way in which it subverts traditional narrative conventions by calling attention to the relationship between the real and the fictional and to the status of the fictional character. Moreover, the Prologue highlights other issues of concern to the reader: the deliberate confusions of the text, its ambivalent tone, its existential preoccupations and, above all, its "inesperado final" which the fictional prologuist challenges. This is the sense in which I mean that there is a connection between narrative fictions and existential fictions. In drawing an analogy between the freedom of the individual and the freedom of a fictional character Unamuno points up a possible dissonance between the world of the novel and the real world, or perhaps between narrative fictions and existential fictions, in the sense that whereas the latter may postulate that man is free, the former of necessity involve the limitation of freedom. Quite simply, a fictional character cannot do what he likes. But in a more general way, too, the prologues explicitly raise the question of man's need for fictions in the face of death: "si nos han arrebatado nuestra más cara y más íntima esperanza vital, ¿para qué no hemos de confundirlo todo para matar el tiempo y la eternidad y para vengarnos?" Fictions, existential or narrative, are the impositions of plots upon the face of reality, the means by which men create patterns in what is only chaos: a novel provides a satisfying order of beginning, middle and end. Yet to the extent that we are aware of its fictionality we are conscious of the void that separates it from the world of common perception. Modernist fiction, of which *Niebla* is a prime example, is enacted in the fertile intermediate terrain of this void. We could say that a novel like *Niebla* frustrates our conventional expectations, but in a way that produces a recognition on our part of something we might have otherwise been unaware of. In order to achieve this, it has had to play with the conventional forms and thereby assume the reader's familiarity with them. *Niebla*, of course, works by emphasising its difference not only from "ordinary reality" but also from the discourse of traditional narrative. *Niebla* signals itself not just as literature but as deviant literature. If traditional realism is held to impose an order on its material, in *Niebla* order is confronted with the random, logic with chance. As Augusto says: "El mundo es un caleidoscopio. La lógica la pone el hombre." Fiction can make kaleidoscopic patterns in an apparently arbitrary way, and so *Niebla*, whose initial story concerns a young man awakening to, and suffering from, the experience of love, looks increasingly inward, as it progresses, at its own genesis, its own narrative tactics. Víctor, in a famous exposition of the theory behind the novel, stresses its freedom of form, created in the process of creating, liberated from the accepted categories of plot. Paradoxically, this entails a rapprochement with life which is itself free (without order) until a plot is imposed upon it. Víctor's *nivola* partakes of the existentialist freedom to create and therefore operates with an absence of character, at least of character in the sense of something fixed in advance. The character of the *nivola* is created as he acts, and therefore the author's presence in the narrative will be diminished as far as possible. Victor thus provides an analysis, in a characteristically Modernist introversion of the text, within the text itself. Moreover, he provides his description of the treatment of character to the novel's main character. Looking back at the way Augusto has been presented confirms Víctor's description. Augusto appears in the opening pages, but his physical appearance is barely alluded to, for the emphasis is placed on his eccentric inner life. Similarly, only marginal significance is accorded to external reality, and indeed the ironical references to it undermine its importance. Augusto is not molded by reality, he appears to be more or less detached from it. Thus those two central features of character definition in fiction — physical appearance and social or environmental context — are virtually eliminated. Nevertheless there is no mistaking that he is a character, so that even if from an existentialist point of view there is no such thing as character, in a novel it seems that there is. And similarly, although it also claimed that there is no plot, a novel is difficult to conceive without one, however unusual. Thus, although the form of *Niebla* appears to confirm Goti's theories, on closer inspection it will be seen that it disproves them. The relation of fiction to reality becomes rather subtle. The nineteenth-century pattern is broken down to create a more modern, more real analogue of life, but the conventions of fiction impose themselves in a manner which undermines the theory. The reader seeks a character; the reader constructs a plot. However, if Augusto is a character, he is still a character without identity, and in his confidences to his dog, Orfeo, he relates his lack of identity to questions of past and future. Here too, then, the novelist must engage in a contract with time, even if it is through the character's wish to project himself onto the future. In any novel, however, a future is only meaningful in terms of a past. In other words, the end of the novel harks back to its beginning. For all the appearance of arbitrariness in the text, there are causal connections which it is possible to make. On the most basic level of plot, Augusto's death is a consequence of his search for identity, and a novel is a novel, not life, precisely because it insists on relations of this kind. Needless to say, this does not mean that the ending is always in some sense predictable. *Niebla* is impressive because of the shock effect of its ending, which is not just unusual by virtue of the logic and coherence of the narrative, but because the very relationship of fiction to reality is intrinsic to its effect. It is a common expectation of readers that novels provide through their order confirmation that experience itself has order, and yet there is simultaneously the recognition that artistic order is not true to experience. Most novels hold the balance between these two perspectives and attempt to disguise the patterns of literature as the patterns of life. Novels begin and above all end, and it is the ending which seems to impart an order which is not present in reality. Hence, in a novel like *Niebla*, the problematical nature of the ending: the author's decision is not the final word. His view had been undermined from the beginning of Víctor Goti's prologue, and the last word, in fact, is left to the dog Orfeo. More accurately, it is left to Ludivina. Before Orfeo's oration Unamuno comments on the classic endings of the nineteenth-century novel in which the destinies of all the main characters are recounted, and he himself refuses adamantly to follow their precedent. This is much more than the conventional open ending which lays stress on life's ambiguities and uncertainties (and is thus paradoxically closer to the texture of real experience than the classic closed ending). It is rather an exposure of the contradictions inherent in the production of the literary text, and therefore it does not seem excessive to argue that *Niebla*, a novel initially concerned with the question of existential choice — the creation of the self through action and relation with the other — explores the problems of working out that question in narrative form. If life is mere contingency, can that be represented in fiction? If man has no character, can a fictional character have none? If man is totally free, can a novelistic character ever represent this? Thus the latter part of *Niebla* grows self-consciously out of the first part. It is not the logical narrative outcome of the plot as it is first presented, but its concerns are entirely germane to it. *Niebla* focusses on the ways in which the real is constructed by language in any text, however realistic, and aims not to reach some final stage of Truth but to deconstruct the conventions of realist practice. It is not for nothing that the unreal nature of language is emphasized in the text. Orfeo says that man "habla, y eso le ha servido para inventar lo que no hay y no fijarse en lo que hay. En cuanto él ha puesto un nombre a algo ya no ve este algo. — La lengua le sirve para mentir, inventar lo que no hay y confundirse." To this extent language itself is unreal, and Orfeo's remark anticipates in a curious way Roland Barthes' later formulation: "Le réalisme, ici, ne peut donc être la copie des choses mais la connaissance du langage. L'oeuvre la plus

34

réaliste ne sera pas celle qui 'peint' la réalité mais qui ... explorera le plus profondément possible la *réalité irréelle* du langage."[24]

It is in this sense that *Niebla* presents itself for what it is: a linguistic fiction, and in the discussion between Augusto and Víctor the invention of fictions, "charlar, sutilizar, jugar con las palabras y los vocablos," is a response to "la conciencia de la muerte incesante." The text is a kind of mirror of itself, not an attempt at imitating the empirical world, but looking inward at its own linguistic and literary reality. The characters' self-presentation as fictional beings prepares the way for the dramatic intervention in the novel of Unamuno himself. But although this is how critics have seen the intervention, the fact is that Unamuno cannot enter the novel any more than Augusto can leave it. The Unamuno in *Niebla* is another fictional character invented by Unamuno and given certain attributes of himself to create an identification between the character and the author, in order to highlight the real nature of his literary production. But despite the apparent non-existence of Augusto, the fact is, as he points out, that once a character is created he escapes the hand of the author and through his interaction with the reader pushes the author in to a peculiar non-existence. Augusto, moreover, attempts to demolish the Great Man theory of literature: the author is not the sole generating force of a text: "No sea que usted no pase de ser un pretexto para que mi historia llegue al mundo." This is a clear enunciation of the structuralist paradox that it is not the writer that writes the narrative but the narrative that writes the writer. In addition, narratives have their own logic of coherence, they operate according to conventions, which is what Augusto means when he says that "Hasta los llamados entes de ficción tienen su lógica interna." In theory, a novelist can do anything, but in practice he cannot put too great a strain on the reader's credulity. A character grows out of what has gone before: he has a past from which the reader will not willingly see him break free. To this degree, the discovery we make about the nature of narrative fiction is dependent upon the shock which is administered to our conventional expectations, but the fact that we are shocked shows how heavily conventionalised the reading experience is. Augusto's suicide is not out of place in the novel, for it is in the very logic of Augusto's progress up to that point. The dissonant element is "Unamuno's" intervention; although it reveals a virtually self-evident truth about the fictional character's freedom, this is a truth which we find convenient to overlook for the duration of the reading experience. *Niebla* contributes to the progressive extension of the limits of the novel by altering the relationships between the paradigms of fictions and what we take to be reality. But in its exploitation of our reading conventions it acknowledges its need for them. However radical or schismatic *Niebla* may seem, it still exhibits a continuity with fictional tradition, and that tradition has rendered difficult the full narrative articulation of its existential message.

Unamuno shows his character to have been created, and the novel itself is inevitably a form which encourages the reader to see patterns in what might only be contingency. The most that can be said is that Unamuno uses formal stratagems to undermine the determinism of plot, the finality of the end, but when he does so he is exploring literary, as distinct from existential, questions.

Niebla, then, shows that concern with theory through the practice of fiction that is characteristic of Modernism. There is within it a movement away from the representation of external reality towards problems of the perception and creation of reality in the light of the inadequacies of language and the weight of novelistic tradition. At the same time, it postulates an opening up of the genre and tilts against the constraints of plot, linearity, and character portrayal and in so doing creates a work characterised by paradox and doubt which makes severe demands on the reader's understanding. *Niebla* partakes of the curiously double-edged quality of many Modernist works which seem to hold out the prospect of intelligibility but never fully yield it up.

Just as *Niebla* has most frequently been read as an expression of the agonic Unamuno, so has *San Manuel Bueno, mártir* been construed as his final statement on immortality and faith, positing the need for simple, if unfounded, faith (or illusion) in the face of the terrible truth of reason. In fact, even at this level, the novel is far from being unproblematical, for in it can be discerned a continuity of, rather than a break with, the central Unamunian preoccupations. But from the point of view of Modernism, it is the novel's capacity to generate a plurality of meaning which will be the prime focus of critical attention. This inevitably raises once again the question of what is truth. Man's deep-rooted desire, his fundamental need to perpetuate himself, are at the basis of his religious feelings, but the will to live, the yearning for immortality, are confounded by logic and reason. Thus a definition of truth can be what we really believe and not the something revealed by reason, which stands against the vital impulse.

That *San Manuel Bueno, mártir* intends to liberate itself from the limitations of specific circumstances is evidenced in the setting of the novel in the mythical village of Valverde de Lucerna, which is not conceived of as a real place. It stands outside history and is associated with a kind of timelessness. Any putative realism which the text might appear to convey is also undermined by the style of the opening paragraph, which is not the natural language one might expect from the peasant, female narrator but rather is studied and formal. The first sentence extends to fill the whole paragraph. Indeed, we might feel that the tone of the narration is hagiographical and the text has some of the resonances of the Evangelical accounts of the life of Jesus, to whom Manuel is constantly likened — by his use of his words, by the linking of his mother to the Virgin Mary, by parallels between his acts and those of Christ. If we are to see this identification as complete, then we are presented with a new version of the Gospel story, one which reveals the appalling truth that Christ himself did not believe but instilled in others the consolations of faith. However, the fact that the novel is mediated by a first-person narrator who is not, apparently, the main character has important consequences. It means, for example, that what we learn of Don Manuel is of necessity at least second-hand and conceivably nothing more than the creation of an individual subjectivity. Angela, indeed, is the principal source of the ambiguity of the narrative. The way in which the narrative is presented reveals firstly the public face of Don Manuel and then hints about something deeper begin to appear. But however much we seem to approach the "inner" Don Manuel, he continues to remain in some strange way remote. What is the "real" Don Manuel, the "yo íntimo" as distinct from the more public "obras" which can both reveal and conceal it? The narrative, moreover, extends its deft exploration to this question of the narrator herself, whose confident opening contrasts with her doubting presence at the end — about her story, about the priest, about herself. In a sense, the narrative does not end; it simply dissolves. But if we consider Angela further, we might conclude that for all that the novel appears to focus on Don Manuel, it is largely about her, and the narrative written "a modo de confesión" is the process by which she sorts out her own emotions, her own relationship with Don Manuel. C.A. Longhurst has convincingly argued the case for a strong sexual attraction on Angela's part towards the priest and suggests that Angela's account, which casts doubt on his sanctity, is connected with Don Manuel's pending canonisation.[25] The novel then can be read as a dramatisation of the conflict between faith and reason, or an allegory of the life of Christ, or as an illustration of the fragility of human personality, or as the distorted account of a girl's emotional entanglement with her priest. It is this latter dimension, grossly simplified in the preceding sentences, which points in the direction of the most suggestive reading of *San Manuel Bueno, mártir*. Angela herself wonders whether what she is writing is totally subjective: as a narrator all she narrates is her own consciousness, and this realisation is followed by a whole series of questions about the nature of belief. Inevitably this raises the question of authority in narrative and, in keeping with the subject of this very intriguing novel, it extends to the question of the reliability of the Gospels themselves. But there is more. Having completed Angela's narrative, behind which he has effaced himself for the rest of the novel, Unamuno himself appears as narrator in the final chapter. The effect of this is to remind us that we are dealing with a work of fiction, and Unamuno characteristically affirms the superiority of imaginative literature over history. The account Angela gives us is a kind of reality, but presumably only for her and for those who believe in it, and so the novel is made to dramatise the process of narrative and highlights the relationship of literary fictions to existential fictions. A fiction is a pattern imposed upon reality, an interpretation, and our interpretations of literary works extend this process of constructing significant fictions. This perception is pre-eminently Modernist.

To this all too brief account of a very complex and rewarding novel we might add something about the way in which the novel is patterned around a small nucleus of symbols, themselves susceptible to varying levels of interpretation. The very elusiveness of these symbols — the lake, the mountain, the wind, the submerged village — give them their poetic force. The lake, for example, is associated with death, with Spain's timeless religious tradition, with "intra-historia," whereas the mountain symbolises faith, illusion, spirituality. Thus the snow falling dies in the lake but lies on the mountain. But these are not opposites: the goatgirl, who seems to embody tradition, stands on the mountainside; the lake, too, can be associated with faith, which for Angela lies like the submerged village within Don Manuel. But for him the village can represent that awful truth hidden by faith and illusion which is the lake. The village and the mountain reflected in the lake can refer, too, to the mysterious nature of personality, forever condemned to insubstantiality. In these ways *San Manuel Bueno, mártir* articulates its own problematic at the level of its own formal structures. Shunning history and the reality of the world of common perception, it confronts the implications of its own fictionality, probes its own meaning as narrative, not in any narcissistic act of self-contemplation, but in terms of the increasingly complex relationship between our conceptions of reality and the forms of our fictions.

This brief and selective examination of some novels produced in Spain between 1876 and 1930 will, I hope, suffice to establish the parameters of the study which follows. While there is little doubt that the new novel of the twentieth century differs from its Realist predecessor, it is not really possible in the case of Spanish literature, even if it is for European literature generally (and this is arguable), to posit a complete schism between the two. We have seen that the Realist novel contains elements which come to artistic fruition in the Modernist novel and that the Modernist novel relies on conventions which are part of the Realist legacy. Moreover, the example and inspiration of Cervantes clearly underlie both modes. What the progression from the Realist to the Modernist novel shows, though, is the increasing complexity of our understanding of reality and the increasing refinement and modification of the fictions which we use to relate to it. In successive chapters this process will be explored through the works of Ramón Pérez de Ayala, the most intellectual and most self-consciously literary writer of the early twentieth century in Spain. These chapters will isolate those features of Modernist fiction adumbrated here: its profound theoretical concern, its search for alternative modes of ordering, its exploration of consciousness, its self-referentiality, its appropriation of and relation to existing literary modes and texts, and its concern with language. We shall thereby see the extent to which Pérez de Ayala both continues the tradition of Realism and deviates from it, and how his own very distinctive fictions conform to and enlarge our conception of Modernism, which for many represents the peak of the artistic achievement of our age.

NOTES

[1]Guillermo Díaz Plaja, *Modernismo frente a noventa y ocho* (Madrid: Gredos, 1959); Donald L. Shaw, *The Generation of 1898 in Spain* (London: Benn, 1975).

[2]A good illustration of this kind of approach is H. Ramsden, *The 1898 Movement in Spain* (Manchester: M.U.P., 1974). A useful corrective is J. Butt, "The Generation of 1898: A Critical Fallacy," *Forum for Modern Language Studies* (1980):136-52.

[3]This classic structuralist definition is enshrined in the title of Claudio Guillén's important work *Literature as System* (Princeton: Princeton University Press, 1971).

[4]*The Education of Henry Adams* (Boston: Houghton Mifflin Co., 1918) 457.

[5]David Lodge, *The Modes of Modern Writing. Metaphor, Metonymy, and the Typology of Modern Literature* (London: Edward Arnold, 1977).

[6]David Lodge, "Modernism, Anti-Modernism and Postmodernism," *The New Review* 4.38 (May 1977):42.

[7]For a good account of Realist theory and practice through the analysis of a number of significant novels drawn from different national literatures, see *The Monster in the Mirror. Studies in Nineteenth-Century Realism*, ed. D.A. Williams (Hull/Oxford: O.U.P., 1978).

[8]In this respect *Tormento* contains some of the features of the narcissistic text: it looks inward at its own processes and makes a statement not only about our moral perceptions but also about our imaginative constructs.

[9]An excellent analysis of the novel in terms of the characters and their moral behavior is provided by Eamonn Rodgers in his critical introduction to his edition of *Tormento* (Oxford: Pergamon, 1979).

[10]Galdós' writing on the novel can be usefully consulted in Benito Pérez Galdós, *Ensayos de crítica literaria*, ed. L. Bonet (Barcelona: Península, 1972).

[11]David Lodge, *Working with Structuralism* (London: Routledge and Kegan Paul, 1981) 22.

¹²Emile Zola, Préface to *Les Rougon-Macquart* (Paris: Gallimard, 1960) I:xix.

¹³G. Genette, "Discours du récit," in *Figures III* (Paris: Seuil, 1972).

¹⁴Wilhelm Worringer, *Abstraction and Empathy: A Contribution to the Psychology of Style* (London: Routledge and Kegan Paul, 1953).

¹⁵This could take the form of the exaggerated realism of the so-called 'tremendistas' or of the extreme of objectivity achieved, say, by Rafael Sánchez Ferlosio in *El Jarama*. A celebrated expression of the ideal of objectivism is that of Christopher Isherwood: "I am a camera with its shutter open, quite passive, recording, not thinking," *Goodbye to Berlin* (Harmondsworth; Penguin, 1965) 7.

¹⁶See Jonathan Culler, *Saussure* (Glasgow: Fontana, 1976), Chapter 4, especially pp. 114-17, and his earlier piece in "Modernism: A Symposium," *The New Review* 10 (January 1975):13-18.

¹⁷José Martínez Ruiz, *La voluntad*, ed. E. Inman Fox, (Madrid: Castalia, 1968) 133. It is interesting to compare this with B.S. Johnson's later and similar remark: "Life does not tell stories. Life is chaotic, fluid, random, it leaves myriads of ends untied, untidily," *Aren't You Rather Young to be Writing Your Memoirs?* (London: Hutchinson, 1973) 14.

¹⁸Miguel de Unamuno, Niebla (Madrid: Espasa-Calpe, 1968) 40.

¹⁹Pío Baroja, *La nave de los locos, Obras completas* (Madrid: Biblioteca Nueva, 1948) IV:326.

²⁰José Ortega y Gasset, *La deshumanización del arte, Obras completas* (Madrid: Revista de Occidente, 1957) III.

²¹Miguel de Unamuno, *Tres novelas ejemplares y un prólogo, Obras completas* (Madrid: Afrodisio Aguado, 1958) IX:415.

²²Pío Baroja, *Camino de perfección* (Madrid: Caro Raggio, 1974) 133.

²³Pío Baroja, *El árbol de la ciencia* (Madrid: Alianza, 1969) 126.

²⁴Roland Barthes, "La littérature aujourd'hui," *Essais critiques* (Paris: Seuil, 1964):164.

²⁵C.A. Longhurst, "The Problem of Truth in San Manuel Bueno, mártir," *Modern Language Review* 76 (1981):581-97. Also his critical edition of *San Manuel Bueno, mártir* and *La novela de don Sandalio* (Manchester: Manchester University Press, 1984).

CHAPTER TWO
THE INTEGRAL NOVEL:
PEREZ DE AYALA AND THE THEORY OF FICTION

While Ramón Pérez de Ayala is one of the most highly self-conscious Spanish novelists of his generation, he wrote remarkably little about the art of fiction. The essays collected under the title of *Principios y finales de la novela*[1] are, on the whole, disappointing in their critical insights, and any compendium of statements which, taken together, might be said to constitute a consistent and systematic view of narrative is the product not of Pérez de Ayala himself, but of critics who have gleaned his theoretical position from his prodigious output of essays and articles.[2] These, of which the most important collections are *Las máscaras* (1917 and 1919) and *Divagaciones literarias* (1958), are mostly *pièces d'occasion* and were provoked by specific plays or works that the author happened to be reading at the time. Nevertheless, it is perhaps surprising that Ayala, with his fondness for constructing elaborate philosophical and intellectual systems, did not try to establish a poetics of fiction. That he did not do so is perhaps an indication of his awareness of the impossibility of such an enterprise, given the wide diversity of forms which proliferate and are encompassed within the term "novel." In fact, writing in *Helios* as early as 1903, Ayala argued for an acceptance of this very diversity. Commenting on the great variety of literary movements motivated by a spirit of "anarquismo estético," he observes:

> En la novela sobre todo se ha llegado al triunfo completo del individualismo atómico a partir de la bancarrota de la escuela naturalista. Hoy cada escritor escribe su novela sin prejuicios de técnica ya definida ni preocupaciones de bando, y el público los alienta a todos. No hay una novela concebida específicamente y que predomine sobre los demás: hay la novela in genere, que cada cual entiende a su modo.[3]

In this climate of novelistic pluralism, no one style is dominant. The most celebrated expression of this in Spanish is, of course, Pío Baroja's oft-quoted assertion that "la novela, hoy por hoy, es un género multiforme, proteico, en formación, en fermentación; lo abarca todo: el libro filosófico, el libro psicológico, la aventura, la utopía, lo épico; todo absolutamente."[4] However, a consequence of the existence of such a situation, intrinsically liberating in itself, is that it tends to create in writers a state of uncertainty or insecurity which manifests itself in the self-consciousness of the works they produce. Ayala was writing at that most critical time in the history of the novel, the turn of the century, when the most basic assumptions underlying the writing of fiction were beginning to be seriously questioned. The novel, both in terms of its formal properties and of its relationship to reality and experience, becomes increasingly problematical. This phenomenon is summarised most succinctly by Bernard Bergonzi:

> The tradition of nineteenth-century realism, which underlies most contemporary fiction, depended on a degree of relative stability in three separate areas: the idea of reality; the nature of the fictional form; and the kind of relationship that might predictably exist between them ... It goes without saying that for many twentieth-century novelists and critics this assumption is no longer credible.[5]

As well as highlighting the nature of the crisis that characterises the movement from the Realist to the Modernist novel, Bergonzi's observation also calls attention to the two central strands that must be written into any definition of the novel. These two tendencies have been categorised by R. Kellogg and R. Scholes in their important work *The Nature of Narrative*[6] as the empirical and the fictional: the empirical mode tends towards the real and approximates to history and mimesis; the fictional mode tends towards the ideal and approximates to romance and allegory. For the former, the novel is essentially an imitative mode portraying the lives, feelings, experiences of people in their social context and inviting confirmation in terms of the reader's own experience of the real world. For the latter, the novel seeks no such confirmation. It does not run parallel to history or sociology, but aims to delight, instruct and create an object of beauty in its own right. The modern novel is a synthesis of these two tendencies, and this imparts to it its all-embracing nature. In the early twentieth century, the latter strand is reinforced by a heavily symbolist bias which is clearly discernible in Pérez de Ayala's pronouncements on the nature of art (for he tended to write in terms of art rather than of fiction as such). Contingency, lifelikeness, realism are set against form, aesthetic wholeness, design and pattern. This broad distinction, which we find in many critics of fiction, and the opposition and ultimate synthesis which it can imply, is central to any consideration of the novels of Pérez de Ayala. He is in every sense, to use David Lodge's suggestive term, a "novelist at the crossroads."[7]

Most of Ayala's ideas on fiction are woven into the texture of the novels themselves, and therefore it is to them, rather than to his critical writings, that one must turn in order to understand his contribution to the poetics of fiction. In fact, the theoretical element in Ayala's fiction has earned him the almost universally applied title of "intellectual" and has led to the coining of the term "novela-ensayo" to characterise his work. He himself, in a celebrated text, affirmed his own view of the essay as being the core of modern literature:

El género literario llamado "ensayo" es un producto del injerto de la ciencia en la literatura. De consiguiente, el ensayo recaba para sí la categoría de punto de referencia con que emplazar y apreciar la evolución de los géneros literarios clásicos en la literatura moderna. Lo típico de todos estos géneros (la acción en el drama, la narración en la novela, el metro y la rima en la poesía) se ha atenuado cuando no se ha esfumado por completo en el estado actual de su evolución, estado de transición, a mi juicio. En cambio, todos ellos se han anudado al ensayo con íntimos lazos conyugales. Y, recíprocamente, el ensayo embebe e irradia, a menudo, emoción dramática, emoción novelesca, emoción lírica.[8]

In the present chapter, Ayala's broad position will be sketched by reference to the most markedly theoretical parts of his novels and to some of his more characteristic pronouncements on art and, less frequently, on fiction, which collectively constitute the basis of his poetics. This is important, for it would be a mistake to conceive of Pérez de Ayala as writing fiction to a previously elaborated formula, as if an idea were separable from its expression in language. In an essay on Juan de la Cueva, collected in *Las máscaras*, Ayala denies that the artist works from an *a priori* theoretical position: "En arte, jamás la teoría antecede a la práctica. El artista sabe lo que hace y cómo lo hace y para qué lo hace; pero lo sabe en el momento de estar haciéndolo, con un conocimiento tan profundo y activo que su manera más adecuada de expresión es la creación misma" (III:265). This notion, apparently paradoxical, that the artist's priorities are worked out in the actual process of creation itself, has been articulated more recently by Malcolm Bradbury in his rejection of the notion of writing as a question of prior content seeking an appropriate form: ". . . we surely must say that the action imitated exists for the writer simultaneously with that which has to be written (that which motivates and directs the compositional process) and that which is worked, achieved, realized in the writing."[9] To some extent, this is the posture I wish to adopt in my analysis of Ayala's fiction, for not only does he, like any writer, choose and change as he writes, but he also, as he writes, consciously works out formal and aesthetic problems through the medium of the evolving fiction.

As we have seen, the period 1900 to 1930 corresponds to the high point of literary modernism which is characterised by its own sense of historical discontinuity with the preceding period. Pérez de Ayala himself shows his awareness of the radical break that occurred between the nineteenth and the twentieth centuries, although he makes no attempt to account for it:

si comparamos los escritos de cualquier autor joven con los de un autor de fines del siglo XIX, hallaremos, con evidencia incontestable, que difieren por la ideología y la estética, por los conceptos y por el léxico, por la manera de pensar y por la manera de escribir.[10]

Ayala is aware of the loss of coherence in the modern world and refers explicitly to "una ruptura en la unidad de las ideas." He refuses, however, to endorse any self-conscious innovation for its own sake, qualifying as "ridícula vulgaridad eso de afanarse en hacer algo nuevo, que nunca se había hecho antes." For Ayala there is a fundamental seriousness about the pursuit of art, just as there is a permanence in art itself which transcends the fashions of the historical moment. Pérez de Ayala's modernism is both innovatory and traditionalist.

There is, nonetheless, in Ayala's view, a fundamental change in both outlook and expression on the part of twentieth-century artists, and the implication is that historical changes in literary fictions correspond to changes in knowledge, that the modes of fiction are constantly modified and adjusted to take account of changing modes of perception, of the changing paradigms by which experience is ordered and made comprehensible. The fact that reality has become increasingly resistant to ordering has made fiction itself increasingly difficult and problematical. Changes in fiction themselves do, of course, meet resistance because of their deviation from traditional modes. In this sense, major novelists are the genuine innovators, for they do not perpetuate the stereotypes but reshape them. To this degree, Frank Kermode is absolutely right in his assertion that "the history of the novel is the history of forms rejected or modified, by parody, manifesto, neglect, as absurd."[11] The most interesting novelists are those who do experiment with the forms, who do strive to adjust the fictional paradigms. Pérez de Ayala grasped this fact too at an early stage in his career:

Cada novela que se escribe (aludo a las novelas genuinas y perduraderas) se diferencia de todas las anteriores y de aquí que la mayoría de los críticos comenten con unaminidad: "Esto no es una novela."[12]

There is little doubt, then, that the problems of writing fiction are an essential concern of Pérez de Ayala as he engages in the actual process of writing itself, and this is nowhere more clearly seen than in *Belarmino y Apolonio*, his major comic introverted novel published in 1921. Indeed, the opening chapters of this novel may serve as a guide to the central preoccupations which underpin the whole of his creative enterprise. That these chapters are written in a half-serious, half-comic tone is an indispensable part of Pérez de Ayala's prac-

44

tice and contributes to the ambivalence of the reader's response. Given the manner in which these ideas are presented, it is not possible to take them entirely seriously, and yet it is undeniable that they are in some way serious. This double-edged character of the narrative, which is repeated in some form in nearly all of Pérez de Ayala's work, is the largest single significant element which contributes to its status as a complex structure. It functions as part of the text's problematical nature. It is interesting to compare Ayala's practice with what Elizabeth Hardwick has written about this and other features of modern, problematical novels:

> Many good novels show a degree of panic about the form. Where to start and where to end, how much must be believed and how much a joke, a puzzle; how to combine the episodic and the carefully designed and consequential ... the mode of the writer is to admit manipulation and design, to exploit the very act of authorship in the midst of the imagined scene.[13]

This observation applies perfectly to *Belarmino y Apolonio*. In the opening paragraphs, a theory of knowledge is developed in terms of the distinctive qualities of boarding-houses in different countries, "una investigación científica de sociología comparada" (IV:13). Don Amaranto's disquisition traces the development of human knowledge from an integrated perception of the universe to the fragmentation of modern science: "Cada ciencia, de por sí, es una abdicación al conocer íntegro" (IV:16). If the universe is a "coordinación de infinitos fenómenos heterogéneos" (IV:16), each science deals with only a small part of it. Using two phases of the Comtian scheme, don Amaranto sees the scientific age following the theological age, bringing with it the discovery that man's secure view of the world was simply an illusion, that life has no meaning and existence is incapable of being apprehended fully. John Weightman draws up the most complete balance sheet of comparison between the old and the modern world-views. The old was "firm and organically structured. People believed in God, in the picture of the universe presented by theology, in the social hierarchy, in the seasonal patterning of life which kept to the same pastoral rhythms, in the wholeness of the human personality, in the meaningfulness of moral codes, in the persistence of aesthetic forms, in the reliability of language to allow man to know his place in the scheme of things, and so on." In the modern view, "God is dead ... the social hierarchies are no longer automatically accepted; all moral codes are seen to be relative; the human personality has exploded through inner pressures and external uncertainties; language, instead of being the rational instrument of the mind, has become a quasi-independent medium whose relationship with reality is more doubtful than ever in the past."[14] Science, for Amaranto, does not offer an answer but provides an escape into meticulous investigation, "no de otra suerte que un despreocupado, por pasatiempo o ansia de olvido, se emplea en coleccionar objetos inservibles" (IV:17). This profoundly skeptical view of science is linked to a nostalgia for that earlier age when "el hombre se había acostumbrado a la presencia de lo absoluto en cada realidad relativa; el mundo estaba poblado de mitos; la esencia de los seres flotaba en la superficie, como la niebla matinal sobre los ríos; y el conocimiento íntegro se ofrecía al alcance de la mano, como la frambuesa de los setos" (IV:17). The whole thrust of Amaranto's remarks points to a radical critique of Positivism in particular and the nineteenth century in general, for if the theological age has been superseded, so too has the scientific-positivist one. Specifically, Amaranto's words are a repudiation of Positivism as a theory of knowledge which holds, in the words of D.G. Charlton, that "science provides a model of the only kind of knowledge we can attain. All that we know of reality is what we can observe or what we can legitimately deduce from what we can observe."[15] Hence Amaranto's illustration of his theories through the example of the young girl whom he wishes to know (IV:18-19) in a way which suggests a rejection of rational, scientific knowledge in favour of a more intuitive or imaginative understanding. Of course, the basic dichotomy postulated here between art and science is itself a fundamentally nineteenth-century one. Elsewhere, Pérez de Ayala draws a distinction between the truth as revealed by art and the truth as revealed by science: "La verdad estética es inmediata, intuitiva, permanente. La verdad científica es transitoria, mediata, discursiva, lógica" (IV:1123). The scientific outlook is linked to the aesthetics of Realism. The clearest example of this is the notion of plot, which relies entirely on the conception of time as a sequence and portrays the connections between events in terms of relationships of cause and effect. The world operates on a mechanistic principle and is verifiable through direct observation. The difference between this kind of Realism and the revolution of Modernism is analogous to the distinction between Lirio and Lario, which is used as the structuring principle of Chapter II.

If the Prologue to *Belarmino y Apolonio* is concerned primarily with theories of knowledge, Chapter II is concerned more specifically with the problems of fictional form. It is significantly prefaced by a note to the "lector impaciente," advising him to pass quickly over it since it merely describes the setting in which the action of the novel is to take place. This is often taken as implying Ayala's contempt for the ordinary novel-reading public interested only in a story. Andrés Amorós has compared this to Julio Cortázar's disdain for the "lector-hembra," the passive partner in the novelistic experience.[16] Within several of the novels there are examples of the ironical use of the term "novel" to imply simply entertainment, excitement or gossip. In *Belarmino y Apolonio* itself, Padre Alesón, talking of Belarmino's putative daughter, says "No hay novela y sí hay novela"

(IV:93), and in *La pata de la raposa*, Teresuca says to Manolo: "Pero a mí me gusta que me cuentes cosas como en las novelas."[17] In the present instance, Pérez de Ayala's admonition to the reader is a recognition of the diminished importance of setting in the modern novel. By contrast, setting was conceded considerable importance in Realist novels, for it was precisely through detailed description that the novel was provided with that "solidity of specification," to use Henry James' term, required to give that sense of the substantiality and reality of the material, phenomenal world which the novel purported to reflect. Of the Moderns, Virginia Woolf is one of the most dismissive in her repudiation of the oppressive weight of circumstantial detail that is so typical of Realist practice: "So much of the enormous labour of proving the solidity, the likeness to life, of the story is not merely labour thrown away but labour misplaced to the extent of blotting out the light of conception."[18] But in Ayala's case, the parenthesis is also a signalling device. The author would scarcely have included the chapter had he not considered it important. He is therefore playing a kind of game, for the chapter turns out to be anything but straightforward Realist description. It is one of the crucial theoretical parts of the novel, dealing as it does with the formal problems inherent in the novel's reproduction of the external world.

Amaranto's first significant remark to the narrator is on the nature of narrative fiction: "A nada menos aspira el novelista que a crear un breve universo, que no otra cosa pretende ser la novela" (IV:33). This can be taken to mean either a world in miniature, an artistic microcosm reflecting in some way the greater reality outside, or an autonomous universe, self-contained and complete in itself, as Pérez de Ayala's other critical writings would seem to confirm. Nevertheless, Amaranto is still concerned with problems of representation or imitation. The novelist's difficulty is that he can only reproduce the world superficially "porque las imágenes son sucesivas en el tiempo, y no se funden, ni superponen, ni, por lo tanto, adquieren profundidad." (IV:33). In other words, the resources of narrative are inadequate to the creation of effects of synchronicity. In Amaranto's words there is a possible echo of Lessing's *Laocöon* as he attempts to define the limits of painting and narrative. The form of painting is spatial and can, even must, be apprehended in an instant as a total image; the form of literature, especially the novel, is linear and temporal. The novelist "no puede pintar: únicamente puede describir, enumerar" (IV:34). This is the "Maldición originaria del novelista," and it derives from the limitations of the medium in which he works. Pérez de Ayala shares with other Modernist writers the desire to overcome this limitation and to replace successive order as exemplified in traditional narrative with a synchronic arrangement. Virginia Woolf, again, aimed to go beyond the "formal railway line of the sentence,"[19] to elude the essential linearity of narrative. Of course, any such undertaking can only be partial and tentative, for no novel can hope to escape time completely, either in the sense of time in which the events narrated take place or in the sense of the time taken to read the novel itself. An Imagist poem could perhaps, as Ezra Pound suggests, present "an intellectual and emotional complex in an instant of time,"[20] but the novelist finds it difficult to halt the flow of narrative time. Joseph Frank's concept of "spatial form" in narrative is helpful here, but only if one recognises it for what it is, a metaphor, for novels do not really have a spatial organisation.[21] Nevertheless, when the temporal flow of a narration is interrupted, the reader's attention is deflected towards the play of relations within the text itself. As we shall see when we analyse the structure of *Belarmino y Apolonio*, the conventional form of narration is destroyed and unity is maintained by play of cross reference. This process is present in any novel — it is in fact a definition of literariness — but Modernist writers call particular attention to this kind of spatial ordering. As Frank shows, we can find antecedents for the technique in Flaubert. In *Madame Bovary* there is the famous scene of the "comices agricoles" in which Flaubert tries to reproduce the effect of many things happening at once within an immobilised temporal space: everything has to be understood as taking place simultaneously. In James Joyce's *Ulysses* the techniques of alternation, juxtaposition and repetition of key-words underline the relationship between the different parts of the whole work. For example, in the "Wandering Rocks" section a phrase from another section is introduced into the dialogue, where it has no relevance except for the fact that it refers to the same moment in time. The dialogue and the incident form part of a single design. Moreover, Modernist novels are characterised by their short temporal duration. *Ulysses* recounts the events of a single day in Dublin; *To the Lighthouse* the events of two days separated by a period of some years; *Mrs. Dalloway* extends from morning to evening; *Belarmino y Apolonio* covers the days of Holy Week. Even Proust's great work, *A la recherche du temps perdu*, in its use of involuntary memory which juxtaposes a present sensation and a past event, frees experience from temporal succession. But the freedom is not total. Pérez de Ayala and other Modernist writers alter the normal chronology of events, make compromises with time, but do not dispense with it completely. In Chapter II of *Belarmino y Apolonio* it is interesting to observe how the discussion slides from the question of consecutiveness in narrative to the question of narrative perspective and thereby construes depth not in chronological terms but in terms of the limitations of any single point of view. The ensuing dialogue between Lirio and Lario, the positivist and the artist, on the nature of the Ra Ruera has a relativising effect, but the difference between the two characters is not about the objective reality of the street, about which there is not disagreement, but on their respective philosophical positions, the merits of their particular view of the world, the scale of values which they espouse. The narrator renounces a single, stable, allegedly objective view of the world and replaces it with opposing views of the impressions made on two contrasting consciousnesses. Chapter II thereby becomes an exemplification of the practice of narrative perspectivism, showing how reality is modified according to the perspective from which it is seen. Faced with a world shattered into "miriadas de imágenes," Pérez de Ayala forges a new unity, the "breve universo" of his novel. Lirio insists on his view that the imagination, through art, constructs the world we perceive: "El Arte vivifica las cosas, las exime de su coordenación concreta y de su finalidad utilitaria: las hace absolutas, únicas y absurdas; las satura de esta contradicción radical que es la vida, puesto que la vida es al propio tiempo negación y afirmación de la muerte" (IV:40). This is an aesthetic view of the mind (elsewhere Ayala wrote that the "única forma de conocimiento es la emoción estética"), and a reversal of the classic Realist/Naturalist position. Pérez de Ayala puts at the very heart of his novel an opposition between two modes of thought and, by extension, two conceptions of art, one Realist, one Modernist. In so doing, he presents his narrative as problematical, structuring it around a technical or formal problem, or a number of technical or formal problems, which he then sets out to resolve.

The solution to problems of this kind is never complete, however, and herein resides the essential radicalness of Ayala's fiction. The novel *Belarmino y Apolonio* can only be fully comprehended in the context of a problematic of writing, in terms of questions of reproduction, communication and intelligibility. The fundamental ambiguity of tone which characterises a novel of this kind, its Janus-like quality, is essential to the making explicit of its inherent subversiveness. In this respect, Sartre's definition of the anti-novel is particularly helpful:

> Les anti-romans conservent l'apparence et les contours du roman; ce sont des ouvrages d'imagination qui nous présentent des personnages fictifs et nous racontent leur histoire. Mais c'est par mieux decevoir; il s'agit de contester le roman par lui-même, de le détruire sous nos yeux dans le temps qu'on semble l'édifier, d'écrire le roman d'un roman que ni se fait pas, que ne peut pas se faire.[22]

Ayala's achievement is to have exploited the duality of the narrative tradition to which I referred at the beginning of this chapter, to have adhered sufficiently to the forms of reality, or more properly, to the conventional and accepted modes of representing reality, while at the same time deviating sufficiently from them to dramatise the dilemmas of writing as an activity and to explore the ways in which our perception of the world is shaped by language and indeed contained by language. The dialogue between Lirio and Lario raises in an acute way the problem of the relationship between the fictional world and the real world, between the world of words and the world of things.

The relationship between art and reality is, of course, a central problem in any consideration of aesthetics, but it is a problem that is posed with special pointedness in the novel which traditionally has been seen as representing reality more directly and more completely than any other literary form. Pérez de Ayala, in his critical essays, approaches the question in a variety of ways. He asserts, for example, that the novel is the genre of maturity because it requires a long process of experience behind it:

> Sin duda la vocación y aptitud de novelista se manifiesta desde primera hora, pero no es posible escribir la gran novela, con todos sus atributos, antes de la madurez ... Una gran novela de juventud no puede ser sino una novela subjetiva, y un novelista subjetivo no está en condiciones creativas de escribir sino una sola novela; la misma con variaciones, si reincide.[23]

To the subjective novel, Ayala opposed the universal novel: "Quizá el soñado ideal de todo gran novelista ha sido escribir una sola novela universal, en el otoño de su existencia."[24] But of course, as the word "universal" implies, Ayala is here referring not only to existential experience but to literary experience, for he was intuitively aware of what is now commonly referred to as intertextuality, the notion that books are inspired less by reality or direct experience than by other books. In fact, he conceives of originality as being measured by the number of resonances that are to be encountered in a writer's work: "El autor es tanto más original — y no hay paradoja — cuanto más remotas son las resonancias que en él se concentran; como si dijéramos que sus raíces beben la sustancia de las tradiciones literarias primordiales" (III:161). The new work is born of the interaction, in T.S. Eliot's phrase, of tradition and the individual talent. Stephen Heath expresses the same idea thus:

> Far from being a unique creation of the author as originating source, every text is always (an)other text(s) that it remakes, comments, displaces, portrays, resumes. A text opens in and from that complex formation of modes of articulation that gives, as it were, the theatre of its activity, a series of settings always already there in its very possibility.[25]

Ayala's insistence on experience, then, is not intended to imply that the novel is a direct imitation of experience, for this is to concede too little importance to the weight of literary tradition and the power of the literary imagination. For Ayala, a work of art stands apart from the reality that may have inspired it or stimulated it, for art itself is a system of conventions above all else. What art offers is

> una realidad superior, imaginativa, de la cual participamos con las facultades más altas del espíritu, sin exigir el parangón con la realidad que haya podido servirle de modelo o inspiración; antes, al contrario, rehuimos ese parangón, que anularía la emoción estética y concluiría con la obra de arte o la reduciría a un tedioso pasatiempo. (III:189)

Artistic creation is not a mechanical copying of external reality, for at every point Ayala stresses the predominance of creativity over observation and claims for the artist the power to transform reality. Art is man's substitution of superior imaginative forms for rudimentary, natural and imperfect ones: "el artista no siempre persigue la verosimilitud. A veces la voluntad del artista se sobrepone a la realidad y deforma y transforma las formas naturales." This artistic will is manifested, for example, by a more poetic use of language, by a conscious stylisation of the characters, by the creation of artistic patterns and designs, in order to create a different order of reality, one that is autonomous, self-sufficient, complex and complete within itself. It is not, therefore, surprising that Ayala dissents from what he takes to be the principles upon which Realism and Naturalism are founded:

> "Novela realista" y más "novela naturalista" es contradicción en los términos o pleonasmo futil. Si realidad en bruto o tal como es, ya no es novela; y si es novela tiene que ser realidad, pero realidad esencial; una proyección o extracto superrealista, y sobrenaturalista, en cierto modo.[26]

In his book *The Fabulators*, Robert Scholes, arguing for a fiction that pursues "fabulation" and rejects Realism, expresses a similar point of view: "Realism exalts life and diminishes art, exalts things and diminishes words."[27] Of course, it is excessive to worry that the gap between reality and novel will be bridged to the extent that the text will ever be mistaken for reality. Being made of words, the novel cannot really imitate reality directly as can, say, sculpture. Writing can imitate ways of writing about reality, and so the Realist novel, as we have noted already, has been based on biography, autobiography, letters, etc., and uses language in ways associated with these kinds of writing. Inevitably, the novel is pulled by the conventional connections between words and things in the direction of Realism. Therefore Pérez de Ayala, although the whole thrust of his thinking on art points to a loss of realism in the pursuit of form, will not sever the links with reality completely. In a characteristic dualism, he sees the created work partaking of both art and life:

Toda obra de arte genuino es un trozo de realidad verdadera, en donde están resumidas totalmente, y como en epítome, dos altas realidades: Vida y Arte. Toda obra de arte
genuina es condensación de realidades múltiples, forma
somera y adamantina donde se compendian formas innu-
merables. (III:42)

For Ayala, then, fiction is poised between the order of the world
and the order of art. However different from nineteenth-century
Realism, there is a Realist basis to this theory akin to the kind of
compromise upon which David Lodge sees the novel as being constructed:

It is realism which holds history, romance and allegory
together in a precarious synthesis, making a bridge between
the world of discrete facts (history) and the patterned, econ-
omised world of art and imagination (allegory and romance).
The novel supremely among literary forms has satisfied our
hunger for the meaningful ordering of experience without
denying our empirical observation of its randomness and
particularity.[28]

Ayala seems to feel that in order to give a complete account of
reality and human experience of reality, the artist must take everything and reshape it into a new synthesis: "Presentemos la realidad
tal cual es, si bien con luz más viva, luz que mana de la síntesis
artística" (III:29). Artistic perfection is the central illumination offering
that illusion of completeness beyond ordinary experience, the very
experience which provides art's many facets.

Literature is not concerned with the surface of reality but with the
ideal structures which may be said to underlie it. Fiction is in some
way analogous to the ideal structure of reality:

Si poesía es creación, y no otra cosa significa la palabra
poesía, hemos de buscar su vivo manantial por bajo de la
dura realidad y amargas verdades cotidianas que de esas
aguas se alimentan; hemos de buscar el manantial de vida
allí donde tienen su origen, como en el acto original de la
creación, las normas eternas y valores vitales, de manera
que al volver a descubrir su verdad original volvemos a
crearlas; volvemos a vivirlas poéticamente, creativamente.[29]

Again Ayala postulates some kind of fusion between poetry,
which for him is a visionary enterprise, and the novelistic, which
deals with the here-and-now as a manifestation of some external
principle:

A este reconocimiento [quoted above] se puede llegar ya sea por la intuición de la verdad, que es lo poemático, o bien por el análisis de la dura realidad y de la verdades amargas y presentes cotidianos que es lo novelesco, espejo fiel de momentos transitorios y fluyentes en el cauce de un presente esencial.[30]

The kind of residual mimeticism which is exemplified here assumes a reflection of some invisible reality beyond the confines of common experience and perception. The creative writer inherits in modern form his triple legacy as priest, poet, and man of science:

en un principio, sacerdote, poeta (vate, vidente o profeta) y hombre de ciencia eran una y la misma persona. En el curso de los siglos se especializaron estas funciones, por división del trabajo. Pero en los descendientes por línea legítima, persiste el árbol genealógico y la unánime savia originaria.[31]

The kind of experience which constitutes the subject matter of many twentieth-century novels is, as we have seen, inner experience. This is what Leon Edel called "the inward turning," the work of novelists who "have turned fiction away from external to internal reality, from the outer world that Balzac had charted a century before to the hidden world of fantasy and reverie into which there play constantly the life and perception of our senses."[32] In fact, this inward turning takes two forms: firstly, the deep and detailed exploration of the author's own consciousness, and secondly, a self-analytical questioning of the fictional world itself. In his consideration of this artistic self-consciousness, Pérez de Ayala lays stress on the inner life, but he particularly appears to see fiction as exploring the nature of inner and outer, of subject-object, relationships:

El arte del novelista consiste en la proporción inexcusable en sus rasgos sustantivos, con que andan enlazados la realidad externa y el mundo interior; lo que es y el como lo siente y piensa cada cual; la visión de los ojos y lo subjetivo, psicología viva de diversos seres.[33]

Art appears to bridge the gap between consciousness and the external world: "Por el conocimiento estético vamos tomando posesión del mundo exterior y de nuestro mundo interior, mediante nuevas formas" (III:565). This perception underlies all of Pérez de Ayala's creative endeavour, so that whatever his apparent theme he remains a supremely self-conscious artist, pondering the very meaning of the creative act, the role of art in interpreting the world, the nature of significance of literary experience. The novelist draws on his own resources as an artistic consciousness, and this leads Pérez de Ayala to posit a tight connection between fiction and autobiography: "Toda obra de ficción es una autobiografía integral. Toda autobiografía es una obra de ficción" (III:996). To talk of autobiography in this way is to push the novel too far along the axis of Realism, given the complexity of the relationship between consciousness and the external world. Fictions are not so much mirrors of the world as mirrors of the mind. After all, Realism purports to represent the individual's experience of a common phenomenal world, but its ability to do this is increasingly challenged by advances in knowledge and psychology which have pushed individual experience deeper into the psyche, making the perception of reality that much more complex and indeed less "common" than hitherto believed. Common experience would appear to be relegated to expression in myths, symbols and archetypes rather than through sense perceptions of phenomena. We can say, then, that the type of realism thus engendered will differ markedly from the nineteenth-century variety; its claim to be real, however, will be no less genuine. From another point of view as well the autobiography analogy is difficult to sustain. Although Harry Levin claims that the "history of the realist novel shows that fiction tends towards autobiography,"[34] the logical conclusion of this would appear to be a total convergence of fiction and fact. Pérez de Ayala certainly uses details from his own experience in the making of his novels, especially the early ones, but he forges them into a *Bildungsroman*, a procedure characteristic of many young authors. Moreover, as I have shown elsewhere, his position with regard to this material is both complex and ambiguous. It is the altering of facts in the interests of art that distinguishes autobiography from fiction presented as autobiography. Both require a distinctive kind of response, and in the case of fiction the demands of universal significance and formal integrity are placed before those of authenticity and veracity.

What I have described thus far is a progressive weakening of the nexus between the novel and reality as it is commonly perceived. Nevertheless, implicit in what has been said is a recognition that the novel offers something in the way of reality, perhaps a truer, more distilled reality than is available in everyday experience. This uncertainty about what really constitutes reality is written into the form of Modernist fiction. The fact is that the whole idea of what is "realistic" is highly problematical, whereas the word "realistic" is used in ways which tend to disguise its problematical nature. Simply, "realistic " posits a complete equivalence between a certain view of the world, taken by common sense to be "reality," and its representation in literature, especially the novel. Reality thus construed assumes the force of an Absolute, whereas in fact the reality which Realism purports to imitate is simply a particular way of seeing reality, and indeed one which the Realism of fiction does much to reinforce. In other words, reality is not something given and natural, but something which is constructed. The Realist novel both feeds upon this and helps maintain it. As Stephen Heath says in his work on the *nouveau roman*:

> the "realistic" is not substantial but formal (a process of significant fictions), and, in connection with the novel, it may be described in the notion of the *vraisemblable* of a particular society, the generally received picture of what may be regarded as "realistic," such a *vraisemblable* being founded in our culture by, amongst other things, the novel itself.[35]

It is the very familiarity of the forms of fiction that makes it reassuring and readable. Pérez de Ayala gently subverts this sense of familiarity. We can construe his frequent equation of artistic and divine creation in this sense. Each work of art is "un pequeño orbe cerrado y esfera completa, que repiten en epítome el acto y el sentido de la creación primordial" (III:564). In other words, things are made to appear, as it were, virginal and free of preconceptions. It, then, removes the normal sense of familiarity, the usual connections and associations, it defamiliarises by restoring things to their supposed primeval state. Pérez de Ayala once wrote that "los libros son despertadores de la conciencia" (IV:948), by which he can be taken to mean that man goes through the world looking at things with the eyes of habit so that awareness is dulled. Art reawakens awareness and enables man to "ver las cosas como por primera vez, cuando despuntan y van formándose en su luminosa originalidad" (III:564). By making access to the fictional world difficult, the act of perception is prolonged and things are made to appear unfamiliar. Reality is seen in a fresh and unexpected way. Indeed for Ayala, man, in the expansion of his consciousness through his experience of art, recreates the world. Thus Ayala deviates from the pattern of the totally readable text, based on expectations and the confirmation of expectations. This familiarity, on which Realism and its offshoots are founded, is undermined in part by breaking the identification of novel and commonly perceived world, as described by Victor Shklovsky:

> Habitualisation devours objects, clothes, furniture, one's wife and the fear of war. "If all the complex lives of so many people go on unconsciously, then such lives are as if they had never been." Art helps us to recover the sensation of life; it exists to make us feel things, to make the stone stony. The end of art is to give a sensation of the object seen, not as recognised. The technique of art is to make things "unfamiliar," to make forms obscure so as to increase the difficulty and the duration of perception. The act of perception in art is an end in itself and must be prolonged. In art, it is our experience of the process of construction that counts, not the finished product.[36]

Thus, for Ayala, "un artista es un hombre que ha consagrado su vida a ver las cosas como por primera vez, en su desnudez paradisíaca, tibia aún del seno de Dios."[37] A novel written from this standpoint will tend to repudiate everyday experience and view established modes of thoughts as being themselves fictions. Seen in this way, history and the physical sciences are themselves fictions, and at a very basic level their claim to factualness is undermined by the constant process of revision to which they are subjected. For this reason alone, Modernism takes its stand as a rejection of Realism, but being influenced, as it is, by Symbolist poetics, it replaces Realism's scientific stance with an aesthetic one, leading it naturally into often extravagant claims that art offers a privileged insight into reality. From this there is only a short step to the idea that art creates its own reality. This shift from the notion of the interrelatedness of form and content to the predominance of form alone finds celebrated expression in Roland Barthes' images of the apricot and the onion:

> ... if up until now we have looked at the text as a species of fruit with a kernel (an apricot, for example), the flesh being the form and the pith being the content, it would be better to see it as an onion, a construction of layers (or levels, or systems) whose body contains, finally, no heart, no kernel, no secret, no irreducible principle, nothing except the infinity of its own envelopes — which envelops nothing other than the unity of its own surfaces.[38]

Such a view postulates a movement from story to discourse, from the depiction of reality to the practice of writing. Pérez de Ayala never really arrives at this kind of formulation, but it is easy to see how his thinking and fictional practice anticipate modern theories of writing. His thinking on the art of literature, and we may assume that the novel is uppermost in his considerations, relates in a striking way to modern genre theory whereby narrative is broadly divided into the real and the ideal, which come together in the novel, itself a synthesis of the empirical and fictional modes. This synthesis can, however, be considered as a kind of tension, a contradiction inherent in the practice of fiction itself. Many critics have, for example, felt an unease at the modern tendency to conceive of the novel as an elaborate structure of language alone. This debate is seen in the contrasting views of two contemporary practising English novelists and critics, David Lodge and Malcolm Bradbury. David Lodge, on the one hand, argues convincingly and in a characteristically non-extremist way that "all good criticism is a response to language whether or not there is any explicit reference to language in the way of quotation and analysis."[39] At the same time, while most critics accept that any novel is a structure of language, many feel that a response primarily in terms of language alone is inadequate, inadequate because fiction seems to be something more than language. The language approach seems more appropriate to, for example, the lyric poem, for narrative has, after all, been founded on its referential dimension. This is the line taken by Malcolm Bradbury, who complains that "a large amount of fictional criticism has devoted itself, often in vulgarised form, to finding stylistic or verbal unities, symbols or motifs, in literary matter more discursive than most poetry and harder to account for in this way." The problem with this type of criticism, argues Bradbury, is that it pays insufficient attention to "fiction's empiricism; its attention to workaday reality."[40] Seen from the point of view of the practising novelist like Pérez de Ayala, fed on both a Symbolist and Realist aesthetic and both unwilling to accept fiction as a more or less faithful simulacrum of reality and reluctant to deny the links between the two, there lurks a potential antagonism between craft and credibility. Pérez de Ayala seems at times to ascribe to fiction the function of holding together all the chaos of experience and to claim for the novelist the responsibility of discovering the hidden pattern of perfection underlying prosaic reality. Novelists are, he writes, "intérpretes, aunque falibles, de un presunto plan providente que rige los destinos mortales; vates o zahoríes de la armonía universal" (IV:946). In practice, this could at worst result in the making of fictions characterised by little more than happy endings on the level of plot and at best lead to the creation of works of great formal beauty with no corresponding point of reference in the reader's experience. In other words, dealing with the complexity and chaos of experience and at the same time offering an image of order and perfection beyond it proved a difficult undertaking. A novel must be the imposition, through the power of art, of order upon chaos, the imparting of form to the merely contingent, and yet the whole exercise could be regarded as nothing more than the mind's fanciful fabrication. an elaborate and elegant deceit: not a mirror of the world, as the Realists would have asserted, but a mirror of the mind or imagination of the author. It would, moreover, be a very special kind of mirror. Just as for Ayala a complete work of art is a compendium of many different forms, so is absolute truth the totality of all possible perspectives. In everyday life this total view is not possible but. by creating an amalgam of unlikely and disparate components and holding them together in a kind of precarious equilibrium, it offers a model or illusion of absolute reality. Underlying Ayala's view of fiction, then, is a philosophical position which glimpses unity in diversity, permanence in change: "El problema doble, insito a la obra de arte, lo había denunciado ya Platón: desentrañar lo uno en lo múltiple y la continuidad en el cambio" (IV:1125). One way in which Ayala accomplishes this is by borrowing the patterns of earlier literature to impart form to his work, and this is also the means by which the ideal solutions, so characteristic of his denouements, are achieved. Such denouements bring pleasure, but they are rarely convincing when judged by "realist" standards. Ayala's fictions make sense of the world on their own terms but not in the terms ordained by common sense. It is in this sense that Ayala's conception most closely corresponds to romance, which he refers to variously as "fábulas de amor" or "eróticas," in which adversity is followed by harmony and fulfillment. This romantic pattern corresponds exactly to that of Ayala's major novels. But rather than being construed, as romance often is, as a flight from reality, these works can be interpreted as a challenge to it. The realism of Ayala's novels resides not in the reflection of external reality, but as reflections of the processes of thinking and writing about reality. That is to say, there is increasing skepticism about the patterns which fiction imposes upon reality, and this skepticism is highlighted by creating fictions which are manifestly fictions, that is, which make no claim to be faithfully mimetic, in order to emphasise that all patterns imposed upon experience are fictions, and perhaps none more so than mimetic narratives themselves.

These theoretical perspectives are, however, not without their difficulties and contradictions. On the one hand, Pérez de Ayala appears to construe art as discontinuous with reality, if only because of its inability to deal with reality in an adequate manner. We have already considered this inadequacy in relation to conveying effects of synchronicity. Narrative language creates difficulties of another kind as well, however. The raw material of fiction, prose, is also the medium of ordinary, everyday, non-literary discourse. To that extent, it is functional and referential, both undermining the novel's aspiration to be an art form and at the same time tending to relate it constantly to the world of everyday reality. Ultimately Ayala deals with this problem by once again realigning art and reality, but on a more absolute plane. By making the language of fiction more poetic, Ayala endeavours to endow it with expressive possibilities and a con- centrated intensity absent in everyday usage. It is through the cross-fertilisation of fiction and poetry that he hopes to create what he has designated the "integral novel," a mirror, or simulacrum, of the totality and complexity of the orders of reality:

> todo gran novelista ha sido — aunque no haya escrito versos — un gran poeta lírico, pues la única manera de otorgar vida psíquica a los personajes novelescos no puede ser otra sino exaltarlos, cuando llega el caso, hasta la más alta tensión poética, y lírica; esto es, subjetiva. Por decirlo así, el novelista-poeta se enajena y vierte en otros moldes de psicología viva. Este es el milagro del gran novelista- poeta. El poeta, nada más que poeta, canta de continuo el aria de su yo. En el novelista-poeta, en cambio, se verifica la multiplicación del yo. Esta multiplicación del yo es perfec- tamente compatible con el tipo de novela integral que se

propone abarcar la realidad entera; o bien, y viene a ser lo mismo, una zona de realidad externa, de perímetro definido, cerrada sobre sí misma, como un orbe autónomo. Aquí esta el toque de la novela, como género literario.[41]

The implications of this quotation for Ayala's view of fiction are wide-ranging. By laying stress on "vida psíquica" rather than on the presentation of objective reality, he points the way to a novel which will portray mental states, that will show an increased interest in the workings of consciousness. What is involved here is much more than the consciousness of fictional characters, for it is on his own resources as an artistic consciousness that the artist draws. The artist creates, rather than reproduces, reality, and this created reality is possessed of a completeness that is beyond ordinary experience. Art is discontinuous with reality only in the sense of reality as commonly perceived. In one of his essays Ayala writes that "el arte es una realidad más verdadera que la realidad tópica" (III:415), and elsewhere he states that "lo que vive en la novela es más vivo que la vida misma; es realidad esencial." By freeing the novel from the limits of empirical observation and representation, the novelist provides it with access to that absolute vision apprehended through the pursuit of artistic perfection. Such a claim will, for many, be exaggerated, but for Pérez de Ayala it will be as valid, even more so, than the claim that Realism can in some way represent the Truth. Realism is characterised by what it omits; Modernism is characterised by all that it strives to embrace. The Modernist novel will be autonomous, self-sufficient, complex and complete within itself. Modernism recognises the chaos and the complexity of the modern situation, but at the same time it creates formal strategies to confront that chaos and complexity. The coherence of art provides the meaning absent in everyday experience. In an essay Ayala wrote that "la unificación de lo diverso y la inmutación de lo mudable son antinomias que sólo se concilian en el acto estético." Such an aesthetics will, of course, tend to destroy the forms and structures of the traditional novel, for it implies that life imitates art. We create reality as we perceive it, but it is art which predisposes us to see it in certain ways. Modes of perception are cultural in origin and are modified by changes in art forms. The most celebrated expression of this view is, of course, Oscar Wilde's *The Decay of Lying* (1899), in the dialogue between Cyril and Vivian on the priority of art over nature. This dialogue, incidentally, is a curious anticipation of the one between Lirio and Lario in Chapter Two of *Belarmino y Apolonio*. Vivian protests against the current Naturalist vogue, the "tedious *document humain*," the cult of imitation, opposing it to the new aesthetics: "Art finds her own perfection within, and not outside of, herself. She is not to be judged by any eternal standards of resemblance. She is a veil, rather than a mirror." Vivian's summary of the new aesthetics is a *locus classicus* of Modernism. Art never expresses anything but itself. Life and

Nature may sometimes be used as part of Art's rough material, but before they are of any real service to Art they must be translated into the forms of artistic conventions: "Life imitates art. Lying, the telling of beautiful untrue things, is the proper aim of art."[42] While Ayala does not hold so defiant an aesthetic position, a similarity of outlook is implicit in much of what he writes. Lirio's assertion, for example, that once Lario has painted the Rúa Ruera, the street itself may just as well be destroyed, is an acceptance of the superiority of art over life, and the whole of *Belarmino y Apolonio* is an extended treatment of the question of art and reality. In his novel Ayala postulates an equivalence between knowledge and creation. The human mind does not simply reflect the outside world but actively constructs it. The novelist's attention is therefore diverted away from the object of knowledge to the processes of knowing itself. If the processes of knowing and creating are seen as related, art appears as one way of apprehending the flux and chaos of reality, creativity as a means of integrating experience. There is here again a shift away from physical reality and in Ayala's case priority appears to be given to the articulation of unifying and integrating ideas over the normal status accorded to observation and the registering of sense impressions. This is a further departure from Realist practice:

> El error de partida de las novelas realistas y naturalistas consistía en que se consideraba fácil suplantar y sustituir la experiencia esencial de la vida vivida por o con la materia impersonal de una observación dirigida y de una estadística improvisada.[43]

Moreover, the tendency to unify and to integrate acts as a counterweight to the tendency to fragment and relativise. As we have seen, Ayala recognises that any truth revealed by reason can claim coherence and validity. In the words of the narrator in the epilogue of *Belarmino y Apolonio*: "El error es de aquellos que piden que una opinión humana posea verdad absoluta" (IV:218), which is entirely compatible with the stance of Ortega y Gasset: "La sola perspectiva falsa es la que pretende ser la única."[44] But Ayala does not adopt a position of out-and-out relativism, for he sees intelligence as being engaged in a process of ordering and understanding: "La verdad flota atomizada y desperdigada por el mundo. La inteligencia procura reunir y conciliar el mayor número de estas verdades fragmentarias, heterogéneas, por lo común contradictorias."[45] In other words, while he rejects the notion that each truth is an absolute in itself and discards any mechanistic view of the world, he still seeks the coherence provided by an intellectual system. Herein resides his essential modernity. Ayala recognises that changes in scientific thinking have rendered impossible a perceivable, coherent world and that modern man is confronted with a world that is not a unity but a multiple. Each age "enfoca al universo desde un vértice de óptica diferente," as each tries to get closer to the truth of "la eterna incógnita" which will never be penetrated (IV:1041). Order can only become possible for modern man by moving away from a belief in individual essences and accepting the world, in all its manifestations, as a structure of relationships. The philosopher A.N. Whitehead crystallises this modern view in his assertion that the "event is what it is by reason of the unification within itself of a multiplicity of relationships."[46] Not only are the narrator's words at the end of *Belarmino y Apolonio* true that "Tan verdad puede ser lo de don Amaranto como lo de Escobar; y entre la verdad de Escobar y la de don Amaranto se extienden sinnúmero infinito de otras verdades intermedias, que es lo que los matemáticos llaman un *ultracontinuo*. Hay tantas verdades irreductibles como puntos de vista" (IV:218), but Belarmino and Apolonio themselves can be defined only in terms of their relationship with one another, and not independently. Relationships confer identity. The problem with any single perspective is that it is limited. Hence, to return to don Amaranto's disquisition, analytical science and rationalism destroyed the integrity of the universe, split spirit and matter, and then by subdividing into ever more specialised sciences fragment the world even further. Only art can hope to overcome the chaos of the modern experience, and this aesthetic position, together with a decline in prestige of reason and science, leads to a progressive fading of realism. Virginia Woolf, again in *Modern Fiction*, points the way forwards for the Modernist writer: "life is not a series of giglamps symmetrically arranged: life is a luminous halo, a semi-transparent envelope surrounding us from the beginning of consciousness to the end."[47] Writers struggle with the eternal conflict between form and contingency. To Rilke, for example, art uncovers a hidden reality that we tend to ignore. For Proust art is the central illumination, making sense and creating patterns out of what appears to be merely contingent. As Jonathan Culler observes, *A la recherche du temps perdu* is "a strenuous attempt to avoid the contradiction of the one and the many by adopting a perspective which makes the varieties of temporal experience fall under the heading of general laws, as elements of a system adumbrated for a single case."[48] For Ayala, art enables man to substitute perfect imaginative forms for natural ones: "la voluntad del artista se sobrepone a la realidad .. y deforma o transforma las formas naturales" (III:327-28). This movement away from reality leads inevitably to a concern with artistic form itself, whose potency contrasts with the poverty of material reality. But there is, nonetheless, a persistent and unsatisfactory dissonance between theory and practice. To Ayala, dealing with shapeless contingency and creating something of formal beauty seemed irreconcilable pursuits, giving an adequate account of human experience while offering an image of order and perfection beyond haphazard reality and at the same time avoiding the appearance of contrivance proved a difficult undertaking. This is the fundamental irony inherent in

Ayala's practice of fiction. A novel must be a whole vision, the imposition of order upon chaos, a means of subsuming contingency into form through the power of art. Any order thereby created could be seen as only a pure fiction, authenticated by reference to itself alone. But, looked at from a wider perspective, it is hardly surprising that the early Modernists tried to find in art an alternative reality. The view of Modernism which underlies this book is best summarised by Edmund Wilson in his seminal work *Axel's Castle,* where he advances the thesis that the history of modern literature is that of the "development of symbolism and of its fusion or conflict with Naturalism."[49] There is, however, another view of the modern movement, a more philosophical one, which sees nihilism as Modernism's defining characteristic. George Lukács, for example, a critic who is very hostile to the Modernists but very perceptive in his evaluation of them, believes that "Kafka's *Angst* is the experience *par excellence* of Modernism."[50] In other words, he identifies Modernism with a general crisis of beliefs and values. We can, however, reconcile these two views by recognising that the Modernists' view of art is intimately related to their *Weltanschauung*: God is dead, life has little meaning, knowledge is fragmented, communication difficult, relationships transitory. It was precisely in the practice of writing that these writers sought those "consolations of form"[51] which were not to be found in the ordinary world. Whatever the problems and contradictions inherent in such a position, art, for Pérez de Ayala and other Modernist writers, provides a harmonious and integrated reality. Order, for the novelist, can no longer be proved, for example, by the coherence of a plot mirroring the apparently causal relationships of external reality, for that reality is increasingly characterised by fragmentation and discontinuity. Any new order will be an artistic one, and the artist is the high priest of this new religion.

Pérez de Ayala, recognising the truth of Schopenhauer's dictum that "The world is but my representation" and that the world is different for each one of us, is confronted with the artistic problem of finding a form that will convey the complexity of reality and yet retain an artistic unity and coherence. This is the real challenge of Modernism, the creation of formal strategies for coping with the chaos of the modern situation. James MacFarlane pinpointed this when he observed astutely that "the defining thing about the Modernist mode is not so much that things fall apart but that they fall together."[52] For Ayala the integrating function of art was realised in the creation of his "orbes autónomos," the autonomous worlds of his own ideal fables.

NOTES

[1]*Principios y finales de la novela* (Madrid: Taurus, 1958).

[2]For example, the two articles of Pierre Sallenave, "La estética y el esencial ensayismo de Ramón Pérez de Ayala," *Cuadernos Hispanoamericanos* 234 (1969):601-15 and "Ramón Pérez de Ayala, teórico de la literatura," *Cuadernos Hispanoamericanos* 244 (1970):178-90, and the piece by Eunice Myers, "Tradition and Modernity in Ramón Pérez de Ayala's Views on Literary Criticism," *Crítica Hispánica* 2 (1980):157-66.

[3]*Helios*, Madrid, 1903.

[4]Pío Baroja, Preface to *La nave de los locos*, in *Obras completas* (Madrid: Biblioteca Nueva, 1948) IV:313.

[5]Bernard Bergonzi, *The Situation of the Novel* (London: Macmillan, 1970) 188-89.

[6]R. Kellogg and R. Scholes, *The Nature of Narrative* (New York: Oxford University Press, 1966).

[7]David Lodge, *The Novelist at the Crossroads* (London: Routledge & Kegan Paul, 1971).

[8]*Pequeños ensayos* (Madrid: Biblioteca Nueva, 1963) 278.

[9]Malcolm Bradbury, "The Novel and its Poetics," in *Possibilities* (Oxford: Oxford University Press, 1973) 286 (see Note 40).

[10]*Tabla rasa* (Madrid: Ed. Bullón, 1963) 88.

[11]Frank Kermode, *The Sense of an Ending* (New York and London: Oxford University Press, 1966) 129-30.

[12]*Ante Azorín* (Madrid: Biblioteca Nueva, 1964) 88.

[13]Elizabeth Hardwick, "Reflections on Fiction," *New York Review of Books* 13 February 1969.

[14]John Weightman, in "Modernism: A Symposium," *The New Review* 10 (January 1975):26.

[15]David Geoffrey Charlton, *Positivist Thought in France during the Second Empire* (Oxford: Clarendon Press, 1959) 5.

[16]Andrés Amorós, *La novela intelectual de Ramón Pérez de Ayala* (Madrid: Gredos, 1972) 94. He adds that "En las novelas de Pérez de Ayala no importa sólo — ni siquiera fundamentalmente — lo que sucede al final. Más que los hechos importa el drama de conciencia, el conflicto humano y moral que se desencadena en el interior de sus personajes." Even this, however, weds Ayala's novels too closely to a human involvement with the text, whereas their field of operation is primarily aesthetic or imaginative.

[17]*La pata de la raposa*, ed. Andrés Amorós (Barcelona: Labor, 1970) 42. The *Obras completas* give "como en los romances de las romerías" (I:241). The idea is the same, but the Amorós text, based on the first edition (Madrid: Renacimiento, 1912) is metafictionally more explicit.

[18]V. Woolf, "Modern Fiction," *Collected Essays* (London: The Hogarth Press, 1966) II:105.

[19]Quentin Bell, *Virginia Woolf, A Biography, Mrs. Woolf, 1912-1914* (London: Hogarth Press, 1972) II:106.

[20]Ezra Pound, "A Retrospect," reproduced in *Twentieth-Century Literary Criticism*, ed. D. Lodge (London: Longman, 1972).

[21]Joseph Frank, "Spatial Form in Modern Literature," in *The Widening Gyre* (New Brunswick: Rutgers University Press, 1963).

[22]Jean-Paul Sartre, Preface to Natalie Sarraute, *Portrait d'un inconnu* (Paris: Gallimard, 1948) 7-8.

[23]*Principios y finales de la novela* 10.

[24]*Principios y finales de la novela* 15.

[25]Stephen Heath, *The Nouveau Roman: a Study in the Practice of Writing* (London: Paul Elek, 1972) 24.

[26]*Principios y finales de la novela* 41.

[27]R. Scholes, *The Fabulators* (New York: Oxford University Press, 1967) 11.

[28]David Lodge, *The Novelist at the Crossroads* 4.

[29]Prologue to the 1942 edition of *Troteras y danzaderas* (Buenos Aires: Espasa-Calpe, 1942) 18.

[30]ibid. 18.

[31]*Tributo a Inglaterra* (Madrid: Aguilar, 1963) 265-66.

[32]Leon Edel, *The Psychological Novel 1900-1950* (London: Hart-Davis, 1955) 11-12.

[33]*Principios y finales de la novela* 25.

[34]Harry Levin, *James Joyce* (London: Faber and Faber, 1944) 36.

[35]Heath 20.

[36]Victor Shklovsky, "Art as Technique," quoted by Robert Scholes, *Structuralism in Literature* (New Haven: Yale University Press, 1974) 830-84.

[37]*Tabla rasa* (Madrid: Ed. Bullón, 1963) 219.

[38]R. Barthes, "Style and its Image," *Literary Style*, ed. Seymour Chatman (London: Oxford University Press, 1971) 10.

[39]David Lodge, "Towards a Poetics of Fiction: An Approach through Language," in *The Novelist at the Crossroads* (London: Routledge and Kegan Paul, 1971) 63.

[40]Malcolm Bradbury, "The Novel and its Poetics," in *Possibilities: Essays on the State of the Novel* (Oxford: Oxford University Press, 1973) 277. Originally published as "Towards a Poetics of Fiction: An Approach through Structure," in *Novel* (1967) I:45-52, as a reply to Lodge's essay referred to in the previous note and also published in *Novel*.

41*Principios y finales de la novela* 24-25.

42Quoted in *The Modern Tradition*, ed. Richard Ellmann & Charles Feidelson, Jr. (New York: Oxford University Press, 1965) 16-17.

43*Principios y finales de la novela* 43.

44José Ortega y Gasset, *El tema de nuestro tiempo, Obras Completas* (Madrid: Revista de Occidente, 1957) III:200.

45*Divagaciones literarias* (Madrid: Biblioteca Nueva, 1958) 217. Quoted by Frances Wyers Weber, *The Literary Perspectivism of Ramón Pérez de Ayala* (Chapel Hill: University of North Carolina Press, 1966) 14.

46A.N. Whitehead, *Science and the Modern World* (Cambridge: Cambridge University Press, 1929).

47V. Woolf, "Modern Fiction" 108.

48Jonathan Culler, in "Modernism: A Symposium" 16.

49Edmund Wilson, *Axel's Castle. A Study in the Imaginative Literature of 1870-1930* (Glasgow: Fontana, 1959) 29.

50Georg Lukács, *The Meaning of Contemporary Realism* (London: Merlin, 1963) 136.

51Iris Murdoch uses this phrase in her essay "Against Dryness," *Encounter* (January 1961):16-20.

52"The Mind of Modernism," in *Modernism*, ed. M. Bradbury & J. MacFarlane:92.

CHAPTER THREE

THE MODERNIST PALIMPSEST:
MYTH AND LITERARY TRADITION IN PEREZ DE AYALA

In his disquisition on knowledge in the Prologue to *Belarmino y Apolonio*, don Amaranto de Fraile, as we observed in the previous chapter, compares the fragmentation of the modern world brought about by science with the integrity of the ancient world unified by mythology:

> Antes, en la edad teológica, el hombre se había acostumbrado a la presencia de lo absoluto en cada realidad relativa; el mundo estaba poblado de mitos; la esencia de los seres flotaba en la superficie como la niebla matinal sobre los ríos, y el conocimiento íntegro se ofrecía al alcance de la mano como la frambuesa de los setos. En un árbol, si era laurel, un antiguo veía a Dafne, sentía el contacto invisible de Apolo, y empleaba las hojas para guisar y para coronar los púgiles y los poetas. ¿Qué más necesitaba saber? (IV:17)

This nostalgia for a myth-centred world which recurs in the work of Pérez de Ayala corresponds to a more generalised return in the modern period to mythical forms which the progress of science has tended to undermine. The work of Frazer, Cassirer, Jung, Lévi-Strauss and others has awakened interest in the study of myths in a systematic and scientific manner, and the Modernist movement in literature is itself characterised by an appropriation of, mainly Classical, myths in the elaboration of new imaginative works. T.S. Eliot, in a celebrated essay, ascribed to Joyce's parallel use of the *Odyssey* in *Ulysses* "the importance of a scientific discovery." What appealed to Eliot's modern classicism were the formal possibilities inherent in Joyce's method for "manipulating a continuous parallel between contemporaneity and antiquity." The method was "simply a way of controlling, of ordering, of giving a shape and a significance to the immense panorama of futility and anarchy which is contemporary history."[1] This corresponds in broad terms to Ayala's practice but he, like Joyce, is interested in myth for reasons beyond form in the sense that Eliot appears to understand it. This whole question is, by its very nature, immensely complicated, and no writer's use of myth is ever simple. It is motivated by a complex of cross-currents which interconnect at various points. For Pérez de Ayala myth lies outside history, at least outside history in the sense of cause and chronology, the piecing together of objective data. Myth is in this sense timeless and therefore relates to two key aspects both of the work of Pérez de Ayala and of the whole Modernist enterprise that we have been considering: synchronicity and originality. In their thinking on the relationship between past and present, Modernists tended to see the whole of time existing simultaneously. The critic G. Josipovici, for example, writes that "the great discovery of Modernism is that the past is not a solid mass, weighing down upon the present, but is itself in need of reinterpretation in terms of the present."[2] Applied to the creation of literary works, such an attitude implies that literature is a system, not a historical process, and this is a notion which is expressed emphatically by T.S. Eliot: "the whole literature of Europe ... has a simultaneous existence and composes a simultaneous order."[3] Naturally, the use of myth and existing literature in the creation of new works is an open acknowledgement of this fact. At the same time, however, such an admission places limits on the author's own originality. The forms and conventions of literature are inherited, and any author is imitating every bit as much as he is initiating. Modern writers tread in the footsteps of their predecessors, in one sense passively, but actively as well, for through them old myths are remade and reborn. Myths embody basic structures of human thought and behaviour, and at the same time they serve as cultural forces moulding the collective life of social groups and communities. These interacting features of myth are relevant to any consideration of its use by Pérez de Ayala, but in the final analysis, it is the literary aspect of myth that is uppermost. Before examining Ayala's first extended use of a myth pattern, in his short novel, *Prometeo*, I wish to look briefly at the current state of critical work on Ayala's use of sources, in particular at the kinds of literary material that had significance for him.

The most basic approach to Ayala's classical vision is that of Andrés Amorós, who sees it as being related in a fundamental way to the temporal dimension of man's existence:

> Observando el devenir humano, Ayala llega a una idea básica: todo se repite, todo es igual a lo que ha sido, aunque sea distinto por vivirlo personas diferentes. De aquí deriva una visión del mundo como encarnación repetida de los mitos clásicos.[4]

At the same time this vision of the world in terms of myth leads to a generalising attitude on Ayala's part, so that the individual, and individual experience, are given a representative or symbolic value for "todo es uno y lo mismo" (II:204-05). Amorós attributes this, on the very first page of his important book on Pérez de Ayala, to his classical education, his knowledge of Greek and Latin, his predilection for classical authors which he maintained to the end of his life, together with that great source of Christian mythology, the Bible. Ayala is a classicist, too, in his notion of the poet improving on Nature, "dando la verdad de las cosas, pero una verdad seleccionada ... una verdad representativa en el más alto sentido" (II:511).

67

I would not, of course, seriously dispute this view, but when one is analysing the use of myth in literary texts, it is surely more fruitful to examine the way in which the mythological pattern is embedded in the text and the effect this has on the production of the text's meaning. In this way the function of the myth within the grammar of the narrative will be highlighted. Such an analysis will of necessity take us beyond the confines of the sources provided by classical literature.

When considering the function of myth in Pérez de Ayala's work, it is important to recognise that a very elaborate and widespread use of literary borrowings is involved and that their function varies according to context. Only two works refer directly to a classical antecedent, *Prometeo* and *Bajo el signo de Artemisa*. In other works, the allusions are more oblique: *Tigre Juan* and *El curandero de su honra* contain parodic echoes of Tirso de Molina, Zorrilla and Calderón. *Los trabajos de Urbano y Simona* recalls Cervantes' *Los trabajos de Persiles y Segismunda*. Other sources, not signalled in this way, but significant in the works in which they appear, are Don Quijote, the myth of Dafnis and Chloe, Odysseus, Adam and Eve, and certain fairy-tales, as well as numerous minor, and sometimes debatable, echoes, for example, Hamlet, Hercules.

In *Divagaciones literarias*, Ayala writes of the way in which traditional works impose themselves upon new writers almost as a kind of cultural imperative:

> Hay obras artísticas que se incorporan de manera tan consustantiva a las categorías intelectuales y perceptivas de una época, de un pueblo, y aun a veces de la humanidad toda, que es punto menos que imposible traducir las emociones o sensaciones directamente recibidas de la realidad, si no es por referencia a emociones o sensaciones semejantes de aquellas obras artísticas, ya sea recordando un episodio de ellas a manera de imagen explicativa, ya citando una frase, que viene a ser como centro luminoso de asociaciones. (IV:838)

The kind of patterning which results from this, moreover, is one aspect of the features that we can use to define "literariness" in a literary text. The most complete study of the use of myth in the work of Pérez de Ayala is the published dissertation of Maruxa Salgues de Cargill, *Los mitos clásicos y modernos en la novela de Pérez de Ayala*, as well as some related articles by her.[5] Salgues de Cargill's studies are essentially to do with the recognition and illustration of sources, but her general approach is also aimed at elucidating Ayala's attitude to Spain. She makes the point that in Ayala's earlier novels classical antecedents predominate, while in the later novels he is more concerned with myths that are specifically Spanish in origin. I shall, of course, refer to Salgues de Cargill's work and to that of other critics, but my own approach to this question is essentially different from theirs. In the first place, it attempts to go beyond the question of influence to consider questions of significance, although in some cases this involves a deeper probing of the sources than has hitherto been undertaken. Secondly, my approach is not to see the question of myth in isolation, but to consider it within the context of the formal strategies of Modernist fiction, of which Ayala is a leading exponent. Finally, it is concerned with myth as an essential feature of literature itself. I shall be concerned less with the author and his beliefs and more with the processes of the narrative itself, on the text as a signifying system. A very simple example will suffice to indicate the general direction of this approach. For critics who relate myth entirely to Pérez de Ayala's ideological position, myth enjoys a greatly diminished literary value. In Ayala's early works in particular mythological allusions abound, often acting as little more than isolated terms of comparison, and frequently pedantic ones at that. Critics who are interested in the "Nihil novum sub sole" idea to the exclusion of all else will not differentiate in a substantial way between these isolated references and more extended uses of mythical parallels. In fact, a systematic use of myth to establish patterns within a novel is very different in kind from an unsystematic use of classical allusions, though individually these may be significant in themselves. Extended uses of mythological motifs must be considered within the context of the formal characteristics of the novel. The placing of these motifs is an important part of the novel's composition, and their function is usually prefigurative. In *Tinieblas en las cumbres*, for example, the narrator draws a simple comparison between Fernando and Rosina and Adam and Eve (I:70), saying that, unlike their Biblical forefathers, they felt no shame at finding themselves naked, since they felt innocent. Naturally, such a reference is entirely different from the use of the Adam and Eve myth in the Urbano and Simona novels, where it serves the purpose of an identification myth: "El y Simona eran Adán y Eva" (IV:344). Here the characters are imitating, engaged in a process of repetition, as indeed is the author. The primeval myth is reborn within them, passively experienced and actively remade, at once inside and outside of time. In the earlier example, the reference is isolated, almost casual. Similarly, it would be necessary to distinguish between the use of the Prometheus myth in *Prometeo*, where motifs from the myths of Ulysses and Prometheus are fused both to structure the plot and to provide a symbolic commentary upon it, and its use in *Troteras y danzaderas*, for example, when Arsenio Bériz writes to Alberto: "aquí estoy yo, como Prometeo, encadenado a la roca conyugal, sin dar ni pie ni mano, y los buitres insaciables del hastío, de la concupiscencia, del ansia del vivir, de todas las pasiones nobles en suma, desgarrándome la tripa" (I:804). Here the major elements of the punishment of Prometheus are harnessed simply to give a hyperbolic description of the frustrations of married life. It is this kind of usage which most accords with Esperanza Rodríguez Monescillo's tripartite summary of the influence of the Greek world upon Pérez de Ayala:

> La influencia del mundo helénico en la obra de Pérez de Ayala se ejerce en tres direcciones fundamentales:
>
> Primera: En el curso de sus novelas, poemas o ensayos el autor, a propósito de cualquier circunstancia o como corroboración de una teoría, trae a colación las palabras de algún literato o personaje histórico griego, que cita textualmente.
>
> Segunda: En las mismas condiciones el autor puede glosar las palabras u opiniones de algún autor griego, no recibiéndolas literalmente, sino haciendo referencia a ellas con lenguaje propio o entreverándolas a veces de citas textuales seguidas del comentario personal.
>
> Tercera: La influencia del mundo helénico se reduce a un ambiente o telón de fondo en el que se mueven los personajes del autor; se trata siempre de comparaciones, alusiones, recuerdos momentáneos, visiones fugaces de mitos, leyendas o paisajes griegos.[6]

This critic's study has at least the advantage of distinguishing between different levels of classical influence, but she tends to leave all of them in the position of a kind of learned supporting material for the main text. I, however, see the phenomenon as a much more fundamental feature of Ayala's literary art, which applies not only to myth in the strict sense but also to any form of extended literary borrowing. There are many reasons why one author should borrow from another, and in the case of the novel one of the most important is that it provides a short-cut to plot unfolding. The author is absolved from being inventive on the level of plot and can divert his attention elsewhere. Myths, after all, are good stories, stories which have stood the test of time. The real advantage of myth is that it offers the author, and the reader, something that is readily recognisable, and that this is an essential ingredient of any art.

This is certainly true of *Prometeo* (1916), the first work in which Pérez de Ayala attempts a full-scale version of an ancient work. In fact, what we find here is the linking of two myths, that of Prometheus, which embodies the principal character's aspiration towards the superhuman, and that of Odysseus, which provides most of the material for the plot. Naturally it is necessary to be aware of the associations of these myths for the work to be fully appreciated. From the point of view of narrative technique, however, what is important is the extent to which the classical analogy is used for the purposes of authorial commentary, for it appears to be no coincidence that the widespread use of mythological motifs in fiction appears to emerge at a historical point in the development of the genre when the use of direct comment begins to be regarded with disapproval by theorists and writers alike. It is tempting to see the mythological parallel, then, as the key to the interpretation of the work and the means by which the author's values are imparted to the reader. In addition to Homer's *Odyssey*, other literary antecedents for *Prometeo* have been suggested. One of Ayala's earliest critics, Francisco Agustín, took up Salvador de Madariaga's idea of the kinship between Prometeo and *El conde Lucanor*, suggesting that the short novel is an "enxiemplo" after the style of Don Juan Manuel in which an exotic element (in this case Greek) is adapted to contemporary Spanish life.[7] More recently, Julio Matas has suggested a close connection between Ayala's "novelas poemáticas" and Cervantes' "novelas ejemplares": both give artistic expression to complex truths. Marco acts against the natural order and his punishment is implicit in his act, for his attempt to create a genius results in the birth of a deformed son. Marco deviates from the norm of moderation which Ayala regards as an underlying law of nature, with the inevitable tragic consequences. Matas then extends his argument by adding that "Marco sintetiza, en lo individual, el embotamiento físico y espiritual de la España de su tiempo."[8] This ideological interpretation, in conformity with the general outlook of the Generation of 1898, has formed the basis of the majority of critical approaches to the work. For example, Donald L. Fabian speculates that in *Prometeo* "Ayala means to suggest that the recovery of Spain will require intelligent, sustained, co-operative action rather than ambitious individual effort."[9] In a similar vein, Norma Urrutia argues that the work is "un nuevo intento de formular el esquema del español ideal."[10] Esperanza Rodríguez Monescillo considers that Ayala's fusion of the myths of Odysseus and Promethus "tiene su raíz en el propósito de ejemplificar y aleccionar a sus compatriotas más o menos responsables del momento histórico desgraciado que España está viviendo, con miras a lograr de ellos un poco de reflexión sobre los males de la Patria y un mucho de voluntad de superación y sacrificio."[11] Other critics, like F.W. Weber, see *Prometeo* not so much as a work of generational ideology but as a "thesis novel that admonishes against prideful attempts to subjugate life to the systems of reason."[12] Andrés Amorós construes it as a demonstration of the "fracaso del superhombre nietzscheano."[13] This variety of interpretations is a consequence of the complexity of Ayala's short novel. That Ayala was interested in the superman ideal there can be little doubt, but I wish to argue that he is interested in it as a myth. Its use is an indication of Ayala's awareness of the essentially literary nature of his undertaking, and critics' underlining of the work's affinities are to my mind simply a confirmation of the existence of literature as a system of conventions. This is further proof, if any were needed, of Ayala's modernism, which the generational approach, bent on ideological interpretation, has tended to obscure.

I have argued the case for a different approach in an earlier article,[14] where I outlined the literary background to the Prometheus myth since its earliest origins, showing how it offers a multiplicity of possibilities for a writer such as Pérez de Ayala to exploit: Prometheus as the liberator of man, the creative artist, the man who thirsts after knowledge, the man of suffering who symbolises the human condition, the champion of individualism and freedom, the superman. The cultured reader, then, will begin with a basic set of assumptions before he reads the work, so that in a very real sense the myth deflects attention away from the characters and their lives towards a concern with the completion of a pattern, the perfection of a form. The pleasure of this type of work could be said to be largely aesthetic in nature. The choice of the myth prefigures events in the narrative. Thus the title of the work, the naming of the mythological characters, the use of well-known quotations and, in the case of *Prometeo* and the other "novelas poemáticas," the introductory poems, all perform a broadly similar function in that they anticipate what will or what may happen in the novel. In modern terminology, they form part of the proairetic code, prospectively opening possibilities. Eric Bentley suggests that an author uses myth because it offers something that is readily recognisable which is an essential ingredient in any art: "The point of any myth is to provide a known element as a starting-point and preserve us from the vacuum of absolute novelty. Art is a matter of satisfying certain expectations, and myth sets up expectations with a minimum of fuss."[15] The reader has a certain set of expectations, a number of possibilities are opened up and, as the narrative develops, a pattern emerges. In fact, in *Prometeo*, despite the title, it is the myth of Ulysses which predominates in the early part of the novel, and the reader is left to speculate on the possible connection between the two myths.

Prometeo spans five chapters of unequal length. Initially the Homeric parallel is rigorously pursued, but increasingly the tone of the work becomes more sombre and the language employed becomes more direct. Thus the whole movement of the novel appears to represent an undermining of the character's heroic ideal. Often in this kind of novel the mythological parallel is a private affair between reader and author and the character is unaware of it, but in *Prometeo* this is not the case. The novel works on the principle of mythical imitation or identification, and the whole thrust of the narrative is justified by the fact that Marco is a professional classical scholar. At the same time, however, there is a difference between our awareness of the myth and the character's awareness of it. The progression of the narrative involves a diminishing number of possibilities, both in terms of the choices open to Marco and of the shape to be given to the mythological material. The reader's hypotheses are gradually reduced until the completed pattern has emerged.

Ayala's short novel is based primarily on Books V, VI and VII of Homer's *Odyssey*, and the summary of Marco's life (II:594-95 and 607-09) uses the main details of Odysseus' story to King Alcinous (Books IX and X). Ayala does not simply borrow the broad outlines of the story but quotes almost directly from the original. The repeated use of the epic epithet, "Nausicaa de los brazos blancos," for example, adds to the epic tone of the novel, but much more extensive quotations are also incorporated into it. The description of Calypso's cave (II:596) is very reminiscent of Homer, as are Marco's shipwreck and the storm at sea (II:597). Nausicaa's dream is taken directly from Homer (II:599) and Marco addresses her in the exact words used by Odysseus in the epic (II:600). All these examples of near-quotation add to the literary-imitative nature of the work and call attention to the act of writing itself. The old quotation is blended into the new work and yet retains a sort of independence from it. It retains its original significance and is modified by its new context. Herman Meyer uses the terms "assimilation" and "dissimilation":

> In general it might be maintained that the charm of a quotation emanates from a unique tension between assimilation and dissimilation: it links itself closely with its new environment but at the same time detaches itself from it, thus permitting another world to radiate into the self-contained world of the novel.[16]

The first chapter of *Prometeo* is recounted in a mock-heroic style in which the ancient and the modern are juxtaposed. Two levels of prefiguration are present from the outset, the overall pattern being dictated by the well-known story of Odysseus while the detail and significance of that story are foreshadowed by the use of the initial poem, which is built upon the associations of Odysseus the traveller. The motif of the journey is easily related to the theme of self-realisation, a vision of man full of latent possibilities which should not be stifled by routine or convention. Marco's spiritual journey finds its correlative in his actual journey from Italy to Spain in search of fulfillment. Dualities of this kind are a prominent feature of the first chapter and are seen most particularly in the blending of the high and low styles, the counterpointing of the heroic and the mundane, both of which give rise to the whole series of anachronisms. The mythical is juxtaposed to the everyday, as the "fábula antigua" is adapted to modern times. The story is no longer taking place in a heroic age; it is narrated not by a bard but by a novelist:

> Así, lo que en las edades épicas fue canto heroico al son de la cítara, es ahora voz muda y gráfica, esto es, palabra

escrita, sin otro acompañamiento que la estridencia lánguida de la pluma metálica sobre el papel deleznable. El aeda ha degenerado en novelador. (II:594)

The Muse invoked, the muse of fiction, is the goddess of gossip and, in the summary of the *Odyssey* which follows, this duality is highlighted: "canta/cuenta"; Florence under the aegis of Ares then John the Baptist (a direct borrowing from Dante); Herod and Pilate as the proverbial equivalents Scylla and Charybdis; "brebajes ambrosianos" / "bebidas alcohólicas" (II:594-95). Later the narrator refers to "rojo néctar y cristalina ambrosía, que el tabernero, hombre lego en asuntos de mitología, denominaba vino y aguardiente" (II:597). The effect of this dual treatment is, of course, ambivalent. These pages could be regarded as an attack on the vulgarity of modern life and as nostalgia for a more noble and heroic past. There could be a suggestion that literature itself has become degenerate. Equally, they could imply that classical values are outmoded in the modern world. In literary terms, we can see here that "compacting of past and present" that is characteristic of Modernism, as well as a foregrounding of the linguistic medium itself.

Chapter II explains Marco's mythical identification with his hero, Odysseus, which is so complete that even the narrator is affected to the degree that he finds himself recounting a "verídica historia en un estilo alegórico, épico y desaforado" (II:601). The principle of imitation works on two levels: the character imitates a mythical hero while the author imitates an older work. Just as in the novel the world of myth is counterpointed with the real world, so too are Marco's aspirations and ideals set against the down-to-earth common sense of his uncle. Marco, in his nostalgia for the past and his monomania, senses his incompatibility with the modern world, and thus the second chapter makes increasing reference to that modern world and contemporary circumstances as the various allusions of Chapter I are explained. The "tierra de los lotófagos" is Seville, where Marco has slipped into a temporary state of oblivion. Circe becomes a Seville prostitute who helps him dissipate his inheritance. The reference to the "morada de Aides" would appear to be an allusion to Salamanca, which would make the reference to "Tiresias, que era un sabio y tenía cara de búho" mean almost certainly Unamuno, coincidentally another Professor of Greek. The city of the sun (Helios) turns out to be Madrid. This conscious literaturisation of reality has led Maruxa Salgues de Cargill to look upon *Prometeo* as "un pequeño juguete literario," and there is a sense in which these parallels are used for short-term comic effect. The same motivation lies behind Ayala's later reincarnation of Don Juan as a stall-keeper in an Oviedo market, but his intention is not limited to this. In Chapter II also Marco's quest for the ideal is for the first time identified as an aspiration towards the superhuman, the Promethean: "El aspiraba al tipo semidivino, al Prometeo, y si a no serlo él mismo, cuando menos a concebirlo, a comprenderlo, a adivinarlo, a ayudar a su gestación" (II:607). The third chapter, dedicated to Nausicaa, marks a change in emphasis from past to future. The process of demythification is continued in the ridiculous surname of Marco's future wife, which effectively undermines any suggestion of the eternal woman contained in her first name, Perpetua. By a careful progression, the title and initial poem of Chapter IV foreshadow the union of the couple. The story now becomes increasingly straightforward as the mythological parallel is kept distinctly out of sight. For example, the bringing of the news of the shipwreck could not be more prosaic. Perpetua's mistress is not spinning, but having her hair done. The possible significance of Marco's nakedness, prefigured in the initial poem, is undermined by "es seguro que habrá cogido un catarro" (II:618).

The collapse of Marco's ideal is prefigured in the poem of Chapter V, ironically entitled "Prometeo." The expectations set up in the previous four chapters are close to fulfillment, but the child turns out to be a "criatura repugnante, enclenque, el cráneo dilatado, la espalda sinuosa. Prometeo" (II:631). The juxtaposition of the description and the heroic name reinforces the irony of the novel's denouement. As Marco turns in upon himself, the novel focusses more and more upon the son, and the tone of the work becomes more direct until it attains the maximum of objectivity in the final paragraph. The stark realism with which the work ends contrasts brutally with the high-flown style of its opening. Prometeo is an exceptional being by virtue of his deformity, not superhuman but subhuman. Homeric prose and literary imitation give way to detached reporting, mediated only by snatches of peasant dialogue: the process of demythification is also carried out on a linguistic level. In *Prometeo*, then, myth is rewritten apparently to demonstrate the futility of pursuing a heroic ideal. Theme and technique go hand in hand: the world of myth is submitted to the test of reality. In a sense there are three levels of narration of *Prometeo*, the fictional/real world where the tragedy unfolds, the mythological world which parallels it, and the vantage point of the author, and the reader, which defines the relationship between the two. The prefiguration contained in the title of the work is doubly ironical in that the significance of it is totally lost on the character himself. However, on a more general level, *Prometeo* exposes not so much the failure of the Superman ideal as a misunderstanding of it. The principal reason for the use of myth becomes clear: myths and symbols take man beyond his immediate situation and enable him to see life in terms of what is possible. As such they ultimately represent aspirations which can never be fully realised or actualised. On a more straightforward level, *Prometeo* could be said to be a lesson in humility. Myth is the patrimony of all mankind and not of one individual. The self can only be realised in and through others. Ayala wrote in an essay on Nietzsche: "el hombre deseoso de realizar la plenitud de su personalidad percibe, si es inteligente, que sus medios son limitados, que necesita de los demás hombres" (IV:1128).

Prometeo, then, does more than simply use a mythological parallel. It explores the whole meaning of myth itself. On one level, the myth is used to provide a commentary on Marco's action, but for most of the narrative it is highly ambiguous, so that the reader is constantly speculating on its possible meaning. While the myth prefigures the action, it is only useful retrospectively in interpreting that action, and indeed any such interpretation can only be tentative. The interpretative function, indeed, largely recedes behind the aesthetic purpose of the myth, which is to shape in advance the narrative material so that the reader anticipates the completion of a pattern. The possibilities set up by mythical prefiguration are gradually diminished as the narrative develops until the completed form emerges. Seen in this way, the reader's attention is diverted away from any involvement with the character towards more formal considerations, towards an interest in the practice of writing. Finally, Ayala counterpoints the world of myth and reality and evaluates the distinctive attributes of each. *Prometeo* can in this way be seen to offer another perspective on the dilemma characteristic of early twentieth-century art: the relationship of life to art, of the subjective, created world to objective reality. By making literature rather than life the prime raw material of his fiction, and by his self-conscious handling of that material, Ayala creates an autonomous, self-contained world in which the thematic is subordinated to the aesthetic. Any ultimate discoveries the reader might make are concerned with the nature and meaning of myth itself.

The second of Ayala's "novelas poemáticas," *Luz de domingo*, is an attempt to create in modern form the tone and atmosphere of the traditional Castilian ballads. However, in general the work has been interpreted in a social sense and universally praised for its realism and its soberly realist technique. For Andrés Amorós, the protagonist, Cástor, "es un ejemplo del liberalismo llevado a extremos de ingenuidad." In his opinion, Ayala is suggesting that "los españoles poseen los gobernantes que merecen" and the final message is that "hace falta un cambio radical de todo el sistema para que los españoles limpios de corazón puedan respirar libremente."[17] We cannot seriously dispute this interpretation of the novel, for it is clear that in it innocence is destroyed by corruption and brutal egoism. But it is not necessary to explain the work in terms of the ideology of the Generation of 1898. More doubtful is the interpretation of Julio Matas that seems to ascribe all the responsibility for the tragedy to Cástor, since the protagonist "peca por 'defecto.' Cástor se aparta de la norma de no llenar cabalmente la función activa que al elemento masculino corresponde." Later, Matas adds that "Cástor, en fin, no ha vivido entre los hombres a la altura de la norma y, por tanto, no puede hallar la felicidad (o plenitud) sino en un mundo patético donde está abolida la esencial condición humana."[18] One of the first critics of Ayala's writing, Francisco Agustín, sees in Cástor "el símbolo de una España nueva y pura, que pugna contra la vieja e impura,"[19] an equally debatable assessment. Eugenio de Nora is more accurate when he speaks of "realidad implacable bañada en tierna y estremecida poesía," but it is difficult to accept his conclusion that the characters and situations are painted "en blanco y negro absolutos," which leads to an "exceso de simbolización simplista, de esquemático idealismo — país maldito de santos y de malvados — que debilita estéticamente la fábula."[20] On the contrary, the novel lends itself to a variety of conclusions, and therein resides its value as a literary work. The tragedy arises from a combination of circumstances which conspire to frustrate human happiness: brutal provincial politics, the innate evil of the Becerriles, man's selfishness, Cástor's meekness, the inscrutable designs of destiny. In this sense, *Luz de domingo* continues the theme of *Prometeo*. In both novels, humans suffer at the hands of an arbitrary and cruel fate. Both novels express the tragic sense of life which Pérez de Ayala appears to have experienced at the moment of writing them. This sense is related directly to the choice of the ballad as the literary infrastructure of the novel.

In a very interesting article, John H. Hartsook finds antecedents for *Luz de domingo* in two Cervantine sonnets, sonnets which criticise the lack of nobility of the Castilian aristocracy and the loss of traditional values.[21] But Hartsook also observes that the use of literary tradition offers the modern writer a form which mitigates the realism and actuality of his tale and creates an essential aesthetic distance for the true appreciation of a work of art. Hartsook claims that "When deeds of great violence, especially those condemned by the taboos of society, are introduced into a literary work, the author must take special pains to achieve form, for then form serves to allay the unconscious guilts and anxieties that are stirred in the reader and detract from aesthetic enjoyment." The initial poems, which Ayala once compared to "las mayúsculas miniadas que encabezan las crónicas antiguas" (II:79), fulfill a similar function, as well as prefiguring the events in the narrative. In this way a certain element of suspense is removed from the narrative, for the high points of the story are anticipated in advance. It is this technique which most imparts to *Luz de domingo* the character of a traditional ballad. Worth recalling at this point is the pertinent observation of Frances Wyers Weber, who views this technique from the standpoint of Ayala's literary perspectivism. In her view, there exist three versions of the action: "A tragic tale passes through the prismatic refraction of three different literary genres, the epic, the street song, the bawdy tale."[22] The most important genre, however, is the ballad.

The tone of the novel is established from the outset by the epigraph from the *Poema de mío Cid*, lines 2741 and 2742. These refer very clearly to the famous episode of the Afrenta de Corpes, an allusion which no cultivated reader of the novel could overlook. The reader is thus prepared for the scene of the rape of Balbina, narrated in Chapter VI. This tone is sustained through the use of typical epic metre that continues to be used in the ballads, evidence of the close relationship between the two genres. In fact, we have here the octosyllable characteristic of romance, although Pérez de Ayala prefers to use lines of sixteen syllables, that is, two octosyllables, a form also preferred by Ménendez y Pelayo in his transcriptions of the ballads, with assonance. The author gives us from the beginning a clear indication of the influence of the ballad in the composition of his novel.

The ballad is essentially narrative in structure and tone, although it usually contains long passages of direct speech and highly dramatic episodes. The method of narration tends to be objective (a quality, in fact, often noted by critics of *Luz de domingo* but rarely attributed to the influence of the ballad or the desire to imitate it), and although there is usually a considerable amount of emotion, this emotion is not greatly emphasised but is suggested discreetly. Similarly, no direct moral evaluation is offered: the facts are allowed to speak for themselves, without being subordinated to any didactic purpose. We can say, too, that the ballad limits itself to giving the facts and the circumstances without analysing the motives and emotions of the protagonists. The language is characterised by simplicity and force. Sentimentality is avoided. Equally, the narrative is simple and direct, concentrating on a single episode or a series of closely connected episodes. Action predominates over description. Ballads tend to have a great variety of themes but in general national themes enjoy less importance than individual dramas. Frequent themes are that of the tragic sense of life and that of justice and revenge, themes which are very important in *Luz de domingo*. Therefore, the epigraph taken from the *Poema de mío Cid* and the ballads which head each chapter would arouse expectations of this sort in a reader with a knowledge of the relevant literary tradition. As is the case with the ballad, *Luz de domingo* begins *ex abrupto*: Cástor is about to get married, and the initial poem evokes the nostalgia for the familiar home which he will soon leave. This poem uses repetition, a device frequent in the ballads, the effect of which is to increase the impression of a literary world, a world of fantasy, which has little to do with the real world. In other words, it is a device to attenuate the realism of the narrative, similar to that found in children's stories: "Erase una vez . . ." A distancing effect is achieved through the use of words which give an archaic flavour to the story. Moreover, Ayala constructs a very conventional plot for his novel: Cástor enjoys a year of complete happiness in Cenciella, which culminates in the day of the wedding, but at the moment of his greatest happiness, evoked in the second poem, which is a hymn both to the dawn and to the plenitude of love, the tragedy is taking shape, and its origins are explained somewhat clumsily in a dialogue between the worldly-wise doña Predestinación and the trusting and ingenuous Cástor. The tragedy is prefigured in the ominous note embedded in the poem: the incipient heat of the spring awakens the sleeping snake. The second chapter ends with a direct allusion to the theme of justice.

The third poem takes up this theme to contrast the power of the rich and the submission of the poor, thereby giving relief to the theme of social injustice, a theme with a long literary ancestry and much favoured by medieval writers. In this way, *Luz de domingo* achieves a fusion of literature and reality: bitter social criticism is filtered through literary *topoi*. The literary tone is evident, for example, in the character of doña Predestinación, whose significant and somewhat comical name indicates her role as seer or pro-phetess of the tragedy that is to come, and also in the characterisa-tion of Balbina, who is clearly idealised, above all in the conventional epithets to denote purity and in the lightly disguised Petrarchan echo: "los nevados dientes deslumbran en la luz del sol." In the poem which follows we encounter the conventional device of the pre-monitory dream (seen already in *Prometeo*), which repeats the images associated with purity and anticipates the rape with allusions to the dove pursued by the seven falcons. Even the number seven has literary resonances which Ayala will evoke again in his later novel, *Los trabajos de Urbano y Simona*. This fourth chapter links the destiny of Cástor and Balbina to the political destiny of Cenciella and introduces again the ambiguous image of Sunday light which will play an increasingly important role in the novel. The rape of Balbina contrasts strongly with the sustained literary tone established by Ayala, but this tone in no way diminishes the emotional impact of the violent event. Indeed, it could be said that the effect produced by the multiple rape of Balbina is greater because of the literary nature of the tale in which it is circumscribed. The realist qualities of the scene are undeniable: the ingenuous protest of Cástor, the sneers of Longinos, the background music played by Alpaca's municipal band, the bare language with which the rape itself is described, without emotion and without comment. After this brutal scene, impersonal and objective, "literature" begins to manifest itself again: Cástor con-tinues to use the conventional epithets of purity, the theme of justice and offended honour comes to the fore, although it is treated in a literary manner in the blind man's ballad which begins the sixth chapter. The traditional device of the birthmark is enlisted to confirm the true paternity of the child, as well as the motifs of the journey and of escape, and finally death brings liberation and final peace, symbolised by the Sunday light which bathes in poetry the final moments of Cástor and Balbina, who depart this valley of tears to seek happiness in the "país de la Suma Concordia" where "brilla eternamente la pura e increada luz de domingo." Like the traditional ballad, *Luz de domingo* ends tragically, and what optimism there is in the final lines is very tentative and undefined.

It is therefore difficult to draw firm conclusions from this second of the "novelas poemáticas de la vida española," for the novel quite simply cannot be reduced to a single interpretation. The causes of the tragedy are various. If Cástor appears to lack masculinity, he also has good qualities, and the ending appears to give a religious orientation to the tragedy. When it is compared to the two novels which accompany it, and bearing in mind the nature of the literary imitation which Ayala has undertaken, one must be on one's guard against seeking a moral or establishing a too simple correlation with everyday reality. In *Luz de domingo* Ayala uses literature as a sort of escape from reality by creating a literary world not unlike the real world but made more bearable by the imposition of a final harmony and peace. The central theme of the three novels would appear to be the pursuit of some unattainable reality, and in each life and literature interact to create a strange sensation of ambivalence on the part of the reader. In *Prometeo*, the mythical world is reinterpreted to demonstrate the futility of pursuing a heroic ideal: the mythical world clashes with the real world. In *La caída de los Limones*, the illusion of the fictional world acts as a mirror of the world Arias inhabits, a world of his own making, fashioned to his own needs. The illusion of this unreal world is shattered by the intrusion of the real. In *Luz de domingo*, the ideal is found only in an unreal world. The world of literature is a world of fantasy, it is a refuge against despair, it offers a momentary joy and consolation, the imposition of the inner world upon the outer. *Luz de domingo* is thus a highly suggestive work in which Ayala has perfectly harmonised form and content, or more properly, form is content, making it a small masterpiece which José María Martínez Cachero is surely right in describing as "el más hermoso ejemplo del dominio narrativo de Pérez de Ayala."[23]

It is not until his penultimate novel, published in two parts in 1923, that Ayala once again makes extensive use of literary tradition. Of Ayala's major novels, *Luna de miel, luna de hiel* and *Los trabajos de Urbano y Simona* have received least acclaim and been the subject of least critical attention. For many readers, a fundamental absurdity of situation and apparent lack of seriousness and artistic purpose heavily outweigh the novel's qualities of fine humour, elegance of style and literary inventiveness. Yet this novel exhibits some of the central concerns of Ayala the novelist, fusing theory and practice into an extended consideration and illustration of the nature and significance of imaginative literature. The undoubted eclecticism of the two works lends support to this view, for they constitute a compendium of literary genres in which the tradition of prose romance predominates. The first part of the novel makes reference to Longus' *Daphnis and Chloe*, and the title of the second part echoes directly Cervantes' *Los trabajos de Persiles y Segismunda*, published posthumously in 1617. Ayala thereby acknowledges his great predecessor no less clearly, if less explicitly, than Cervantes himself when, in the 1613 Prologue to the *Novelas ejemplares*, he referred to the *Persiles as* a work "que se atreve a competir con Heliodoro." Heliodorus' Greek romance, the *Ethiopic History of the Loves of Teagenes and Cariclea*, was first translated into Spanish in 1587 by Fernando de Mena. Although Ayala refers to two other romances, *Daphnis and Chloe*, which I have just mentioned, and Achilles Tatius' *Leucippe and Clitophon*, he makes no allusion to Heliodorus. His familiarity with the tradition is, however, clear, and his debt to the tradition of prose romance extends beyond the incorporation of specific material or the borrowing of specific incidents. In fact, these tend to act as signs to the reader that the novel is not to be judged by contemporary literary standards, for in it Ayala can be seen to be grappling with certain literary problems which were also the concern of Cervantes. In this respect, the combination of "creación y crítica," the development of a fiction alongside a commentary on that fiction, is one of the important ways in which Ayala attempts to recreate the spirit of Cervantes' work. While Ayala's use of classical sources is widely acknowledged, affinities between him and Cervantes are less easily recognised. As far as *Los trabajos de Urbano y Simona* is concerned, many critics have pointed out the obvious Cervantine echo in Ayala's title, but none has elaborated on its possible significance. As soon as the novel appeared, one critic emphatically denied any connection between it and the *Persiles*:

> es comprensible que el recuerdo de Dafnis y Cloe haya acudido a los puntos de la pluma de los que han tratado de la novela de Pérez de Ayala con más razón y título que las novelas de trabajos y aventuras, como los *Trabajos de Teagenes y Cariclea* o los de *Persiles y Segismunda* con los cuales no tiene más relación que la del título de la segunda parte y la que nuestra imaginación quiera añadir.[24]

G.G. Brown makes a similar point, though with more caution: "comparing the works does nothing to illuminate any obscure meaning in Pérez de Ayala's version, nor even to indicate how he interpreted Cervantes' rather enigmatic novel."[25] In a later chapter on narrative introversion I shall look more closely at the question of Cervantine influence. For the present, suffice it to say that Cervantes offered Ayala a model of a work which would combine imagination and public acceptability in much the same way as Heliodorus offered an example to Cervantes himself three centuries earlier. The Urbano and Simona novels derive from Ayala's interest in literary problems, and the plethora of literary references within them serves to divert the reader away from any realist evaluation of them. Insofar as the theme of inadequate sexual education has a thematic importance in the novel, it is secondary to and consequential upon Ayala's desire to depict the growth of primeval love which, because of the manner in which Ayala justifies his admittedly incredible situation, leads to a degree of social criticism aimed mainly at austere religiosity and the harmful effects of clerical influence upon people's lives. Of more interest to us, however, are the literary paradigms offered by prose romance.

Romance is a prose narrative in which the subject matter is preponderantly fictional rather than historical, as is the case with the epic. Whereas the only subjects fit for the epic are politics and war, romance deals with the theme of love, and the fundamental unreality which characterises it is reinforced by the absence of any clear historical setting. Basically, the plot of romance centres on a pair of lovers who are confronted with a series of external obstacles which are placed in the way of the fulfillment of their happiness. Despite all adversity and hardship, the lovers remain faithful to one another and, aided by Providence, their love triumphs. The hero and heroine of romance are thoroughly idealised, and the outcome of the story is invariably happy. Not surprisingly, this pattern would have appealed to the optimism which underlies Ayala's mature philosophy. For the first part of the novel, Ayala looks to Longus' *Daphnis and Chloe*, as the text itself makes clear. Doña Micaela, in her very first words, likens Urbano and Simona to Adam and Eve (IV:225) and emphasises that her comparison is based on her belief in the couple's innocence: "Insisto en que los chicos son como recién nacidos. No cabe mayor inocencia. Son igual que Adán y Eva. Segura estoy que los dejaríamos en un jardín, por su cuenta, y no sucedería nada malo" (IV:226). The final word is a reminder of the other dimension of the Biblical myth of innocence: banishment into the world, the knowledge of good and evil, the experience of guilt. Don Cástulo, who has been entrusted with Urbano's education but, more importantly, is given the role of expounding some of the literary ideas in the work, finds the Greek romance of *Daphnis and Chloe* a more fitting comparison:

> Pues eran dos pastorcillos, lastimados de mutuo y ardiente amor, que vivían a solas, devaneando y triscando a lo largo del día por bosques y praderas; pero aunque Natura, no más allá de los rebaños que ellos mismos apacentaban, les ofrecía doctrina y ejemplo, su inocencia de las prácticas amorosas eran tales que no acertaban a satisfacer el deseo. ¡Egloga deliciosa, pulquérrima! (IV:228)

Cástulo's summary is a reminder of how *Daphnis and Chloe* differs slightly from romance convention. The couple's love is a gradual growth and not the more usual instantaneous passion. Progressively, the goatherd and shepherdess become aware of their love, first Chloe and then Daphnis. It is this which interests Ayala above all in *Luna de miel, luna de hiel,* for the novel is a re-enactment of the myth of primeval love, of love which is unique. Thus, when Cástulo shares Urbano's experiences, he is able to comprehend how Adam's love was unique, like that of a prince kept in a cave: "a fin de que un día conociese a una sola mujer, la Mujer por excelencia, y que gustase el amor, Amor Unico, como nadie lo había gustado desde Adán" (IV:260). Ayala acknowledges this interest in an interview with Luis Calvo: "En *Luna de miel* me serví de una fábula para ver cómo se presenta el amor en su primer germen."[26] In the novel, references to Eden and Paradise are assimilated to the pastoral ideal. The first description of El Collado (IV:253-54) recalls the etymology of a "paradise," meaning garden in which "nature" is preserved and which symbolises the natural, self-reliant life: "Dentro del recinto, a más de parques y jardines, había anchos huertos de legumbres, con linderos de frutales varios, pomaradas, praderíos donde pastaba un gran rebaño de vacas berrendas, gallineros, conejeras, colmenares" (IV:253). There are literary precedents for such a description, in the garden of King Alcinous in the *Odyssey,* for example, and in the Greek romances of Achilles Tatius and of course of Longus himself. The pastoral seems to represent civilised man's constant yearning for the simple and the natural as a reaction to the refinement and complexity of society, implying a belief in man's perfectability through adherence to the laws of nature. In his novel Ayala links the idea of pastoral to Urbano's Edenic experience of love, first glimpsed in the couple's early morning work in El Collado (IV:301-02). Urbano and Simona mirror the ignorance and frustration of Daphnis and Chloe, the only significant difference being that in the Greek romance it is Daphnis who takes the lead, whereas Urbano's inexperience leads to the initiative being passed over to Simona. Another difference from Longus is that Ayala adopts the *in medias res* technique which we find in both Heliodorus and Cervantes. The first section of the novel is largely concerned with the education of Urbano and the stages through which he passes on the journey from innocence to knowledge and begins to come to terms with the inherent opposition between nature and society, an opposition which is explored in the philosophical debate between Cástulo and doña Rosita (IV:286-87). This discussion also recalls the rhetoric of argumentation which is a feature of romance, a learned quality which can also be seen in Cástulo's displays of erudition as, for example, when he explains the etymology of "ósculo." These digressions are related to the central themes of the novel in much the same way as the digressions in *Daphnis and Chloe* are connected to the main action. For instance, in Longus' romance the stories of the doves of Pan and Syrinx, and of Echo, are all pastoralised, bear some relation to music, and foreshadow the outcome of the main narrative by ending happily. Ayala sets the love of Urbano and Simona against other love relationships: Micaela and Leoncio; Cástulo and Conchona; doña Rosita and her "capitán de fragata"; Paolo who, at the age of fifty, is too young to marry yet has an illegitimate child; Micaela's mother and her lover. But it is the progressive enlightenment of Urbano which predominates. An important incident in his development is the fishermen's ritual of betrothal, followed almost immediately by the washing up on the shore of the corpse of the drowned man. Urbano makes a connection between love and death. Love appears as an instrument of being, a means of affirming the self. What most resembles *Daphnis and Chloe*, however, is the physical aspect of love. Starting with the overheard remarks at home, then the enigmatic words of Antón de Munda, the apparently conflicting explanations about the mare and the bull and their roles in procreation, Urbano begins to come to terms with the physical side of his passion. Similarly, Daphnis and Chloe, despite the examples of the animals around them, are unable to overcome their ignorance. Philetas' advice that the only cure for Eros was "kisses and embraces and the meeting of two naked bodies side by side," is echoed in Cástulo's solution: "no veo otro desenlace racional sino meter a Simona y Urbano, juntos, dentro de un cesto, por toda una noche, como se hace para casar un palomo y una paloma. Y luego, que obre la Naturaleza" (IV:285). In both cases, the male is initiated by a third party. Daphnis is seduced by Lycainion and is distressed by what he learns of the effects of initiation on the virgin Chloe. In Ayala's modern version, the role of Lycainion falls to the distasteful cleric, don Hermógenes Palomo, and Urbano's reaction echoes exactly that of Daphnis: "No quiero ser hombre. Que me devuelvan mi niñez" (IV:411). This scene takes place in the early part of *Los trabajos de Urbano y Simona*, shortly after the couple have been separated and the bailiffs have taken steps to have the family evicted from El Collado. The fact that this is intended to be a version *a lo profano* of the banishment from the Garden is made clear when Urbano is able to relate what is taking place to his reading of *Genesis*. This scene has also certain resemblances to the despoiling of the garden in Book IV of *Daphnis and Chloe*, which is intended to represent the symbolic death of man and nature. When he is banished from Paradise, Urbano's "trabajos" begin. The external circumstances which keep Urbano and Simona apart are the equivalents of Dorkon, the pirates, the Methymnaens, and Gnathon in Longus' romance. A final point of comparison, on a purely structural level, is the composition of four books. *Daphnis and Chloe* is characterised by symmetry and an antiphonal principle of arrangement. This would, of course, be natural in a story dealing with a pair of lovers, but the parallelism of the romance extends far beyond this, as W.E. McCulloh observes.[27] Ayala's fondness for parallelism and symmetry is well known, as is evidenced in the two-part structure of the novel and its patterning around the phases of the moon. The loves of Urbano and Simona are paralleled, in grotesque counterpoint, by the loves of Cástulo and Conchona. The *Persiles*, as it happens, is divided into four books. I and II are different in character from III and IV, and this difference has helped scholars to date the composition of Cervantes' work. In particular, the second half is notable for the frequent interventions of the author, which are rare in the first two books. In Ayala's case the different titles point to differences in intention and technique. In fact, *Luna de miel, luna de hiel* follows the pattern of a classical tragedy, though of course the often comic treatment of the theme robs it of any real tragic potential. Nevertheless, the recurrent mention of fate in the opening pages creates a sense of inevitability associated with tragedy, despite the element of pastiche. Julio Matas argues that in *Luna de miel, luna de hiel* Ayala adheres to the Aristotelean unities of time, place and action.[28] Urbano is brought to a recognition of his tragic weakness, and the novel ends in catastrophe. The tragic element is consistent with the symbolic death of the hero through banishment from Paradise. The second part of the novel, *Los trabajos de Urbano y Simona*, follows the pattern of romance and traces the account of how obstacles are overcome and love emerges triumphant. The two parts of the novel are inverted images of one another, and in both the literary framework is exposed for the reader to see. In the second part plot and incident play a larger role in a kind of para-melodrama of which Conchona's confrontation with the thieving servants towards the end of the first part gives a foretaste.

By the time the final part of the novel is reached, Ayala has let his fondness for literary pastiche take over. Firstly, Simona is kept in seclusion by seven ugly sisters who epitomise the petty jealousies and obsessive behavior of women without men. Then she is kept in a convent for fallen women from which Urbano has to rescue her. These are the "trabajos" the lovers are now made to face for, no longer frustrated by their own innocence, they are confronted with a series of external obstacles. Urbano, having mastered the arts of riding, fencing and handling firearms, projects himself as the Romantic hero who, on learning of Simona's seclusion, plans "un rapto lleno de poesía y peripecias a la luz de la luna" (IV:523). On the night in question the appropriate atmosphere is evoked: "Era noche de luna llena. Las doce. Al pie del ciprés ... En lo alto destacó un hombre con antifaz negro" (IV:530-31). When he fears Simona will die, Urbano, in true romantic fashion, sees death to be the only solution. In all their tribulations, "se había comportado heroicamente, como un héroe del sentimiento" (IV:543). Ayala is engaging in a playful parody, but not for any thematic purpose, such as revealing Urbano's inauthenticity and stock responses, but merely to continue his imitation of literary genres. The whole escape scene is in dialogue form, which increases its affinities with Romantic drama of the "comedia de capa y espada." And lest it be taken seriously, there are self-reflexive comments. When Simona falls unconscious, Paolo observes: "¿Cómo querías que fuese? Otra cosa sería vulgar e impropia de esta aventura" (IV:533-34). Urbano, on the honeymoon, deliberately chooses to adopt a literary pose by pretending that he and Simona are brothers, "porque en las comedias clásicas sucedía con frecuencia que las enamoradas iban disfrazadas de hombre, y éste es el más lindo epílogo de la aventura" (IV;544). There are other literary echoes as well of which the characters are not aware. The ritual of the fisherman's wedding in *Luna de miel, luna de hiel* recalls the Golden Age motif of the "bodas rústicas" which we find, for example, in *La Galatea* and in *Don Quijote*, Book II, Chapters 20-21. More significant, from our point of view, is the fisherman's wedding in the *Persiles*, which is related to Ayala's novel through the theme of conflict between paternal authority and the wishes of children in the arrangement of marriages. More significant, even, is the neo-Platonic notion that the beauty of the soul is more important than the beauty of the body. This is expressed in more down-to-earth terms by the doctor, don Arcadio Ontañón, when praising Conchona's qualities: "si los mozos mirasen en las mozas más las cualidades que la cara bonita, tú ya tenías galán, y el mejor de todos" (IV:422). It ties in, too, with a later incident when Simona loses her beauty because of typhoid. In the *Persiles* Auristela is transfigured by the sorcery of the Jewish magician. In *La española inglesa*, sometimes considered as a *Persiles* in miniature, Isabela is transformed by the poison of the Queen's servant. In both cases the lover's loyalty is rewarded by the restoration of the beloved's beauty. In similar fashion, Ayala's novel enjoys a "desenlace feliz."

We can see, then, that the Greek romances and Cervantes' imitation of them in the *Persiles* attracted Ayala because of certain literary problems they raised. This is a point I shall develop further in a later chapter. Their essential eclecticism offered a model for the modern non-realist writer who wishes to dramatise the actual creative process itself, to dramatise, indeed, the conflict between artistic rules and artistic pleasure and freedom. In the *Persiles*, Periandro's narration is justified on one level as a desire to display "la grandeza de su ingenio y la elegancia de sus palabras." Ayala's novel can be justified on a similar basis. Older forms of fiction enable Ayala to display ingenuity of style and invention, to indulge in variety without being concerned with artistic unity, and to combine the aim of entertaining with that of providing insights into human nature and experience. The novel combines the imitation of pastoral, pastiches of other genres, the aesthetics of the grotesque, into a distinctive fiction underlying which is a philosophical theme. The final message is that of the continuity of human life: "somos dos llamas de la misma hoguera. Antes de apagarnos habremos transmitido a otros la antorcha encendida" (IV:547). There could be no clearer justification for reviving the legacy of the past in the literature of the present. The unmistakable optimism of Ayala's novel is comparable to that of the *Persiles*. Both novels are philosophical journeys, though naturally Cervantes' Christianity is more evident. In the *Persiles*, there is a clear progression towards perfection: the novel begins in the barbarous regions and then, in terms of its geographical setting, becomes increasingly civilised, culminating in Rome, "el cielo en la tierra." *Daphnis and Chloe,* likewise, is a kind of mythical interpretation of existence. The pagan Greek celebrates in his romance the transcendent in nature. In all three authors there is a quest for a deeper meaning to human life, and to read these works properly the reader must distinguish between the universal and the particular, between poetic and historical truth. The Golden Age theorists who drew distinctions between the verisimilar and the true, between the ideal and the real, who asserted the necessity of the marvelous, the capacity of imaginative literature to arouse wonder, are in a sense resurrected in Ayala's novel. In the wake of Realism, Ayala claims that lies have pleasure and value, that fictions are a peculiar kind of truth. In *Luna de miel, luna de hiel*, Ayala asserts the supremacy of the creative imagination and forges out of a variety of literary sources a highly original fiction designed to portray, with characteristic self-consciousness, not some allegedly objective reality, but the dynamic processes of the creative act itself.

In writing his last novel, *Tigre Juan* and *El curandero de su honra*, Pérez de Ayala returns to the *comedia* of Spain's Golden Age, in particular to Tirso de Molina's *El burlador de Sevilla* and Calderón's *El médico de su honra*. The distinctiveness of this aspect of Ayala's work lies in his linking of the archetypal figure of Don Juan to the honour code, in his comic and irreverent treatment of the two themes, which the parodic title of the second part foreshadows, and finally in the original interpretation of Don Juan himself. Although my main concern here is in the literary aspect of these myths, both have, of course, profound social and psychological implications, so that Ayala is also concerned with the role and position of woman in society, especially Spanish society, and with the wider phenomenon of human sexual attraction.

The myth of Don Juan Tenorio, though typically Spanish, is of course universal. Since his first appearance in *El burlador de Sevilla*, Don Juan has fired the imagination of many different writers, including Molière, Byron, Shaw and Zorrilla, who wrote the best-known Spanish version. In Spain, in the early part of the twentieth century, he attracted the attention of several famous writers, including Azorín, Ortega y Gasset, and Marañón, as well as Pérez de Ayala himself.

Although we know that the "convidado de piedra" element in Tirso's play comes from folklore, and Don Juan's motto "tan largo me lo fiáis" has been traced to popular tradition, there are no known sources for Don Juan himself. *El burlador de Sevilla*, therefore, seems to have been the original for others who followed. In Tirso's play Don Juan is highly mobile, hurrying from one conquest to the next, a supreme actor, undoubtedly promiscuous, unscrupulous and deceitful. He seduces several women of different social classes, kills the father of one of them and then invites his memorial statue to dinner. The statue returns the invitation and finally carries Don Juan away to Hell. Thus Tirso's play is about divine retribution. Whereas the popular image of Don Juan has rested more on his fame as a great lover, in Tirso's play he is characterised as a "burlador," who flouts the honour code: "el mayor gusto que en mí puede haber / es burlar una mujer / y dejalla sin honor" (Act II, II:313-15). Ayala's version of the myth is therefore faithful to the original in seeing the interrelatedness of Don Juan's exploits and the honour code.

Broadly speaking, *honor* is one of the great motifs of Golden Age drama, first used by Tomás Naharro, and is frequently the main theme of the *comedia*. Honour is a social code which supposedly protects the integrity of society and, at its most basic level, means the opinion that others have of one. Honour is usually associated with noble status and derives directly from that status. Anything that might lower one's esteem in the eyes of others is an affront to one's honour and must be avenged. The dramatic possibilities of such a code are obvious and were most fully exploited in the realm of sexual relations. But it did undoubtedly have a basis in social reality. Ayala seemed to sense instinctively that without the honour code and its insistence of keeping women protected and secluded Don Juan could not exist. In his view, an excessive preoccupation with fidelity and virginity leads to a distorted relationship between the sexes. It can lead to cruel and inhuman acts of violence and encourages immature displays of *machismo*, an aggressive pseudo-manliness which consists in constantly proving oneself to the opposite sex. For Ayala this unhealthy state of affairs, the product of complex social and cultural factors, impedes the growth of a mature, stable and loving relationship between individuals. It is more likely to produce instability and neurosis, or worse. In his last novel, Ayala undertakes the demythification of Don Juan and of the code of *pundonor*. Most of the ideas found in *Tigre Juan* and *El curandero de us honra* had been put forward earlier by Ayala in *Las máscaras* (III:339-90). He takes a largely negative view of the "tenorio" figure, but the central feature of Ayala's interpretation of Don Juan is his questioning of his alleged masculinity. This theory of the "feminoid" don Juan is exemplified in the novel through the character of Vespasiano Cebón, and indeed the very ideas expressed in the earlier essay are repeated in the discussion between Juan and his adopted son, Colás, early in the first part of the novel.

In a sense Ayala in this novel employs similar techniques to those he had used earlier in *Prometeo*. He uses ordinary people in ordinary circumstances to undermine the status of the aristocratic code, to make it appear ridiculous and empty. Thus the Calderonian husband becomes a provincial stall-keeper, while Don Juan appears in the guise of a travelling salesman. Juan, the "fánatico del deber y del honor," revels in the role of the Calderonian husband which he plays for the local amateur theatre group, for in it he finds the literary correlative of his own experience. His life is made to conform to a literary model. At the same time he feeds upon another literary model, the "tenorio," and Ayala thereby shows the interdependence of the two archetypes. But the events of the narrative are designed to show how Juan's faith in Don Juan is put to the test and shown to be a symptom of his own inadequacy with women. Don Juan is the myth to which men misguidedly aspire. Although most of the discussion about Don Juan takes place in the first part of the novel, Vespasiano himself does not appear until the second part. Until then he has existed only in the minds of Juan and Herminia, for each of whom he fulfills a need. The description of him given by Colás and doña Iluminada nevertheless seems to confirm his lack of masculinity. The second part of the novel explores the consequences of his flight with Herminia so that, although the Don Juan myth is still present, it is the honour motif which predominates. Indeed, the juxtaposition of Vespasiano's return and the performance of Calderón's *El médico de su honra* emphasises the interrelatedness of the themes of *donjuanismo* and *pundonor*. The production enables Ayala to give a summary of the play and bring out those aspects which have relevance for his novel. Ayala moves away from the technique of treating his themes conceptually, as he had done in *Tigre Juan*, and begins to highlight them through the conscious reworking of the literary model. There is an analogy between the representation of the Calderonian play and the composition of Ayala's own novel. Just as Juan's portrayal of don Gutierre, despite its impact, is undermined by his extravagant costume, so Ayala's twentieth-century version of Calderón's play is made comic by being enacted in a provincial town by very down-to-earth characters. Humour points up the disproportion between the horrible demands of the aristocratic honour code and the realities of modern provincial life. On a more technical level, the mingling of two literary modes creates a certain incongruity of anachronism, for each seems to mock the other. But there is at the same time a curious osmosis in that while the mythical is contaminated by contact with the mundane, the ordinary is somehow endowed with archetypal significance. Traditional concepts and archetypal literary figures are demythified, while the modern story of love triumphant acquires something of the status of new myth.

The *Adagio* of *El curandero de su honra* is built around details borrowed from Calderón's famous play. The situation of Gutierre and Leonor is repeated in the lives of Juan and Engracia, for both husbands are deceived by appearances and both exact vengeance for an imaginary wrong. Apart from the basic situation, however, Ayala's most important borrowing is the central motif of blood-letting, which generates a whole complex of associated images centred on the basic conflict between love and honour, which itself constitutes the main theme of *El médico de su honra*. This conflict is most clearly expressed in the lines "El amor te adora / el honor te aborrece," which Juan takes up and repeats obsessively in his mind. The use of the double column enables the honour theme and the myth of Don Juan to be worked out side by side. As Juan reflects on the multiple meanings of honour and reaches a new level of understanding which will form the basis of responsible conduct, Herminia is confronted for the first time with the true image of Vespasiano and his inability to establish a stable relationship with another person. As Herminia makes this realisation, Juan, in the other column, is beginning to realise just how problematical a concept honour is. As well as a semantic discovery about the number of meanings the word contains, practical and ethical considerations are also raised. If his wife were to deceive him, he should kill her and cleanse his honour. But this would not erase his dishonour, which would still remain, and it would conflict with his feelings. He could kill himself or seek to be blind to the truth. But this would conflict with his duty. Neither course of action would repair his wife's dishonour. As Juan weighs up these conflicting possibilities, as he acts out in his mind the archetypal literary role, the action is interrupted by a comic interlude, the anecdote of the peasant beating his wife. This sudden switch of perspective provides a humorous and pragmatic approach to marital honour — the peasant beats his wife not for infidelity, but for sharing his food with other men — which contrasts with Juan's stereotyped reaction. The crucial difference, however, between Ayala's couple and Calderón's is that Herminia is expecting a child, and this brings with it new responsibilities. When this news is conveyed to Juan, he accidently cuts himself. This is a further conscious echo of Calderón's play. The blood motif was present from the outset in Juan's occupation, it becomes a symbol of his guilt, of the crime of murdering his wife. Here it is introduced in a different context, that of paternity: "Sangre. Sangre. Mi sangre mezclada para siempre con la sangre de Herminia" (IV:722). It was present, too, in the image of the bleeding feet of Herminia and it will recur, finally, when Juan attempts to purge himself of his bad blood. Another echo of Calderón's play is the contrast between light and dark, which serves as a metaphor for blindness and illumination. This is implied in the creation of the college for the blind and the deaf and dumb run by don Sincerato, which acts as an emblem of man's incapacity for discovering the truth and perceiving the world through the senses. Light and darkness are present too in the characterisation of doña Iluminada and are reproduced, most importantly, in the rituals of St. John's Night. The bonfires illuminate the darkness, and in Sincerato's words "El Dios de la luz vence al príncipe de las tinieblas" (IV:726). In a hallucinated state, Juan sees superimposed images of Herminia and Engracia as the multiple associations of blood are evoked: "curandero de tu honra, purga tu mala sangre. Purifícate" and "No quiero un hijo de tu sangre. Asesino de mujeres" (IV:737). Juan progressively comes to realise that dishonour is brought, not by the wife, but by the husband's desire for vengeance. Wife-murder is a greater crime than the offence it is intended to punish. Ayala alters significantly the tragic outcome of Calderón's play: Juan bleeds himself in an attempt to commit suicide, thereby adopting the very attitude he has condemned in Colás earlier. The blood-letting is a symbolic purging of his former self. The old Juan has died and a new one is born: "Don Juan, el Tigre ha muerto. Bien muerto está. Ha renacido otro Don Juan" (IV:756).

The novel has effectively ended at this point, but Ayala continues it with the addition of a *Coda*, which serves to show the consolidation of Juan's and Herminia's happiness after the birth of their child, and a *Parergon*, which takes the form of a discussion between the principal characters on the major themes of the novel. In the context of *pundonor* the *Coda* is significant, for it portrays Juan as completely indifferent to public opinion and ends with a poem, a hymn to paternity and to the grandeur and mystery of human life. The *Parergon* enables him to expound his views on honour, which now place the emphasis on personal dignity rather than on social appearances: "El honor es la suprema libertad ... El honor es el sentimiento de la propia responsabilidad ... El honor es fidelidad para con uno mismo. El honor es bravura en arrostrar las consecuencias de los propios actos" (IV:776). This modification is paralleled by a similar modification of his views on Don Juan. Through him Juan discovered his true self. Don Juan has a place in the overall scheme of things, and his punishment lies in the fact that he is his own victim. Thus the two themes, *donjuanismo* and *pundonor*, are brought together at the end of the novel, having been explored in all their varying facets, their significance and relationship to one another radically re-defined.

Ayala's treatment of the two myths, then, is related to the central theme of the novel, the passage from incomprehension to understanding, but at the same time it raises inevitably the whole question of the artistic representation of reality. If we conceive of fiction caught in a debate between history and poetry, this is because the novel contains more of the contingent, the accidental, than any other genre and at the same time seeks to justify itself, not only as imitation, but

91

also as an art of language. Ayala's use of existing literature serves to heighten our sense of fiction as art. All the characters, in fact, detach themselves, at least momentarily, to discuss some aspect or other of literature. Tigre Juan, clearly, is totally engrossed in the *comedia* to the extent, as Weber observes, "that real emotional transport can only be compared to the effects of theatrical catharsis," as when he experiences "una manera de dichoso embobamiento, como ante una apoteosis escénica de gran tramoya." He quotes phrases from *Othello* and *El médico de su honra*, blending together his own lines with those of famous dramatic characters. Colás comments on the story of Werther which enkindles his own nascent romanticism. Doña Mariquita, on the other hand, dismisses works of literature as "majaderías inventadas para pasar el rato" (IV:684). Doña Iluminada makes frequent references to fairy-tales and romances of chivalry and seems to see her own role in life as in some way analagous to literary creation. She describes Colás as a "cabellero andante" (IV:613) or as an "arquetipo de donceles y príncipe de amadores perfectos" (IV:693). When things go wrong, she describes her part in the tragedy as that of an "egoísta maese Pedro de este aflictivo retablo, momumento de nubes, tan presto levantado como venido al suelo" (IV:740), evoking, in Weber's words, "the classic Cervantine example of the deceptive boundaries of reality and art."29

In making literature out of literature, Ayala calls attention to his own creative role, to the interplay of subjectivity and objectivity which is characteristic of all fiction. The various literary transpositions in *Tigre Juan* and *El curandero de su honra* show the essential fictionality of the work, as the literature of the past acts as a mirror for the new work. As well as *donjuanismo* and *pundonor*, we find a whole series of Golden Age motifs and themes. There are *conceptista* word plays, puns, the use of the comic anecdote, the intercalated tale, and major themes such as the fugitive and illusory nature of life and the idea of the world as a dream which is elaborated in the poem of the *Coda*: "Todo huye y se desvanece. / Vivir. Soñar. La vida es sueño. / El mundo es el sueño de Dios" (IV:700). Therefore, although the novel is a comic deflation of two literary archetypes, its attitude to literature generally is more complex. Life and literature are constantly seen to interfere with one another and through conscious manipulation of the narrative, parody and artistic transpositions the novelist directs attention away from external reality towards the intricacies of the novel's own making.

We therefore can see how Pérez de Ayala's use of the paradigms of existing literature involves much more than a recognition that "todo se repite," to use Amorós' phrase. His practice has, in fact, less to do with his vision of the world than with his conception of literature. He is a classicist in the sense that he believed that novels are based less on life than on other books and that the body of literature is a system of interrelated texts, just as the text itself is a system of interrelated elements. Ayala's practice is to conform to or to deviate from existing models, and this is the practice of all writers whether they acknowledge it or are even aware of it. In order to create works of literature and in order to understand works of litera- ture it is necessary to have assimilated the conventions by which they operate. Ayala therefore interprets true originality not as novelty, but as the acknowledgement of sources, of origins, "las tradiciones literarias primordiales" (III:161). Here is the keystone of Ayala "classicism," the exact opposite of the Romantic idea of the writer turning personal experience directly into words. We could conclude, even, that Ayala comes close to saying, perhaps without articulating it fully, that it is not man that creates literature, but literature that creates man.

NOTES

[1]T.S. Eliot, "Ulysses, Order and Myth," *Dial* 75 (1923):482-83.

[2]G. Josipovici, *The Lessons of Modernism* (London: Macmillan, 1977) 101.

[3]T.S. Elliot, "Tradition and the Individual Talent," in *Selected Essays* (London: Faber and Faber, 1975) 38.

[4]Andrés Amorós, *La novela intelectual de Ramón Pérez de Ayala* 66.

[5]Maruxa Salgues de Cargill, *Los mitos clásicos y modernos en la novela de Pérez de Ayala* (Jaén: Instituto de Estudios Giennenses, 1971); "Mito de don Quijote y Sancho en *Belarmino y Apolonio*," *Insula* 274 (Sept. 1969):16; and with Julián Palley, "Myth and Anti-Myth in *Tigre Juan*," *Revista de Estudios Hispánicos* 7 (1973):399-416.

[6]Esperanza Rodríguez Monescillo, "El mundo helénico en Ramón Pérez de Ayala," *Actas del II Congreso Español de Estudios Clásicos* (Madrid: Sociedad de Estudios Clásicos, 1961):511.

[7]Francisco Agustín, *Ramón Pérez de Ayala. Su vida y obras* (Madrid: G. Hernández y Galo Sáez, 1927) 162-164.

[8]Julio Matas, *Contra el honor. Las novelas normativas de Ramón Pérez de Ayala* (Madrid: Ediciones y Seminarios, 1974) 46.

[9]D.L. Fabian, "Action and Idea in *Amor y pedagogía* and *Prometeo*," *Hispania* XLI (1958):32.

[10]N. Urrutia, *De Troteras a Tigre Juan* (Madrid: Insula, 1960) 44.

[11]Esperanza Rodríguez Monescillo 512.

[12]F.W. Weber, *The Literary Perspectivism of Ramón Pérez de Ayala* (Chapel Hill: University of North Carolina Press, 1966) 41.

[13]Andrés Amorós, *La novela intelectual* 258.

[14]"Myth and Meaning in Pérez de Ayala's *Prometeo*," *Belfast Spanish and Portuguese Papers* (Belfast: Queen's University, 1979) 79-94.

[15]Eric Bentley, *The Life of the Drama* (London: Methuen, 1955) 53.

[16]Herman Meyer, *The Poetics of Quotation in the European Novel* (Princeton: Princeton University Press, 1968).

[17]Andrés Amorós, *La novela intelectual* 267-68.

[18]Julio Matas 46-48.

[19]Francisco Agustín 167.

[20]Eugenio de Nora, *La novela española contemporánea 1898-1927* (Madrid: Gredos, 1958) 488-90.

[21]John H. Hartsook, "Literary Tradition as Form in Pérez de Ayala," *Romance Notes* VI (1964):21-25.

[22]F.W. Weber 100.

[23]José María Martínez Cachero, "Prosistas y poetas novecentistas. La aventura del ultraísmo. Jarnés y la 'nova novorum'." *Historia general de las literaturas hispánicas* (Barcelona: Vergara, 1968) VII:406.

[24]"Andrenio" (E. Gómez de Baquero) writing in *La Esfera*, 2 June 1923.

[25]G.G. Brown, *A Literary History of Spain. The Twentieth Century* (London: Benn, 1972) 43.

[26]Luis Calvo, "El día de Ramón Pérez de Ayala," *ABC*, 23 November 1930.

[27]W.E. McCulloh, *Longus* (New York: Twayne, 1970) 63-64.

[28]Julio Matas 88.

[29]F.W. Weber 94.

CHAPTER FOUR

ALIENATION AND INTEGRATION:
PEREZ DE AYALA AND THE NOVEL OF CONSCIOUSNESS

An interest in psychology is not in itself a defining feature of Modernism, for the great nineteenth-century novelists showed an enormous interest in the psychological mainsprings of human behaviour and traced out in fine detail the complex of motivation and personal interaction that characterise the actions and choices of individuals. On the whole, however, their interest centred primarily on conscious behaviour, and they saw their role as that of an observer looking from the outside on the manifestations of behaviour which they attempted to approach in a broadly "scientific" manner. A clear distinction existed between the observer and what he observed. The Modernist conception of consciousness, on the other hand, departs from the essential stability of this largely traditional viewpoint and, broadly speaking, involved a marked shift from outer to inner, accompanied by an awareness that consciousness itself was unstable, problematical and essentially unknown. Modernists concern themselves less with the external manifestations of consciousness and more with its obscure, beguiling and potentially dangerous outer limits. As with so much else in the Modernist panorama, their response to new psychological ideas is one of challenge and crisis. Unlike the Realist, the Modernist could not take for granted that he was what he seemed to be or that others were as they seemed to be. Virginia Woolf seems to hit the right note in her perceptive and eminently quotable *Modern Fiction*:

> for the moderns ... the point of interest lies very likely in the dark places of psychology. At once, therefore, the accent falls a little differently, the emphasis is upon something hitherto ignored, at once a different outline of form becomes necessary, difficult for us to grasp, incomprehensible to our predecessors ... there is no limit to the horizon, and ... nothing, no "method," no experiment, even of the wildest — is forbidden, only falsity and pretence.[1]

Shifts in ideology and ideas meant that traditional frameworks of assurance were collapsing, the institutions which provided meaning were under threat and, above all, that ultimate guarantor of Absolute meaning and purpose, Religion, had lost its unique sense of authority. To be alive became not a cause of rejoicing and exhilaration, but a source of anxiety, insecurity and despair. The discovery of the unconscious was at once enslaving in that it postulated a self greater than the merely conscious, but it was also potentially liberating for the creative artist in that it revealed a whole reservoir of material

beyond the processes of reason which would both inspire and valid-
ate his creative enterprise.

It is not my intention in this chapter to trace the influence of any
particular psychologist on the work of Pérez de Ayala. That is not to
say that there are no such influences acting upon his work. An
examination of what remains of his library shows a special interest in
works of psychology and, as I shall demonstrate, there is a remark-
able affinity between the ideas of Carl Gustav Jung and the vision
embodied in Ayala's mature works. My intention, though, is to trace a
pattern of concern with the workings of the mind, in a way which
involves an overlapping or interaction of philosophy and psychology,
throughout Ayala's fiction, and to suggest that it follows some of the
most significant developments in the thinking of psychologists in the
twentieth century, the century in which, of course, psychology came
into its own as a separate science. In a way, we are considering the
most recent phase in the development of modern scientific knowledge since its initiation in the seventeenth century through the works
of Newton and Descartes, among others. As I have implied, the
central preoccupation in the modern period is man's sense of alienation from the world around him, a dilemma explored in Ayala's early
proto-Existentialist works, and man's attempts to reintegrate himself
within the overall scheme of things, a process explored in Ayala's
later works. Underlying this development is a sense of the dichotomy
between man and the world, between consciousness and reality,
between subject and object, between perceiver and perceived, and a
need to bridge that dichotomy, to destroy the dualism of mind and
body, to close the gulf between the individual and the world, between
self and other. Pérez de Ayala is particularly interesting in this
respect, for he had a fundamentally dualistic cast of mind and at the
same time strove for that sense of harmony which is produced by the
fusion of opposites, the balancing of antitheses, the bringing together
of polarities. This differentiates him from other fictional explorers of
the depths of consciousness, and it is interesting to note how he distanced himself significantly from the work of two great twentieth-
century novelists, James Joyce and Marcel Proust, of whom he
wrote "son el tope postrero, el *nec plus ultra* de aquel callejón sin
salida de la novela psicológica."[2]

It is not possible to consider the question of psychology in narrative without making some observations on the notion of character or,
more properly, on the relationship between character and plot. Most
Realist novelists would have subscribed to the view that novels exist
to portray character and that it is usually a character — real or imaginary — who inspires a novel. Henry James refers to Turgeniev's
practice for whom "the fictive picture ... began almost always with
the vision of some person or persons."[3] Pío Baroja extends this to
include setting as well: "A mí, en general, es un tipo o un lugar el

96

que me sugiere la novela."[4] The fact is that we have become accustomed to the idea that in narrative character takes precedence over the action (or story or plot). Indeed, we read novels to acquire insights into character and have become adept at reading narrative indices of character. Much of our criticism involves character-study, and our assumptions about human individuality are virtually indistinguishable from our concept of character in fiction.[5] In an important sense, the novel reinforces our sense of individuality, but of course it can be argued that such a way of conceiving character is not natural but cultural in origin. It would not have made much sense to Aristotle, for example, for whom the action is paramount and the characters necessary only as agents. In such a view, characters lack autonomy and are merely functional within the narrative. Structuralist critics, too, see characters as manifestations of deep plot functions, although one cannot help feeling that the best studies of this kind are based on primitive forms such as folk tales, where there are actants such as Hero, Villain, Helper, which are essentially functional. However, once the basic type is elaborated, it acquires "individuality," acquires attributes which we use to construct what we know as character. We seem to have a cultural compulsion to do so, and it is well to acknowledge this. At the same time, however, the indices of character cannot exist without plot, however rudimentary, that is to say without the support of a structure of narrative. It is well to bear this in mind when dealing with Ayala's fiction. However much he is influenced by psychological ideas, these are predominantly ideas, and therefore his psychological dispositions of narrative are structural in origin: they function as part of a system. To be convinced by the characters, one must to some degree be convinced by the framework of ideas underlying them. What makes Ayala a modernist in his treatment of the mind is his espousal of a system of framing ideas which underlie his exploration of states of consciousness.

Pérez de Ayala's early novels, the so-called autobiographical cycle of *Tinieblas en las cumbres* (1907), *A.M.D.G.* (1908), *La pata de la raposa* (1912) and *Troteras y danzaderas* (1913), linked by the presence of Alberto Díaz de Guzmán, can easily be accommodated to the general pattern of the fiction of the period. Alberto's spiritual brothers are Pío Cid, Fernando Ossorio, Antonio Azorín, Augusto Pérez and Andrés Hurtado. The traditional approach to this fiction is, as I have already noted, to consider it in ideological terms through the notion of the Generation of 1898. The most convincing and influential work in this area is that of Donald L. Shaw, who emphasises the philosophical crisis experienced by young intellectuals of the time and their search for new value-systems to replace their shattered ideals and lost illusions. I have insisted that to isolate the ideas of a character in a novel and equate them with the ideas of his creator for the purposes of constructing an ideological biography is to do violence to the literary text as text and is not the proper task of the

97

literary critic. This is not to say that Shaw's assessments of individual characters are in some way wrong, for they are clearly not. They are deficient, however, in that they do not elucidate the meaning within the text except at the level of apparent content. To imply that the vision embodied in a text corresponds exactly to what an author "believed" in reality requires a leap over logic and a descent into speculation that is surely unjustifiable. In what follows, therefore, I am concerned with the biography of Alberto Díaz de Guzmán as a manifestation of certain psychological ideas prevalent at the turn of the century which have implications not only for the modern conception of consciousness but also for the Modernist's approach to the art of fiction. We can observe this in the portrayal of the protagonist in Ayala's very first novel.

The presentation of Alberto in *Tinieblas en las cumbres* hints in a somewhat stereotyped way at his psychological complexity ("complejidad," "torbellino de fuerzas confusas," "tediosa seriedad" [I:114]), a rift between the inner and outer selves. When he first looks at Rosina (I:122-23) he appears detached, distanced, so that his inner dissociation is complemented by a dissociation in his personal relationships, a dissociation, moreover, which relates to his relationship with women: the prostitute is treated as a "distinguida damisela." This ambiguity in the male's reaction to woman is something which recurs in Ayala's work and is not unlike Freud's description of the Madonna and the Prostitute. Here Alberto is restrained by "pudor," he has a "purísima afición," attitudes which he retains throughout the journey. Alberto's outlook appears moulded by his religious upbringing and particularly his fear of Hell, which gives rise to emotions of fear, guilt and anxiety (I:131). In his subsequent behaviour, Alberto's external actions contradict his inner feelings, he fails to achieve full integration as an individual, even on a basic level ("aun cuando quería aparecer sereno e indiferente, no las tenía todas consigo" [I:141]). His remarks on painting (I:163), and the narrator's distinguishing of him and Travesedo from the others, prepare the way for the "Coloquio Superfluo" where the main implications of the work are discussed, namely the relationship between nature and consciousness. Yiddy's words about the "vida falsa y convencional" of outer expression already call to mind the discrepancy between the fundamental self and the social self later formulated by Bergson, and his comments on the suffering induced by awareness are markedly Schopenhauerian and anticipate Pío Baroja's *El árbol de la ciencia*, published in 1911. Yiddy has gone beyond the experience which Alberto is at present undergoing, a feeling of dissolution before nature: "confundido y asi como disuelto en un espíritu o gran alma universal" (I:182-183), on the verge of total communion, of total knowledge, the moment of blinding insight into "el gran enigma del mundo, el pensamiento del orbe" (I:183), a sense of revelation that is unique, a precious and unrepeated moment of illumination. For Yiddy these are now "extravagantes ideas de misticismo y panteísmo" (I:186), graphically illustrated in his hallucinatory experience in which the tree symbolically figures. Indeed, Yiddy virtually becomes a tree ("Yo fui un árbol"). For Alberto such an experience is akin to an experience of the divinity to which life should aspire. Interestingly, Yiddy had equated this with the putative *nirvana* of Buddhist endeavour but abandons it in favour of a resigned skepticism and a sustained despising of humanity. In other words, he rejects any notion of ever reaching a sense of total transcendental meaning, whereas Alberto adheres to his view that "el hombre es el sentido de la tierra" (I:191), a humanist affirmation of anthropocentrism. It soon transpires, however, that human mortality is the real basis of this spiritual quest, the desire to remain and survive beyond the limits of temporal existence. Art, which holds out the prospect of eternal fame, offers that possibility. Moreover, although Alberto has outgrown the superstitious elements of popular religion, he remains a religious spirit in his belief in "algo misterioso, de sutilísima esencia que, infundido en nuestro cuerpo, lo anima y le ha de sobrevivir" (I:195). Yiddy is a naturalist in the sense that he believes only in the mind as a set of neurological processess: "La conciencia es un fenómeno nervioso. Muerto el perro, se acabó la conciencia" (I:195). This is a theme which Alberto takes up soon afterwards: "Acaso la conciencia no sea otra cosa que fenómeno huidero; pero por él todos los átomos del inmenso conjunto han de pasar, a su vez, sólo con el fin de que posean y afirmen esta verdad sublime: 'Soy la conciencia del universo.' Y cuando el hombre lo comprende así, es realmente parte de Dios en el Universo" (I:213).

Consciousness is an essential element in the development of mankind, and this accords him his uniqueness in the natural world. But man is aware of the distinction between his consciousness and that of which he is conscious. This consciousness — which, as Alberto reminds Yiddy, was for Pascal the source of man's greatness — makes man aware that he and the world are distinct, and makes him aware too of his own frailty in the face of the natural world. Hence Alberto's desire to fuse with the world and his sense of some all-pervading spirit or power presiding in all things: "¡Espíritu Misterioso, Ciega y Terrible Potencia, seas quien fueses: piedad para este guiñapo de carne efímera y bestezuela inmundamente orgullosa!" (I:214). There is, of course, a dualist concept here of spirit and matter, but also an acceptance or a hope that some superior consciousness governs everything. This makes bearable the limitations of human experience, the fact that man sees his world, in Kafka's words, "with the terrestrially sullied eye."[6]

The primarily interesting thing about Alberto is that he is not concerned with interpersonal relationships but rather more with questions of purpose and finality, hence the religious nature of his experience. Such a position already shows a Jungian predisposition in Ayala's work, as opposed to a Freudian one which is concerned with personal relations and sexuality, and regards the concern with the meaning of life as an abnormality in itself: "He who asks the meaning of life is already sick. The meaning of life is life itself."[7] Religion, for Freud, had been a kind of universal neurosis, and art, to which Alberto is attached in a quasi-religious manner, is akin to it. The sense that life is without meaning and the normal human desire to attribute meaning to it are at the root of the oppressive weight of consciousness. Alberto is obsessed with the prospect of the advent of death at any moment, with the feeling that life is a blind force over which man has no control, and with the horror of the precariousness of human personality, bereft of all possibility of permanence: "El que no seamos nada; el que no sepamos nada; el que sospechemos que el Universo es una cosa ciega, estúpida y fatal; el que pasemos por la vida como la sombra ha pasado sobre las montañas, sin dejar nada detrás de sí" (I:216). As Alberto's entry into the church shows, his desire is to regress to the security of his childhood, the clarity of vision, the strength of faith. His psychological disorientation ("no sé lo que hago" [I:224]) derives from the fact that God has either ceased to exist or at least is forever hidden. There is here the beginnings of an existential crisis, but at the same time Alberto's experience bears a close relation to Modernist theories of art: the artist's finest perceptions are irrational in origin, but they seem to contribute to the healing of the rift between man and nature, if only for a time. The central psychological problem for Alberto in *Tinieblas en las cumbres* is that of relating himself, as a rational but powerless being, to the rest of nature which appears blind, irrational and powerful. Nature exhibits qualities which man, having evolved, does not share, at least consciously. However, the legacy of naturalism has left an awareness that man is still controlled by the forces of nature, by instinct. We can therefore interpret Yiddy's assimilation to the tree in two ways. On the one hand, it represents a desire to fuse with nature and apprehend the meaning of life, but, on the other, it can be seen as a manifestation of the Freudian death-wish, "the most universal endeavor of all living substance — namely to return to the quiescence of the inorganic world."[8] Ayala's evocation can be linked directly to his poem: "¡Quién fuera árbol! Mejor, ¡quién fuera piedra!" in "Canción del hombre macilento," which also refers to Pascal, and which echoes Rubén Darío's "Lo fatal" from *Cantos de vida y esperanza* (1905). The same idea recurs in *La pata de la raposa*. This is a desire to abdicate consciousness in favour of a state of unawareness, of self-forgetfulness. In *Tinieblas en las cumbres*, it must not be forgotten, there is a deflationary element in Ayala's approach to Alberto: he never lets it be forgotten that during most of this experience the character is drunk. Nevertheless, Alberto's search, in common with that of many twentieth-century thinkers, for total explanations is due to the legacy, in Freudian terms, of earlier systems of thought, in the midst of our present scientific one. Man had formed "three great pictures of the universe: animistic (mythological), religious and scientific."[9] These are notions which will recur in Ayala's work, and the fragmentary and limited nature of scientific knowledge will be set against the comprehensiveness of myth. In the first novel, Yiddy exhorts an abandonment of the quest for meaning in favour of a reduction to knowable areas of activity, his "pequeño jardín" (254). In the 1942 Prologue to the Argentinian edition of *Troteras y danzaderas* Ayala takes up the notion of science as modern man's religion:

> ¿Podría acaso supervivir la ciencia, que en el siglo XIX un hipócrita había querido profetizar como "La religión del porvenir"? Pero, aniquilados los demás valores vitales ¿qué sentido o validez ideal podrá conservar la ciencia? Supuesto que fuera factible la conversión de todo lo vital en valor científico, y viceversa ¿de qué nos servivía un amor científico, una belleza científica, una religión científica, una ética científica, un arte científico y una poesía científica?[10]

Yiddy has approached a stage of total skepticism. Alberto seems to seek a regression into an unconscious life, free from pain and contradictions. This involves some acceptance of the fusion of the individual with some universal spirit, an instinctive rejection of the persuasive force of materialism with its purely biological concept of human life.

The general intention behind the early novels is explained by Pérez de Ayala himself in the 1942 Prologue alluded to above. There are reasons, which should be stated at the outset, why this Prologue needs to be approached with some reservations. In the first place, Ayala was writing some thirty years after the completion of his early work, in exile, and in the immediate aftermath of the Spanish Civil War. One of his principal aims was to defend himself against the charge that he had painted a negative, and hence unpatriotic, picture of his country. The Prologue therefore strives to give a more positive orientation to his thought by insisting that the series was left unfinished. At an early stage in his argument Ayala tries to identify his work with the recognised literary movement of the 98 by stating as its aim that of "analizar y reflejar la crisis de conciencia hispánica desde principios de este siglo." Moreover, the close identification of author and character, which was soon taken for granted, may have encouraged Ayala to give Alberto's dilemma a more universal, and therefore less directly personal, meaning. This possibility, together with Ayala's well-known fondness for constructing elaborate abstract systems, casts some doubt on the prologue as a guide to interpretation. Nonetheless, some of the points it makes give an indication of how Ayala conceived his novels and of how they relate to the wider shifts in fiction and philosophy that are characteristic of the period in which they were written.

The most interesting statement made by Ayala in the early part of his Prologue is his assertion that novels are concerned with states of consciousness: "Quiero decir que una novela se compone de las reacciones de conciencia de cada personaje frente al presente vital." Thus minor characters serve to "provocar o estimular en el protagonista reacciones de conciencia" and to represent the variety of basic attitudes to life. It is from this point that Ayala develops his theory that the Spanish crisis anticipated the European one (a theory which can be substantiated), but on the question of the relationship between the individual and the nation to which he belongs Ayala's emphasis is rather different. The crisis which Ayala appears to identify is a crisis of internationalism and a reawakening of the spirit of nationalism. The whole thrust of the prologue is to place the early novels in the context of the individual as an expression of the nation to which he belongs and to explain how the completed process, the individual's "integración y liberación en la conciencia nacional," was never given full expression because the series was never completed. Ayala argues that the nineteenth century, especially the late nineteenth century, was the century of internationalism and that literature in Europe, outside Spain, reflected this in its treatment of consciousness divorced from a national context in the belief that it was confronting universal problems, generally those of the "hipertrofía del yo." The European post-war crisis, as it happens, is a consequence of a collective loss of direction and led to the realisation that a man's experience is universalised only through the nation to which he belongs. Ayala emphasises this unitary perspective when he extols "la cultura unitaria del mundo helénico" and argues that in the twentieth century "la conciencia individual ... ha ido centrándose sobre el eje de la conciencia nacional, con un solo polo magnético, que es la unidad universal de la cultura, la vida del espíritu en sus raíces milenarias, hacia su destino, no menos remoto." Ayala is interested in tracing a disintegrated consciousness in evolution towards an integrated consciousness, that is, with its national present and past, so that the individual is defined only by the greater whole. In other words, an individualist psychology is outgrown. Whatever the justification for this assessment of his early creative endeavour, the 1942 Prologue does provide an insight into the psychological dimension of the fiction, which motivates its peculiar texture:

> Estas novelas ... no debían ni podían ajustarse a un rígido, y desde luego artificial método cronológico ..., sino más bien tendrían que ir fluyendo, como la vida misma, conforme y al par de las contingencias y peripecias que iban presentando aquellas diversos medios ambientes, los cuales

había de precisar y determinar el proceso evolutivo en la psicología de algunos personajes representativos.

Ayala clearly reveals himself as being interested in states of consciousness, "este fluir y reaccionar de la conciencia," as he describes it. This overall psychological evolution is the Ariadna's thread, which must guide the reader through the labyrinth of the early novels so that he can perceive the progression "desde lo caótico en la conciencia individual hasta la ordenación en la conciencia nacional." What remains most vividly, however, from a reading of the novels is the sense of chaos and crisis which characterises the portrayal of the principal character of the series, Alberto Díaz de Guzmán, "en cuya alma iban tomando cuerpo los síntomas de la psicología europea, a fines del pasado siglo y comienzos del actual; la actitud individualista, supernacional y antihistórica, frente a los problemas fundamentales de la vida; la conciencia criticista y disolvente, 'el universo soy yo.'" This crisis results in the loss of faith in all absolutes (love, beauty, religion, art, morality), with the result that there remain often only two alternatives: either the acceptance that everything is without value, or the belief that all must be made again and restored to its original value. This leads Ayala into his exposition of the three phases of consciousness which correspond to the poematic periods of his projected work: *Las formas, las nubes, las normas.* In the first phase, corresponding to adolescence, the world appears passive and made only for the individual who may take possession of it. In the second phase, the visible form of this world resists possession, becomes evasive, bewildering and dissolves into nothingness. The self feels alienated and divorced from the world. The third phase, corresponding to maturity, brings the realisation that the forms are only the visible manifestations of eternal norms to which man must become attuned. He cannot create these norms himself but lives them in all their originality.

In one sense Ayala is being untrue to his original vision, which depicts a fallen world, mistrusting history and progress, and relying on the subjectivity of the artist himself as an alienated consciousness. But in another sense he exemplifies the integrating tendency of Modernism, which seeks to replace the shattered consciousness of modern reality with the unitary vision which it superseded. That vision founds itself, however, not on religion, philosophy or science, but on fiction itself, and to that extent there is a consistency between the notion of our integrating fiction and that of a plenitude of consciousness which exists beyond time and history. We can see the origins of this development in *La pata de la raposa*, which, although it is Pérez de Ayala's third novel, is the chronological sequel to *Tinieblas en las cumbres* and continues Alberto's quest for the meaning of life. That quest is increasingly bound up with the practice of art, and it has implications not dissimilar from those of Existentialist philosophy. Pérez de Ayala's use of his own experiences and his imaginative recreation of them appear to confirm Keith May's observation that "the writer of serious fiction builds his life upon the supposition that the imagination working through the written word is — apart, possibly, from religion — the best way of making sense of things."[11] In the case of *La pata de la raposa*, the connection between the fictional life of Alberto Díaz de Guzmán and the real-life biography of his creator suggests an attempt on the author's part to impose upon his experience a kind of artistic coherence. We can perceive here already the integrating tendency of Modernist fiction, but it is hardly surprising that Maruxa Salgues de Cargill suggests that Ayala's fictional recreation of his adolescence has a mythical significance for him: "Pérez de Ayala, en sus novelas de juventud, y en especial en *La pata de la raposa*, nos ofrece una visión de su propio aprendizaje de la vida por medio del personaje de Alberto. El escritor logra a través del retrato que nos ofrece lo que Thomas Mann había llamado 'identificación mítica.'"[12]

Generally recognised as a *novela de protagonista*, *La pata de la raposa* traces the attempts of Alberto to make sense of existence and forge satisfactory human relationships. The structure of the novel, characterised by spatial and temporal dislocation, reflects the erratic nature of his journey through life. The progression of the narrative is broadly linear in that it spans five consecutive years: from the first edition, we know that Part One, which occupies just over one half of the novel, opens in September 1905; Part Two, which occupies about one third, in February 1907, and Part Three in September 1910. Several intervening years are left unrecounted, so that three short, decisive periods in Alberto's life are juxtaposed. Similarly the action of the novel moves from place to place: Pilares, Cenciella, Villaclara, London, Lugano, the north of Spain and, indirectly, Madrid. This movement, representing both quest and flight, is a prominent feature of the novel and, just as temporal and spatial fragmentation mirror the disorder of the character's life, so too is the alternation of moods and tones in the novel's composition a reflection of his instability. In a sense, the movement of the novel is circular: it could continue in the same way forever with an accumulation of incidents and experiences. A consequence of this type of structure is the relative imbalance between the three parts. If Alberto's life and experience are represented as a continuous cycle of impasses, the author is obliged to introduce some variety into his work through the addition of secondary stories (the life of the Mackenzies, for example), and descriptions that are interesting in their own right (the life of the circus, the music-hall, the Swedes in London), though in all cases these have a function in the main narrative, deepening and developing for the reader Alberto's emotional crisis. Another consequence, which is in the very nature of the theme treated, is a certain inconclusiveness, which Ayala counters by patterning Alberto's quest around the movement of the day. This gives the work an overall shape through the imposition of a tripartite structure based on an elementary symbolism of light and darkness. Alberto will progress from total darkness (*la noche*) to a new dawn (*el alba*) only to relapse into the sunset heralding a new darkness (*la tarde*). The appearance of Alberto in Chapter 2 marks the beginning of the novel proper, and the description of Alberto's awakening is, *pace* Shaw, markedly ironic. All the philosophical or Existentialist watchwords are there: "alma," "conciencia," "arbitrariamente," "un universo ... sin sentido," "ajena," "voluntad" (I:245), but are placed very firmly in the context of a hangover. The fundamental detachment implied by such a perspective is characteristic of the treatment of Alberto throughout the novel. Although the text appears to move on to a more serious level, it is difficult not to see Alberto's self-contemplation and his growing awareness in terms of his physical state. Nonetheless, Alberto's *malaise* is given a metaphysical dimension. Stripped of all "mentiras vitales" and "ilusiones normas" at an early age, he is made aware of the absence of absolute values and of the transience and futility of life's endeavors. The most enduring of his illusions had been his belief in the value of art, "un abrigaño adonde acogerse a la vida" (I:246-47), but the destruction of his works of art (with the exception of the Mona Lisa, whose enigmatic smile appears as a "velado emblema del sentido y la expresión del orbe" [I:247-48]) mark the death of this illusion, just as his throwing out of his books marks his rejection of intellectualism. But these illusions are replaced by another: "Pensaba olvidarse de sí propio" (I:248), so that the novel marks a new beginning for him.

The novel traces this evolution and, in addition to its basic tripartite form, imparts coherence to Alberto's experience by a series of structural devices such as the opposition between light and dark, the use of contrasts, parallels and analogies between different incidents and different sets of experiences, and the succession of high points or epiphanies in the character's experience. These structuring devices enable the reader to apprehend patterns of behaviour in a novel which appears to have no adequate resolution in terms of plot. A salient feature of this behaviour, in my view, is Alberto's aesthetic response to stimuli. This is not merely a phase through which Alberto passes but a consistent characterising tendency, and it is surely no coincidence that *La pata de raposa* itself is impregnated with references to works of art and to literature. This is seen in the use of epigraphs, literary and artistic allusions, scenes reminiscent of the *sainete*, passages which have all the flavour of the *folletín*, and a more general parodic tone. The opening pages recall directly the beginning of Alas' *La Regenta*, also set in Oviedo, and the graveyard scene echoes that of *Hamlet*. All these features will have to be considered in more detail later in relation to the metafictional dimension of Ayala's novels. The novel proper opens with Alberto's recognition of the transience and futility of all life's endeavours, and also of the inadequacy of the last bastion of his defences against life, art itself. There is thus an important psychological dimension to his involvement with art: it offers an alternative reality, a refuge. His abandonment of it, together with his rejection of intellectualism, marks a new phase in his spiritual quest, but the reality is that Alberto is never able to free himself sufficiently from his own consciousness of self to engage purposefully with life. A perfect illustration of this is offered by the poems of Chapter VI, not just the fact that they are artistic transpositions of experience but also that they are based on his readings. Alberto cannot experience first-hand: all is filtered through his cultural experience, and real emotion is confused with aesthetic emotion. This in turn leads to the adoption of the pose, the hallmark of inauthenticity, witnessed earlier when his reactions in the *chigre* are motivated by previous artistic experiences, "esa forma de ver las cosas con ojos ajenos, y en metáfora" (I:258). He needs to strip this away if he is to find his "alma niña," or his "personalidad recóndita, virgen, auténtica" (I:262), and it is the process which is charted in the novel. Alberto's progress is fitful and fragmentary, as is his relationship with Fina, which nevertheless appears as the only point of stability within his life. His rapprochements with her produce periods of expansiveness and serenity, as at one point "comprendía difusamente, entre turbios vapores espirituales, que en su alma germinaban a lo sordo las ideas matrices y las normas morales de una vida renovada, toda serenidad y aplomo" (I:279). But, as I have shown elsewhere, Alberto is really only capable of intellectualising his emotions, of theorising about ideal situations.[13] His view of a love relationship is, in short, literature-inspired, and he himself is the victim of a very particular kind of *modernista* sensibility. Indeed, in a later article, not connected with *La pata de la raposa,* Ayala described this phenomenon in the following terms:

> El reaccionar voluptuosamente sobre las emociones, gozándose en ellas con morbosa delectación y procurando transfundirlas en formas artísticas y sentimentales, tengo para mí que es el peor síntoma de decadencia, poquedad de espíritu y bajeza de ánimo. Además, esta manera de emocionarse no entraña verdadera emoción. Es, en puridad, conato de emoción, emoción fingida. El hombre que por su costumbre y deleite se abandona a estas emociones rumiadas e incubadas artificiosamente en los senos obscuros de la sensibilidad, suele ser hombre incapacitado para recibir la herida saludable y vivificante de la verdadera emoción.[14]

Fina represents one phase of Alberto's spiritual quest; she acts as a kind of Ariadna, leading him through the labyrinth of his confusions. As such, she enables him to abdicate personal responsibility. But there are other phases as well: belief in friendship, the desire to act rather than think, a refusal to take life seriously, "vivir el humoris-mo," a need to react to life in all its totality. In the end Alberto is shown not to have resolved the basic dichotomy within him, the split in his personality which is manifest in the dual perspective of his poem, "La dulce Helena," which reveals his own alienation from himself. In an essay written in the 1950's Ayala put forward some ideas on psychic dissociation:

> .... la psique, cuando tiende y deriva a lo anormal y dese-quilibrado, se polariza hacia dos tipos extremos de actividad interior: el introverso y el extroverso. Estos dos tipos suelen ser intercambiables. El introverso se trueca de súbito en un extroverso desaforado, en un modo de carga y descarga alternadas. A esta psicología inestable se llama ciclotímica; o sea de alma alterna, que se muda, sin estadios interme-dios, del más hondo abatimiento, a la más violenta exalta-ción, del ensimismamiento a la enajenación, o enajenación de sí mismo.[15]

In *La pata de la raposa* Ayala has not formulated a theory of art which can be reconciled with genuine experience of life. Literature and life are to some degree seen as antitheses, and this is a reflec-tion of the wider pattern of polarities which remain unresolved. The integrating function of art will emerge as a theme in his later work, just as the theme of the integration of the personality will assume a major importance. On a psychological level, the dualist principle con-tinues to play a significant role, as we can see as we turn to Ayala's most celebrated novel, *Belarmino y Apolonio*.

While *Belarmino y Apolonio* is striking for its bold experimenta-tion with narrative structure, it nonetheless deserves mention in the context of our present discussion of the psychological *donnés* of Ayala's fiction. For some critics it has the qualities of a *Bildungs-roman* and is therefore something of a piece with Ayala's earlier cycle of novels. Sara Suárez Solís, for example, is of the opinion that ".... esta novela .... en muchos aspectos, tiene incluso no poco de *Bildungsroman*, de novela-aprendizaje, cuyos protagonistas .... sufren un proceso de transformación espiritual, de humanización cre-ciente, de purificación anímica, semejantes (aunque sin perder su valor de parodia) a los que caracterizan a este tipo de relatos."[16] However, the really interesting feature of this novel, which is related to its innovatory structure, is the obvious pairing of characters so that, in psychological terms, it is impossible to see them in isolation one from the other. Thus Wilma Newberry uses the novel as a demonstration of the role of the *Doppelgänger,* or double, in litera-ture. By this term she means, firstly, "a very special relationship between characters that cannot be totally explained in realistic terms. There is a mysterious feeling of affinity for and obsessive awareness of the other, sometimes accompanied by intense and unmotivated antagonism." However antagonistic these characters are towards one another, the reality is that neither is complete in himself and needs the other for fulfillment. Secondly, there is doubling "within characters or within the author, victims of a split psyche, or governed by opposing forces producing the illusion that they are more than one person."[17] An example of this kind of doubling was to be found already in *La pata de la raposa,* where Alberto dramatises his conflict "desdoblándose en dos personas." In moments of crisis the personality disintegrates, following a natural "instinto de bifurcación." The second type is more easily seen in Ayala's last novel *Tigre Juan* and *El curandero de su honra,* whereas *Belarmino y Apolonio,* by and large, accords more attention to the former. From their initial encounter, it is clear that the relationship between the two shoemakers is complex in nature. Apolonio's new store outshines Belarmino's, and yet, although there can be no possible serious commercial competition, Apolonio has a sense, despite his triumph, of being humiliated: "sentíase humillado, adivinando que la verdadera rivalidad entre ellos no era zapateril, sino de otro orden más íntimo y personal, y que en aquella larvada e inevitable rivalidad acaso Belarmino saliese vencedor" (IV:70). It is precisely as his external world is destroyed (the social world) that Belarmino embarks upon his own journey of self-discovery, so radical that it involves a reappraisal of language itself, a repudiation of the outer world and a withdrawal into a world of silence. From the outset we had seen Belarmino cut off from others by his special language and, as he has less work, he has more time to devote to endowing words with his own meanings, to create his own private language. This phenomenon, as Leon Livingstone has recently demonstrated, is related to the question of novel-writing and reading.[18]

For the author, the act of writing narrative involves the creation of alternative selves. Ayala's notion of the "multiplicación del yo" is not dissimilar from Unamuno's idea of the multiplicity of personality in which each person is "todo un pueblo"[19] of contradictory personalities. Both raise, inevitably, the question of how far one can know the authentic self and the extent to which language acts as an obstacle to that knowledge. Moreover, there exists a barrier between self and other, a relationship which is both necessary for a sense of identity and at the same time potentially destructive of it. Thus conflictive tendencies within the individual are mirrored in conflictive tendencies between individuals. The division within the self is a product of consciousness, by virtue of which the self is both subject and object, and for Unamuno "la conciencia es una enfermedad."[20] And the unavoidable consequence of the "terrible tortura de nacer doble"[21] is the conflict between authenticity and falsification. All men wear a mask, put on an act, and their greatest ally in this theatricality is language itself; language is in a sense the creator of consciousness. For the writer, language is the means of self-exploration or of the exploration of reality, but it is also the instrument of exhibitionism, the medium for the displaying of individual talent. Thus language is dual: pose and sincerity are inseparable. This duality is represented in the conflicting personalities of Belarmino and Apolonio. In Ayala's novel, an artistic elaboration of don Amaranto's observation that "el drama y la filosofía son las únicas maneras de conocimiento," there is a paradoxical reversal in that the dramatist is seen as impassive, whereas the philosopher is more emotional than intellectual. Belarmino and Apolonio form an apparent antinomy who are in reality complementary, as is testified in the final chapter of the novel: Apolonio proclaims "Eres como mi otra mitad," to which Belarmino replies, "Sí, y tú mi otro testaferro" (IV:212). The inadequacy of the one is mirrored in the qualities of the other, and the coming together of the two characters represents a healing of the psychic split each has undergone and which is represented in the other. Otherness provides the key to selfhood, and indeed Apolonio's desire to kill Belarmino was in reality a kind of suicide of the second self, a desire to do away with that with which he could not come to terms. Their union at the fountain is a kind of symbolic resurrection as the fragmented psyche is reintegrated. This pattern, of course, extends throughout the whole novel in a series of complementary pairs: don Amaranto-Escobar, Pedro-Augustias, Anselmo-Felicita, Lirio-Lario, and so on. Ayala persistently refers to the doubling tendency of the psyche. He says, "me doblegaré," he creates two complementary and contrasting personalities, just like Amaranto and Escobar, of whom he writes, "¡Qué unidos y qué opuestos los dos personajes!" (IV:215). All of the characters in the novel are like the author's possible selves, and the fiction has the purpose of integrating them. It is not for nothing that of Belarmino and Apolonio he writes: "han existido por mí y para mí," and this gives a totally new and unexpected meaning to "Existir, multiplicarse, y amar" (IV:219).

The interest in doubles extends to Ayala's next novel. *Luna de miel, luna de hiel* and *Los trabajos de Urbano y Simona*. There is a duplication in the characters, for example, in Cástulo and Urbano, which Cástulo himself recognises: "En los trances en que Urbano se halla, me hallo yo asimismo imaginariamente," and there is additionally an inner doubling within the characters. Cástulo "vivía dos vidas paralelas, autónomas y sin mutuo contacto entre sí, una vida real y una vida imaginaria." The novel, as I have demonstrated elsewhere,[22] combines elements of romance and realism, the former to be found in plot and situation and the latter undeniably present in the psychological portrayal of the principal characters. A case in point is doña Micaela.

Doña Micaela dominates the opening pages of the novel, just as she dominates the lives of those around her. One of Ayala's most successful female characters, she is what Amorós calls "un verdadero cuadro clínico."[23] Her principal trait is an absence of sensuality. In church she is attracted not by the richness and sensuality of the decoration and ritual but rather by the cold, dark atmosphere which pervades the interior. In this way her religious experience is characterised: for Micaela religion means a sense of duty, control over life and instinct, a puritanical frigidity which inspires in her "entereza para sobrellevar las iniciaciones conyugales sin repulsión, con sumisa pasividad" (IV:244). Clearly her own particular awareness of sexuality lies behind her very unusual education of her son. Allied to this is her social ambition, manifest in her clear-sighted determination to attain precise objectives and in her desire not to be dominated by circumstances: "Doña Micaela, por el contrario, no admitía la realidad tal cual espontáneamente se ofrece, sino que, antes de aceptarla, pretendía convertirla en lo que ella, doña Micaela, quería que fuese y creía que debía ser" (IV:235). Amorós likens Micaela to don Quijote and to Galdós' Isidora Rufete; a more likely antecedent might be doña Perfecta. Micaela's own experience of life's sordidness at an early age moulded her very distinctive psychology, which can be seen as the product of the interaction of heredity and environmental factors. Her belief that all men are "niños asquerosos" induces her to make of her son "el primer ejemplo del hombre perfecto," an undertaking which relates her to Marco in *Prometeo*. In addition, the birth of a son provides Micaela with an opportunity to indulge her own inner desire to be a man. Ayala, therefore, offers a very Freudian interpretation of doña Micaela: she feels repulsion for men, yet at the same time her own character and behaviour are very masculine. Thus Ayala joins the literary motif of education in a state of innocence to his knowledge of modern psychological theories to create a highly memorable character and to set in motion the plot of his modern version of romance. The novel is poised between the mimetic and the artistically self-conscious.

In the opening pages of *Los trabajos de Urbano y Simona* Cástulo recapitulates the story so far and concedes considerable importance to the role of doña Micaela, "elemento primordial, fuerza que domina todas las demás" (IV:387). In this part of the novel Ayala details the progressive mental disintegration of Micaela. Ayala conceived of the mind as balanced between two extremes, two opposite poles in which psychic energy is created by the tension between them. If there is a tendency to go too far in one direction, there is a reaction and psychic energy suddenly flows the other way. In Micaela's case, one extreme, coldness, determination, masculinity, predominates for the first part of her life. Then, under the impact of an intense emotional shock, her psychic energy is channelled in the opposite direction. Given her psychological make-up, however, she retains a mental integrity which enables her, initially at least, to act in a consistent manner. As Cástulo observes: "Mujer de una pieza. No se dobla ni se rompe. La han vuelto cabeza abajo y es la misma de antes; siempre perpendicular" (IV:399). She clings to her new ideal of poverty and dignity with the same tenacity with which she had pursued her ambition to rise in society. By making her new pattern of behaviour consistent with certain established psychological traits, Ayala shows his own fine psychological understanding. Micaela's firmness of conviction permits her to justify her new course of action, which is just as extreme as her original one. Just as no obstacle was to be placed in the way of the marriage, now no obstacle is to be placed in the way of its annulment. Moreover, her emotional relationship with Leoncio undergoes changes from superiority and cruelty to an almost fawning devotion. Her sexual awareness is rekindled and is accompanied by a general loosening up of her whole personality, an abandonment of the rigidity of which her mode of dress was a symbol: "ropajes austeros, casi sacerdotales, el peinado liso y unos justillos o coseletes que le dejaban raso el pecho" (IV:457). Yet the nature of their married life thus far, with its absence of physical contact, had shaped Leoncio's affection into "un amor espiritual, una pasión del alma" (IV:458). Leoncio, too, we might note in passing, is an interesting psychological case. Suffering from a kind of mother-fixation which is translated into his conception of motherhood as the *summum* of femininity, he needs to seek erotic pleasure outside his marriage. The sexual difficulties of the marriage have physical manifestations. Leoncio's repressed repugnance for sexual contact with his wife is revealed by certain physical symptoms. Her entreating voice sounds like "estridencias de un instrumento de metal, le arañaba los oídos y le daba dentera" (IV;461). To return to Micaela, however, it is easy to see that her sexual longings, made more intense by virtue of their being repressed, produce certain psychosomatic disorders:

> Unas veces decía que el cuerpo le había dejado de pesar y que se sentía subir, como el reflejo del quinqué, hacia el cielo raso; otras, que sus piernas eran sacos de arena y que no podía levantar el pie del suelo. Ahora se sofocaba, enrojecía, se asfixiaba, sudaba; luego palidecía, se arrebujaba en un mantón, tiritaba, con castañeteo de dientes. Acometíanle acaso insólitas formas de dolor, que expresaba siempre con imágenes inquisitoriales. (IV:460)

Unfulfilled, doña Micaela's illness worsens until it verges on real madness. She is beset by all sorts of fantasies and illusions, becomes obsessively preoccupied with her own body, craves to give birth to a daughter. Urbano is able to make some sense of his relationship with his mother in psychological terms: her love for him had only caused him irritation, her absence of love causes him pleasure. Her love is seen as engulfment, an overwhelming force which threatens to submerge Urbano's own identity. He himself sees it as the working of "una ley de compensación psicológica" and observes that the workings of the mind, by virtue of their mystery, are problematical. No clearer definition of the subconscious and the need to understand it is to be found in Ayala's novels. Firstly, he recognises what Jung described as the archetype of the "shadow": "¿Es que llevamos todavía en la caverna de nuestro pecho al hombre primitivo, estúpido y sanguinario? Evidentemente. Oh, ¡qué alegría descubrirlo, conocerlo! Porque en cuanto un cosa está conocida, está asimismo dominada" (IV:472). This discovery is elaborated at once into a theory of mental life which, though very simply expressed, is nonetheless psychologically valid:

> Paréceme que si siempre pudiéramos comprobar cómo funciona el mecanismo de los telares con que nuestra alma teje sus ensueños, sus ilusiones, sus codicias, sus odios, sus desabrimientos, sus envidias, sus vanidades, sus recelos, sus espantos, la mayor parte de los conflictos de conciencia desaparecerían. Teje el alma unas engañosas tapicerías, con figuras que parecen de verdad, y nos pasman o nos amedrentan; si las viésemos del revés, cesarían el pasmo y el susto.   (IV:472-73)

Urbano now interprets his mother's behaviour as a regression to childhood or, more properly, as a living out of the childhood she never had. The *Novilunio* of *Los trabajos de Urbano y Simona* ends with the spectacle of Micaela completely deranged: Urbano has become her daughter and Cástulo is, in her eyes, a woman. It is a spectacle which, though potentially ridiculous, contains its share of pathos. This very realistic character portrayal relates to a wider theme in the novel, the way in which desire can loosen a person's grip upon reality. The theme of madness is related to the theme of fiction, for both are the illusions, or delusions, of the mind. However, as Ayala embarks upon his final novel, the role of art in coming to terms with the burden of consciousness is refined in that the imagination is accorded a more positive and purposeful role.

A persistent theme in the Realist novel was the way in which the real world resisted both the power of thought and the processes of individual consciousness. By the end of the nineteenth century and the beginnings of the twentieth, it became commonplace for artists to adopt a defiantly aesthetic attitude to this phenomenon: the aesthetic attitude offered a relief or an escape from their social maladjustment. Such was the attitude to be found in Alberto Díaz de Guzmán in the early novels, novels which exemplify such fashionable *fin-de-siècle* themes as the antithesis of life and art, the artistic consciousness as superior to what is merely "life," life as simply the subject matter of art and little else. Even in the early novels we were able to perceive an ironic detachment from this perspective on Pérez de

112

Ayala's part, and his later works progress from this somewhat decadent, alienated view of art to a more positive approach to consciousness and its role in coming to terms with "real" experience. Nowhere is this more clearly apparent than in Pérez de Ayala's last novel, *Tigre Juan* and *El curandero de su honra*, a complex work whose diverse facets are integrated by the set of psychological ideas which underpin it. Although Pérez de Ayala uses these ideas, he is not a novelist who delves into subtleties of motivation and feelings. Indeed, he points to the limitations of such writers:

> En las novelas que recaen demasiadamente hacia la tendencia psicológica, los análisis de motivaciones y las distilaciones quintaesenciales de sensaciones y sentimientos, por parte del novelista, tienen siempre algo de imposibilidad e inverosimilitud, de la parte del lector, y muy rara vez consiguen fundirse y consustanciarse en auténtico flujo vital, con la descripción del ambiente, la narración de los hechos y el choque externo realista, del diálogo.[24]

It is interesting that Ayala should refer to the importance of dialogue. In *Tigre Juan* and *El curandero de su honra*, the prolonged and very elevated dialogues between the characters are the means whereby the major themes of the work are articulated. More importantly, however, from our present point of view, they have the function of raising the experience of the characters to a higher level than the merely personal, so that it takes on a mythical or archetypal significance. A very ordinary man becomes the vehicle for heroic feelings, and this is made acceptable by the transmutation through language of the apparently mundane. The full significance of the characters becomes clear only if the existence of a mythic substratum to experience is acknowledged. This also accounts for the use of poetry in the novel as an alternative to detailed psychological description, for we know from his remarks in "Alegato pro domo mea" that Ayala thought poetry had a synthesising or crystallising function: "Sucede también que el personaje novelesco atraviesa a veces trances de compleja tensión o sutilidad psíquica, los cuales son por sí inefables, como las intuiciones de los místicos. El minucioso análisis psicológico (que ha tiempo estuvo de moda en la novela) no sirve sino para acarrear fatiga y confusión. Por parte del novelista no hay sino apelar a la poesía" (II:79). To do so, furthermore, reinforces the perception that character is an interaction of the individual and the common. *Tigre Juan* and *El curandero de su honra*, of all Ayala's novels, is the one which most relies on the notion of character, because it is concerned with the impulse of the self to realise itself, but which refuses to submit itself to the notion of the "convincing" character. There may be at work here a phenomenon noted by Keith M. May: "A great many novelists would find it difficult to accept a scheme in which, apparently, the bases of human individuality are

113

not themselves individualised. The traits and quirks of an individual rest, it seems, on an undifferentiated foundation."[25] Tigre Juan partakes of a characteristic Ayalian dualism, both individuality and foundation, presented in literary terms of both mimesis and myth.

Insofar as Juan's psychology is explored in the early stages of the novel, it is seen purely in terms of the uneasy calm he has imposed on his life and which is disrupted by the first crucial dialogue with Colás. This aspect of Juan's personality is revealed only gradually, firstly as speculation about his past (IV:557), his misplaced paternal feelings (IV:558), his sensitivity on questions of marital honour (IV:554, 559, 560), doña Iluminada's thoughts on his fear of the opposite sex (IV:564), and, of course, Juan's own forthright pronouncements on women. By challenging his views on women, Colás attacks Juan at his most vulnerable point and throws him into a state of mental turmoil. In a sense, one could see the novel as an exercise in psychotherapy by means of which the patient confronts his obsession as a first step to overcoming it. The views of the other characters could be interpreted as projections of his own doubts and anxieties which have been repressed. The key to Juan's character is understanding the nature of his repression. His repressed feelings are not of a specifically sexual kind, though they have sexual associations, and they are not to be thought of as necessarily bad in themselves. The fact is that Juan has expelled from his mind painful memories of his first marriage and has constructed a world-view governed by a rigid set of principles and ideals which have real value in maintaining stability in his emotional life. The image of reality which Juan nourishes is a false one, a delusion, but it is a way of adapting, of coping with the fact that he has become stuck in a particular phase of emotional development. The novel describes the process by which he overcomes this emotional block.

It must be stressed from the outset that there is no concrete evidence that Ayala wrote *Tigre Juan* and *El curandero de su honra* with the work of any particular psychologist in mind. At the same time, it is impossible to read the novel without being aware of its many psychological insights. An obvious case is the delusion, common to schizophrenics, that everyone knows their innermost thoughts. In the presence of doña Iluminada, Tigre Juan was convinced that "la viuda leía dentro de él todos sus pensamientos como escritura clara, y que le veía, de bulto y en forma sensible, todos sus sentimientos" (IV:562). The same phenomenon is described later in terms of the well-known dream: "A veces tenía en sueños una estrafalaria pesadilla: que, sin saber cómo, había salido de casa en paños menores y en traza tan bochornosa se hallaba a la vista de todos los del mercado. Ahora sentíase como si estuviera peor que en paños menores, *in puribus naturalibus*, en cueros, como un recién nacido" (IV:583). The Swiss psychologist Carl Gustav Jung, whose psychological theories are generally applicable to the character of Tigre Juan, would interpret this as the unconscious compensating for the conscious. The man who is emotionally isolated invents the idea that everyone knows his innermost thoughts. After all, Juan in the market is described as "insulado, solo, tan próximo a los demás hombres y, sin embargo, tan distante" (IV:606). The psychological treatment of the characters in the novel is linked to the literary motifs of truth-falsehood, reality-illusion, which form a web through the whole work. An outward sign is really an indication of its opposite. Juan's aversion to women is "una confusión de amor ciego y de pavura" (IV:564); his bursts of anger "eran inofensivo disfraz de un alma tierna y tímida" (IV;600). This suggest a division of the personality into different parts. These can be in conflict with one another or they can function as an integrated whole. For this reason, although some of the novel's psychological insights appear Freudian in inspiration, such as the Oedipal nature of the Juan-Herminia-Colás relationship, the novel, both in detail and in overall vision, is totally explicable in Jungian terms as a quest for integration and wholeness. The psychological integration attained by the protagonist is mirrored in the artistic integration of the novel itself. Jungian psychology is interested above all in the development and growth of the individual personality so that it achieves a balance within itself and establishes a harmonious relationship with the whole of life. Such a view is admirably suited to fictional treatment, for it can naturally be construed as a progression towards some objective or goal. The supreme goal is that of self-realisation, in Jung's words, "a consciousness detached from the world," an attitude of acceptance which is in some way religious. Man discovers his own myth and achieves a reconciliation between the conflicting sides of his own nature. As we shall see, Juan's conflict between emotion and social constraint is resolved by transferring it onto a higher level of experience. The poem of the Coda sees reality from this superior perspective and acknowledges the existence of God. This is not necessarily the conventional Christian God, but a spiritual, inner experience which Jung would term the Self. This all-embracing concept can be described in religious terms but it can also be represented in art, which offers a synthesis of the inner subjective world of the author and external reality. In art man resolves the contradictions of life. There is therefore a close correlation between Ayala's approach to the life of the mind and his thinking on the art of fiction. Man relates to the external world by means of concepts, abstract thought and symbols which manifest themselves in religion, culture and art. Man's image-making capacity, his inner world of fantasy, is essential to successful adaptation to reality, and in this respect there is little essential difference between so-called objective myths, works of fiction and apparently subjective delusions. The unconscious plays an important role here, for it is complementary to consciousness, which requires its co-operation for the full development of the personality. This unconscious is divided into the "personal unconscious," which is unique to the individual and contains his forgotten experiences, subliminal perceptions and so on, and the "collective unconscious," which is common to all mankind and is the source of universal myths and symbols. It is here that primordial images referred to as archetypes originate. It is easy to see that all three parts of the mind are taken into account in the characterisation of Tigre Juan. The use of existing myths in the novel is an acceptance of Jung's idea of the collective unconscious. Myths, known to be similar in widely different cultures and periods of history, express man's basic experiences and try to offer explanations of the world in which he finds himself. Myths and religious ideas are therefore closely linked. In trying to give Juan's experience this archetypal quality, Ayala has had to create a figure who is larger than life. This has been recognised by several critics. Francisco Agustín wrote "reconoceremos en él al personaje de un bello mito novelesco"[26] and "Andrenio" (Eduardo Gómez de Baquero) commented in an early review of the novel: "Personaje mítico llamo a Tigre Juan, no porque sea fabuloso, sino porque estando henchido de humanidad, excede de la talla vulgar humana."[27] The use of myth and archetype, the quest for wholeness, the reconciliation of opposites, and concepts such as individuation, the self-regulating psyche, and the Self, make *Tigre Juan* and *El curandero de su honra* highly susceptible to Jungian analysis.[28]

Juan's problem is his relationship with the opposite sex, and his attitude to women is characterised by the very dualism we find in Jung, the opposing images of woman as destroyer and woman as protector. In mythical terms these are represented respectively as Eve and the Virgin Mary, both of whom are mentioned in the novel. In terms of the character's own experience, the images are projected onto Iluminada on the one hand, and on the negative side onto a complex cluster including for a time both Engracia and Herminia. Frequently these images take the forms of the fairy godmother and the evil witch. In the novel Iluminada is referred to as the "hada madrina" (IV:654), and in a moment of rage Juan calls la Güeya "bruja" and "barragana de Satanás" (IV:603). Juan, culturally conditioned and guilty for his crime, represses the good image and develops the bad. The crisis comes when this particular structure is upset. Jung conceived of the psyche as a play of opposites with psychic energy running, as it were, between two poles. These have a regulating function, for when one extreme is reached the energy passes over to its opposite, a phenomenon known as *enantiodromia,* in which, for example, anger suddenly gives way to calm, hatred to affection, and so on. This is what Jung designates the "self-regulating psyche," a concept which in psychological terms corresponds to the accepted physiological fact that the body is regulated by an

116

elaborate system of checks by which a tendency to go too far in one direction, in the production of a hormone, for example, is automatically compensated and a proper balance maintained. In this respect, it is significant that Juan can be seen as curing himself, as suggested, albeit humorously, by the title *El curandero de su honra* and his practice of homeopathy (IV:555). If this is true, Juan's sudden transformation is psychologically valid and not in the least surprising. It undermines the objections of critics like Norma Urrutia, who writes: "No nos convence, pues, ese Tigre Juan, que odia a la mujer durante ciento ochenta páginas y, bruscamente, como por arte de magia, sucumbe al amor de Herminia."[29] Ayala stressed how unreal the misogynist phase actually is, a device designed to disguise the truth. Juan's outspoken condemnation of women is a need to justify and protect himself ,and the manner in which everything is reshaped and made to conform to his own interpretation of the world is an elaborate delusional system. It is one of the many paradoxes of the novel and in keeping with Ayala's ceaseless probing of polarities in his work. Belarmino and Apolonio are the complementary halves of the same person, the introvert is balanced by the extrovert. Jung himself refers to cases of alternation between introversion and extroversion and even cases where lifelong introverts have become extroverts in middle age. In Juan's case the "good" image of woman had never been completely submerged (IV:61), and it is in the unconscious that latent possibilities of new life are to be found. What is not present in the conscious attitude is lurking in the unconscious and is sometimes manifested in dreams and fantasies. This aspect of unconscious life is given little attention by Ayala, and it is true to say that in the novel unconscious feelings are rendered with more precision than may be thought desirable. However, we join the drama at a point where unconscious emotions are beginning to surface and are therefore experienced in a way that is not, strictly speaking, unconscious at all; they are rather a surge of wild and chaotic feelings and thoughts which burst into consciousness, "ansiedades y zozobras, largo tiempo sumisas, amordazadas, y ahora rebeldes de pronto" (IV:581). So painful are these memories that when they well up Juan tries to rebury them:

> Aquella noche, rebulléndose desazonado, hubo de ser sincero consigo mismo. Apenas, en un momento de abandono de la voluntad y pérdida del dominio de sí, hizo esta confesión íntima, cuando saltó del camastro, cayó de rodillas y, dándose de puñadas en los ojos, murmuraba roncamente. Creyó ver primero una gran mancha roja, y luego un negror poblado de estrellitas rutilantes: Aun bramas por la mujer, insensato, como ciervo sediento por el manantial ... Señor de justicia, Señor de misericordia, ciégame. (IV:582)

This craving for blindness is the clearest symptom of Juan's repression. It might be more appropriate to use the term "dissociation" rather than "repression," as this would include both conscious and unconscious mental contents. Thoughts and feelings which are considered alien to the personality are rejected or denied. In this respect, it is interesting that men condemn in others what they cannot accept in themselves. Thus Juan is vehemently opposed to Colás' idealisation of women, his desire for freedom from restraint, his assertion of the primacy of instinct. Juan's fears are represented in an image dominated by the colour red, which has connotations of passion and violence and is connected to the motif of blood which recurs in the novel. Together they contain suggestions of death and sacrifice, and this is reinforced by the parallel established between Juan and the Christ figure. This mythical parallel of the death and subsequent resurrection of the hero indicates a turning point in life, the transition from one state to another. The arguments with Colás, the suggestion that he should remarry, the conversations with doña Iluminada bring Juan to a point where he recognises that important aspects of his personality have been neglected and the life he created may well prove unsatisfactory. The trauma of the departure of Colás signals the collapse of his former life: "Acabóse ayer. Soy un cadáver que anda" (IV:604). He is born to a second life which is a re-enactment of the first, as several lines make clear: "Parece como si escomenzase a vivir, o séase a desandar y recorrer de nuevo el mismo camino" (IV:611). The vital link with the past is provided by the letter from the wife of his former captain in the Philippines which unlocks the secrets of the past: "Todo había concluido para él. Sólo cuando algo está definitivamente concluso, su pasado revive y se hace actual, perenne e incorregible. Su propio pasado, que Tigre Juan suponía abolido, se restauraba íntegro, cuajado en una eternidad de infierno" (IV:623). Juan becomes Juanín as the story of Engracia and the origins of Juan's obsession are recounted in flashback. The structuring of the narrative in this way enables the reader to undergo a process of enlightenment similar to that of the character. Viewed thus, the novel is essentially dramatic in that both reader and character are brought to the point of recognition. By acting out his own drama, the character comes to a proper understanding of the real nature of his role. Re-enactment has a psychological value as the character, hallucinated or hypnotised, envisages his past as a grotesque dance of death in which characters parade before his eyes, taking on their true significance which he had consciously repressed: "Era, para él, como el derrumbamiento y catástrofe de un mundo falso, perecedero, mundo de apariencias vanas, por él mismo fabricado, en el cual vivía dormido, trasvolado en un duermevela, tomando por realidades tangibles, los sueños de inmaterial urdimbre" (IV:629). The recognition that he had created a false view of reality to make it conform to his own inner needs begins the

118

slow and painful process of individuation which is completed only at the end of the novel. The recognition itself has been achieved by the end of the *Adagio* of *Tigre Juan*, that part of the novel that had revealed the basic split in Juan's character. A highly emotional man, Juan is deeply mistrustful of manifestations of sentiment, "que no gusto de zalamerías, arrumacos y garatusas" (IV:590). His whole life is a struggle for control: "me arrebata tal vez una fuerza irrestistible que destruye aquello que más amo" (IV:599). What we are discussing here is the importance of unconscious desires and emotions and the difficulty experienced in bringing these into the domain of consciousness. Rather than come to terms with his feelings, especially about women, Juan chose to repress them, with the result that his relationships with others have tended to be frictional or conflictive. Juan's natural instinct is to withdraw into himself: "Déjenme solo, como apetezco" (IV:610). Buried in his personal unconscious, his emotions gain in strength and intensity and, in a situation of stress, they sweep away reason. Juan's "murder" of Engracia is a case in point. Placed where it is in the novel, this incident, though a flashback, seems a logical consequence of Juan's attitudes and behaviour in the *Adagio*.

Because of an inner contradiction, Juan's motives and even the very nature of his actions are unknown to him. As he rushes impulsively towards Colás, the narrator observes: "¿Iba a abrazarle o a estrangularle? ¿Qué sabía él? Lo mismo podía resultar lo uno que lo otro" (IV:603), or earlier, "La onda colérica que le henchía había llegado a un punto de plenitud e inestabilidad, indecisa entre reventar con violencia o replegarse y evaporarse en humedad de ojos" (IV:600). This instability, intensified by the cataclysmic vision with which the *Adagio* ends, so radically alters Juan's psychological make-up that Ayala suggests that he is another person, though unaware of it. Juan had always been aware of the dark and powerful forces deep within himself: "Aunque oprimido y a medias domesticado, tigre soy y seré hasta que muera" (IV:571). Jung calls this the "shadow," which is his archetype for all that primitive, uncontrolled, animal part of man which, in a moment of crisis, can overwhelm the rest of personality. In the first half of the novel, Juan had repressed this aspect of his personality because he felt threatened by it; in the second part he is able to come to terms with it. Thus the second part provides an alternative solution to the problem of adultery which becomes possible because Juan's conscious and unconscious have established a different relationship one with the other. It is not achieved without considerable struggle and suffering.

The recognition of Engracia's innocence, the subsuming of his first wife into the person of Herminia, and his psychological transformation create a transitory state of consciousness in which Juan continues to act in accord with a false, self-engendered, though now altered, vision of the world: "En el estado de semialucinación en que Tigre Juan se hallaba, no le era hacedero acomodar los sentidos a la realidad de fuera; antes, por el contrario, deformaba y transformaba los datos del mundo externo a fin de incorporarlos al espejismo de su visión interior" (IV:637). At the centre of this is love for a woman. Men fall in love with what seems to be lacking in themselves. The image of the beloved is therefore initially the expression of a subjective need. Jung's psychology is decidedly woman-centred. In his writings he refers to the *anima*, man's image of woman, as one of the central archetypes of the mind. This archetype seems to come from three sources: the collective, primordial image of woman which man inherits, man's own experience of woman, and the feminine qualities in himself. The *anima* is frequently associated with water or the earth, she appears to have great power and is endowed with spiritual value. Woman, by fascinating man erotically, teaches him about emotion and its value and provides a link between the conscious and unconscious minds. The power of the *anima* may explain the transference of Engracia to Herminia in Juan's mind: he projects his *anima* as the very soul of man, the essence of his personality. A curiously similar observation is made by Ayala at the beginning of the *Presto*: "Tigre Juan . . . quedó suplantado en su ser interior e inconsciente por otro ser ajeno: el de Herminia. Y ya de allí adelante no fue él en sí mismo, sino Herminia fue del todo en él" (IV:637). The *Presto*, then, traces in fine psychological detail Juan's growing love for her, or at least for the resurrected image of Engracia he has projected onto her. A complex of emotions is gradually and unconsciously rearranged to allow Juan to maintain a proper psychological balance, as Ayala carefully explains:

> Para él, creer que continuaba odiando a Herminia equivalía, en una inversión sofística del sentimiento, a gozarse en la certidumbre de que Herminia había rechazado a distancia a otro pretendiente, y como éste era Colás, casi su hijo, necesitaba mantener aquel falso odio por no dejar de deleitarse en la certidumbre de su fundamento. (IV:638)

This love–hate equivalence parallels in a striking manner Herminia's subsequent experience: "El odio a Tigre Juan, aunque de buena fe, ¿no sería mentido, más bien de pasión de amor, miedosa de sí misma, que se resiste a manifestarse?" (IV:665). In Juan's case certain symptoms do manifest themselves: he tries to dissuade Colás from thinking any more about Herminia, he becomes more generous, his appearance is subtly modified, he treats Carmina with exaggerated courtesy. Under the influence of his unconscious love, Juan enters a new phase of "optimismo cósmico" in which "Todas las cosas le seducían; era llevado hacia ellas por un modo de amor nacido de la comprensión. Todo era hermoso. Todo era útil. Todo era bueno" (IV:647). Juan's love unlocks a whole world not previously apprehended as he finds his place in the total order of things. The earth takes on womanly forms; Carmina becomes a symbol of womanhood. When man represses his feminine side, the *anima* is largely negative. When Juan begins to appreciate woman once again, the feminine side of his nature is developed. Thus he wishes to participate in childbirth, remembering the old Asturian custom of the *covada*, and he takes an active part in caring for his child to the extent of attempting to breast-feed. This acknowledgement of the feminine side of man, and by implication of the masculine side of woman, is of course the basis of Ayala's interpretation of the Don Juan myth. Don Juan is an archetypal image in this sense. For Juan he is a saviour or redeemer and is specifically described as such. When a man feels threatened he instinctively seeks someone to blame and at the same time someone to protect or avenge him. This primordial tendency finds expression in Juan's case in his attitudes to women and to Vespasiano. Vespasiano represents something deficient in himself, "su otra mitad ideal; el otro yo, que él hubiera preferido ser" (IV:677). Juan's relationships with Vespasiano and with Colás are reverse images of one another and are both immature. In a way, he is emotionally identified with Vespasiano in that he aspires to be like him. He negates his own personality and is absorbed into Vespasiano. On the other hand, he attempts to incorporate Colás, to so dominate him that he destroys his individuality. The novel shows how Juan's process of self-realisation involves the attainment of more mature relationships in which one neither absorbs nor is absorbed by the other. In the *Presto*, then, a subtle readjustment of conscious and unconscious elements takes place. Juan's apparent "sistema de venganza" is really an elaborate courtship, as the narrator makes clear and doña Iluminada explains in her analysis of the nature of human love. Juan is directed to Herminia via Colás, and a bizarre triangle is created. Were Herminia to marry Colás, Juan's love might be sublimated and expressed as paternal affection, but if this did not take place tragedy would be inevitable. Herminia's rejection of Colás, which she ascribes to her fear of Juan, is an instinctive acceptance of this fact. Herminia appears to be repelled by Tigre Juan, but this is a defence against being attracted to him: "Lo que Herminia siente es vértigo hacia Tigre Juan; un poder de atracción que la domina y que no puede contrarrestar si no es encastillándose en una proporcionada voluntad de repulsión" (IV:653). This repulsion-attraction contradiction must be resolved. Herminia has an instinctive fear of sex which is symbolised in the fairy-tale of Beauty and the Beast. Her *animus*, woman's image of man, is projected onto Vespasiano, who is, significantly, mysterious, alluring and mostly absent. Since he is shadowy and distant, it is easy for Herminia to project an image onto him. When she finally confronts him, he loses his power over her and she

121

is able to live with her husband free from her fantasy and infatuation. In a more general sense, Ayala accepts the existence of the *anima* in his observation that women are attracted by what appears strange, remote or inaccessible: "es propio de la naturaleza femenina inclinarse hacia lo fuera de lo común y perecerse por lo temible y misterioso" (IV:556). Herminia is fascinated by Juan's enactment of the role of the Calderonian husband, and the news of his dark past is a further incentive to marry him. In the *Presto*, Herminia is able to disentangle her emotions and to categorise the attributes of her various suitors into various aspects of masculine love. Colás, the "chiquillo," would satisfy her need to dominate; Juan, the "hombre," her need to be dominated. Vespasiano, meanwhile, offers an escape towards the unknown, and his ambiguous sexuality holds out the prospect of seduction without terror. Ironically, the *Presto* ends with Juan eagerly awaiting Vespasiano's return. Gamborena's words recall the theme of the paradoxical nature of reality and seem to underline the irony. But, as events prove, the words have a more profound meaning than at first appears, for Vespasiano's role is eventually interpreted positively as being a necessary stage in the growth of love beween the two spouses. The first part of the novel, then, is a study of repression, but by the time the full story is known that repression is seen to have a temporary value. Juan's delusional system, in which every woman is made to conform to his view, is part self-justification, part self-defence, and is interpreted positively as adaptive. In the *Presto*, Juan is moving from one state of consciousness into another. There has been a fundamental change, but the mind copes with it only slowly, through subterfuge and symbol. *El curandero de su honra* begins with Juan's recognition of his love and the fixing of the date for the marriage. The initiative, paradoxically, is passed to Herminia, whose outer calm is only a mask. The archetypal woman, clearly implied in the references to Eve, Eden, and seduction by the serpent, frustrates man's plans. In this way the novel is made to transcend the particularities of time and place and functions as an account of universal experience expressed in Christian and pagan mythology. The myth of Adam and Eve was one of the principal sources for Juan's belief in the perfidy of woman and her role in mankind's fall. Now that his opinion is changing, now that he is overcoming his obsession, Herminia is about to act in complete conformity with the Eve archetype. Vespasiano insinuates himself into Juan's potential paradise, in which the past is obliterated. Locked in his own world. Juan is oblivious to the danger and, unable to express his love for Herminia, entrusts Vespasiano with the task. He faces a double betrayal by wife and friend. The security which appears to surround his new life is seen when he claims that Isabel Semprún means nothing to him: "Su nueva vida era tan densa que al pronto le tapaba el pasado. Su presente era un paraíso con altísimo cerco, cuya entrada defendía una esfinge" (IV:686). The complexities of his emotions are most clearly seen with regard to the return of Colás. Once the initial readjustment of relationships is made and the characters recognise the Oedipal implications of their love and overcome them (IV:693-98), matters appear reasonably simple. Colás gives Juan an outlet for his emotion, which is inhibited in the presence of Herminia. Colás' departure had been instrumental in leading Juan to Herminia; now his return breaks Juan's spiritual isolation. For Herminia, Colás' return is a welcome distraction in her married life, but it is also a possible link between her and Tigre Juan. At the same time, Juan notes Herminia's natural gravitation towards Colás and secretly hopes he will leave. He will not, of course, admit this to himself and even transfers his desire to Colás and reprimands him for thinking of leaving (IV:700). This kind of psychological insight reveals the contrary impulses to which human beings are frequently subject. A simple example is when Juan is both fascinated and frightened by his conversation with doña Iluminada: "Le corría por el cuerpo un hormiguillo o anhelo acucioso de marcharse, pero no acertaba a poner punto final a la charla" (IV:591). When Colás and Carmina elope, Juan is "henchido de un sentimiento promiscuo, entre la satisfacción y la contrariedad" (IV:702), a characteristically dual response. For Herminia, on the other hand, Colás' flight arouses her own latent desire to escape, a desire which becomes a veritable obsession. The pattern traced by the novel, then, is one of alternate bouts of tension and relaxation, of revolt and resignation, crisis and contentment. We see underlying this an archetypal pattern of departure followed by return, initiated now by Colás and imitated by Herminia, which represents a phase in life's spiritual journey.

As if intuitively aware of Herminia's absence, Juan, in the *Adagio*, reflects on the related ideas of death, loss and free will and works his way through the varying interpretations of honour. He begins to shift the centre of gravity of the male-female relationship from the man to the woman. He appears as a soul in conflict, seeking both blindness and enlightenment, unable to find peace within himself. This psychological instability reveals the need for a more intense or severe therapeutic shock to reintegrate his personality completely. His anxiety and excitement reach a feverish pitch on hearing of Herminia's pregnancy, and Nachín de Nacha warns him of he danger of ending up "en el malicomio o el presidio" (IV:723). The shock of Herminia's departure initiates a phase of regression. He returns to a state prior to that of loving Herminia: "Vuelto estoy en mi antiguo ser, que yo mismo me asusto y apenas me reconozco" (IV:730-31). Psychological theories are curiously set alongside traditional ideas and pagan superstitions. For example, the close connection between the physical and the mental is seen in the idea of blood-letting, which acts as an emotional purgation, and in Nachín de Nacha's reference to the humours, which can be vomited out (IV:731). Juan's final emotional release comes, of course, on

St. John's Night, when the whole theme of blindness-enlightenment is given its fullest expression. The feast of St. John (24 June) has special significance for Tigre Juan, as it is his saint's day (San Juan Bautista), but in addition to this the night before the feast is traditionally associated with lovers. In Asturias particularly, rituals, essentially pagan in origin and related to love and fertility, are performed. Fire and water are prominent elements signifying male and female respectively. The young men jump through the flames of the bonfires courting death and then re-emerge transformed, while the young girls seek out the cool natural water to which they offer a red rose.

Then, at the end of the ritual, male and female unite as all the elements interpenetrate in an image of harmony and completeness: "los contrarios elementos, tierra y aire, fuego y agua, se penetraban y trasfundían en amoroso consorcio: la tierra se evaporaba y el aire se adensaba: el fuego se atemperaba y el agua hervía" (IV:733). These natural forces signify the depth of passion existing in Juan and Herminia, and their fusion prefigures their eventual reconciliation as parts of the whole of creation. One feature of characterisation in the novel is the association of certain characters with a specific natural element. Thus Colás is in various ways related to the wind and the air: "Hijo del aire. ... el viento reclamaría sus derechos de paternidad" (IV:581). Juan himself is associated with fire: "el fuego que me consume" (IV:730), "Soy un volcán" (IV:731), "devorándose a sí propio como una pira" (IV;732). The Midsummer ritual, with its sexual symbolism, represents an irrational union of opposites and therefore offers an image of wholeness. In Las máscaras, Ayala recalls the myth, discussed in Plato's Symposium, that there were originally three sexes: male, female and hermaphrodite. When Zeus decreed that each should be split in half, the sexes were left incomplete and each felt the desire to seek out the other half. Sexual union therefore becomes an image of completeness (III:367-8). Juan's moment of illumination comes at midnight when, hallucinated, he speaks to images of Engracia and Herminia, while reality appears as a "sueño evanescente" and the world "se desintegraba y fluía, fluía con fugitivas mudanzas." The process of destruction and creation which the whole universe seems to undergo is an image or correlative of Juan's psychological disintegration and then re-integration: "Contemplé el cielo por una rendija y volvíme del revés. El rayo de la revelación hendió mi carne" (IV:739). Juan arrives at this state not by any rational means. Illumination seems to have come from a source beyond consciousness. Juan is purged of the past as Nachín, in a further Midsummer ritual, baptises him in the early morning dew, long thought to have curing powers. Pagan and Christian symbolism combine to link an individual moment of psychological insight to primitive forms of cultural expression. We can see, therefore, that Juan's whole experience has a religious dimension in the sense that its inspiration seems to come from a source outside himself or at least outside consciousness. In Jung's account of the individuation process, the attainment of a new level of psychological insight brings with it a feeling of unity with the whole of life, an acknowledgement of the existence of something beyond or greater than the individual. There is, in fact, a background of religious imagery and allusion to the novel which is clearly apparent in the close connection established between love, suffering and sacrifice. When Colás leaves for the first time, Juan interprets this as the collapse of his whole life: "Acabóse ayer. Soy un cadáver que anda" (IV:604). A religious parallel is evident here, death followed by resurrection. Juan climbs the neighbouring hills "como si aspirase llegar por último a la cima de su calvario y epílogo de su redención" (IV:605). In the mountain hermitage, he acts out his own "Agony in the Garden," using the words from the Gospel: "Señor, Señor, ¿por qué me abandonaste?" (IV:606). When Juan first recognises his guilt, religious vocabulary is again employed: "¡Condenado estoy! ¿Habrá salvación para mí? .... infierno .... purgatorio .... Colás redimió .... expiación .... arrepentimiento .... confesión .... absuelvas" (IV:630-1). Carmina's kiss on Juan's cheek is like "un divino estigma visible" (IV:612). Nachín de Nacha, on a more superstitious level, tries to convince Juan of the existence of another world, a "país encantao," peopled with "ánimes y criatures del otro mundo, xanas, trasgo, duende, huestia" (IV:610). Images and figures are created by man to represent common human experiences. Herminia's life, although treated in much less detail, also undergoes significant change and the Cross acts as a symbol of this. On her wedding night, "Herminia estaba caída sin sentido en el lecho, cara al cielo, abiertos los brazos como crucificados al tálamo." The next sentence seems to confirm that the archetypal pattern of death and rebirth is present here: "Moría la luz artificial del quinqué y nacía la aurora" (IV:691). In an early morning scene soon afterwards, Juan's kisses fix her "a los leños del tálamo igual que en una cruz" (IV:707). Birth and death are, of course, brought together, as I have indicated, in the St. John's Night ritual. It is the image of blood which fuses the idea of death and sacrifice with love and fulfillment. When Juan hears of Herminia's pregnancy, he accidentally cuts himself and thinks of their blood being mingled in that of the child. Juan's occupation as a "curandero" leads him, in a parodying echo of Calderón's play, to bleed himself, first as an attempt at suicide and then, more positively, as a purgation of his own bad blood: "necesitaba sangrar y descongestionar su alma" (IV:754). As doña Iluminada makes clear, Juan undergoes a symbolic death and re-birth: "Don Juan, el tigre, ha muerto. Bien muerto está. Ha renacido otro Don Juan" (IV:756). Juan's search for meaning in life requires the co-operation of both the conscious and unconscious parts of the mind, so that after a prolonged period of suffering and struggle, of progression and regression, he reaches an inner understanding, a sense of wholeness, the realisation of the archetype of the Self which is akin to the experience of God. Thus, as well as harmonising all the contradictions of his nature, he experiences an intimate relationship with the whole of life: "Su conciencia se amplifica, se infiltra y diluye en las cosas, se confunde, con un escalofrío sagrado, en la conciencia cósmica" (IV:769). The unity and continuity of life is seen in the fact that as one life, don Sincerato, is departing the world, a new life, Mini, is being born. Indeed, the union of the individual with the totality is present also in the song of la Güeya to Mini: "dirigiéndole desesperados requiebros de amor—amor a la vida—que parecían dilatarse, en un eco inextinguible, desde la noche de los siglos. La vieja rugosa y el tiernísimo infante formaban un grupo comparable al pámpano y el sarmiento, o bien la vida naciente en el regazo de la tradición" (IV:761). The profoundly religious nature of this concept is the subject of the poem with which the *Coda* ends. Human and divine love are equated and paternity is compared with divine creation. All elements of human life are purposeful. For Juan to reach this state of awareness and acceptance, a long and mysterious process had to be undergone. The culminating experience characterised by a sense of purpose and fulfillment is not capable of being explained in rational terms but manifests itself in paradox. In the poem we read that "Lo torpe guía hasta lo honesto. / El dolor desemboca en la alegría. / La fealdad empuja hacia lo bello" (IV:770). The exploration of paradoxes and contradictions is continued into the *Parergon*. Colás, considering that man is rational and irrational at the same time, argues that reason is common to all men, whereas what is unique to the individual is his "razón de ser; y esta razón de ser es en cada caso la razón de la sinrazón" (IV:785). There seems to be a convergence here between the ideas of Juan and Colás. Colás aspires to the discovery of his "arquetipo congénito, la idea original, el ideal de mi existencia, mi irracionalidad, mi vida" (IV:786). His life is a quest for origins, Juan's is a pursuit of ends; "En la distancia que cada criatura se aproxima más o menos a la perfección, encierra, al respective, más o menos razón de ser. ¿Cuál es la razón de ser del hombre? Hacerse lo más hombre posible" (IV:789). This dynamic conception of personality is what emerges most strongly from the story of Tigre Juan, and when Juan's and Colás' ideas are put together, man is seen as both archetype and potential, created out of some common mould but capable of developing his own unique characteristics.

We can see, then, that the characterisation of Tigre Juan is twofold. He is presented initially as a recognisable human being, living in a specific environment and having a framework of human relationships. On one level, his story is that of a man obsessed with fidelity in marriage who overcomes his obsession through the transforming power of love. In the course of the novel, he acquires archetypal significance as his experience is raised to a higher plane than the normal. Mundane reality is transformed by the power of art into something transcendent, for Ayala treats his theme on a realistic and social level and then refracts it through literature and myth. It is the psychological portrayal of the principal protagonist which fuses the two levels of reality and myth. The split in his personality is healed by symbolic means as he draws on the resources of his unconscious mind, which is partly expressed through archetypal images and collective rituals. The final aim of the individual is the realisation of his total personality, which involves recognising and coming to terms with characteristics in himself that had been consistently rejected. Juan's attempt to be other than he was led to internal conflict, inner disharmony and emotional isolation. On St. John's Night he recognises this: "Yo permanezco a solas, como una roca, sin alteración y sin existencia" (IV:734). In other words, isolation inevitably leads to the disintegration and death of the personality, for paradoxically one is most truly oneself when one accepts the need for a relationship with others. The awareness that one is valued and accepted by others is a prerequisite for self-esteem and self-acceptance. The story of Tigre Juan's search for love involves a rejection of any idea of man's self-sufficiency. It is an assertion that man needs others if he is to be fully at peace with himself.

The treatment of psychological concerns in Pérez de Ayala's fiction, then, can be seen to form a kind of progression. An initial divergence between artistic and real experience is bridged as man is seen as coming to terms with reality through the power of the imagination. Ayala appears to ascribe to art the function of integrating experience, of bringing man's inner world of imagination into a more harmonious relationship with external reality. In *Tigre Juan* and *El curandero de su honra*, the theme of love is explored in psychological terms as a quest for integrity within the individual personality through the development of a mature relationship with another person. When this state has been attained, the individual experiences a sense of fulfillment and inner harmony which is often accepted as characteristic of aesthetic experience. Ayala appears to come to the view that art should serve not to loosen man's grip upon reality but to tighten it. The art of fiction provides a means of linking consciousness and external reality: "El arte del novelista consiste en la proporción inexcusable, en sus rasgos sustantivos, con que andan enlazados la realidad eterna y el mundo interior; lo que es y como lo siente y piensa cada cual; la visión de los ojos y lo subjetivo; psicología viva de diversos seres."[30] Fictions enable man to make sense of the world and adapt it to his inner world of fantasy. The work of art, in which conflicts are resolved and opposing forces are brought into harmony, offers a momentary liberation from the contradictions and tensions inherent in reality. Faced with the chaos of consciousness, such a view of aesthetics implies an acknowledgement of the human mind's incessant striving for order and meaning to which the world of art gives access. It is in his intimate linking of psychology and the art of fiction that Pérez de Ayala differs so radically from the psychological novelists of the nineteenth century and embodies so perfectly the spirit of twentieth-century Modernism.

NOTES

[1]Virginia Woolf, "Modern Fiction," in *Collected Essays* (London: The Hogarth Press, 1966) II:108.

[2]*Principios y finales de la novela* 44.

[3]Henry James, Preface to *The Portrait of a Lady* (New York: Scribner's, 1908) vii.

[4]Pio Baroja, *Páginas escogidas* (Madrid: Calleja, 1917) 12.

[5]Catherine Belsey observes that "within the existing ideology it appears 'obvious' that people are autonomous individuals, possessed of subjectivity or consciousness which is the source of their beliefs and actions," *Critical Practice* (London: Methuen, 1980) 58.

[6]Franz Kafka, *Dearest Father* (New York: Schocken Books, 1954) 66.

[7]Quoted by Keith May, *Out of the Maelstrom* (see Note 11).

[8]Sigmund Freud, *Beyond the Pleasure Principle* (London: Hogarth, 1950) 86.

[9]Sigmund Freud, *Totem and Taboo* (London: Routledge, 1950) 73.

[10]Prologue to 1942 edition of *Troteras y danzaderas* (Buenos Aires: Losada, 1942) 16.

[11]Keith May, *Out of the Maelstrom. Psychology and the Novel in the Twentieth Century* (London: Paul Elek, 19779) 115.

[12]Maruxa Salgues de Cargill, *Los mitos clásicos y modernos en la novela de Pérez de Ayala* (Jaén: Instituto de Estudios Giennenses, 1971) 37.

[13]"Literature and Experience: the Problem of Distance in Pérez de Ayala's *La pata de la raposa*," *Bulletin of Hispanic Studies* LV (1978):129-41.

[14]*Pequeños ensayos* (Madrid: Biblioteca Nueva, 1963) 112.

[15]*Principios y finales de la novela* 31.

[16]Sara Suárez Solís, *Análisis de "Belarmino y Apolonio"* (Oviedo: Instituto de Estudios Asturianos, 1974) 242.

[17]Wilma Newberry, "Ramón Pérez de Ayala's concept of the *Doppelgänger* in *Belarmino y Apolonio*," *Symposium* XXXIV. 1 (1980):57.

[18]Leon Livingstone, "Lenguaje y silencio en *Belarmino y Apolonio*," in *Simposio Internacional Ramón Pérez de Ayala* (Gijón: University of New Mexico, 1981) 71-90.

[19]Miguel de Unamuno, *Tres novelas ejemplares y un prólogo, Obras completas* (Madrid: Afrodisio Aguado, 1968) IX:L420.

[20]Miguel de Unamuno, *El sentimiento trágico de la vida, Obras completas* (Madrid: Afrodisio Aguado, 1968) Vol. XVI.

[21]Miguel de Unamuno, *El otro, Obras completas* (Madrid: Afrodisio Aguado, 1968) Vol. XII.

[22]"Romance and Realism: Pérez de Ayala's Urbano and Simona Novels," *Neophilologus* (1980):208-26.

[23]Amorós, *La novela intelectual* 326.

[24]*Principios y finales de la novela* 23.

[25]Keith M. May, *Out of the Maelstrom* 36.

[26]Francisco Agustín, *Ramón Pérez de Ayala. Su vida y obras* (Madrid: G. Hernández y Galo Sáez, 1927) 214.

[27]"Andrenio," *El Sol* 13 March 1926.

[28]The ideas of Jung which are used in this analysis are well known, and therefore I have not attempted to support my views with specific reference to Jung's writings. The relevant sources are the *Collected Works* (London: Routledge and Kegan Paul, 1953-71). Helpful summaries are Anthony Storr, *Jung* (Glasgow: Fontana, 1973) and Freida Fordham, *An Introduction to Jung's Pscyhology* (Harmondsworth: Penguin, 1953). The material in the remainder of this chapter has been published in my Critical Guide to *Tigre Juan* and *El curandero de su honra* (London: Grant & Cutler, 1981). I am grateful to the editors of the series, Professors Alan Deyermond and John Varey, for permission to reproduce it.

[29]Norma Urrutia, *De Troteras a Tigre Juan* (Madrid: Insula, 1960) 101.

[30]*Principios y finales de la novela* 25.

CHAPTER FIVE

THE WINDOW AND THE GARDEN:
NARRATIVE INTROVERSION
IN THE NOVELS OF PÉREZ DE AYALA

In Virginia Woolf's *To the Lighthouse*, Lily Briscoe despairs of being able to achieve "that razor edge of balance between opposite forces: Mr. Ramsey and the picture, which was necessary."[1] In this sentence Virginia Woolf crystallises the essential dilemma of Modernist art, that of balancing, as it were, the claims of the real with the claims of art, and which leads inevitably to a concern with art moving to the centre of the work of art itself. This dilemma is most acutely felt in the novel, which moves in that indeterminate space between the orders of form and the orders of reality, whatever that may be. The whole thrust of the nineteenth-century novel, the Realist novel, had been outwards towards reality, which it explored in all its fullness and circumstantial detail. The twentieth-century novel, by contrast, looks inward towards its own reality, explores in a highly self-conscious way its own genesis, techniques and even meaning. The emphasis shifts from the product to the process. While the nineteenth-century novel did not seriously question its ability to apprehend reality, the Modernist novel incessantly probes the complexity of this relationship, enquires into the paradoxes of the real nature of fiction and the fictional nature of reality. As such, it merely brings to the fore what is true of all fiction, namely that it is linguistic and of course fictive in nature. The achievement of nineteenth-century Realism was to disguise the conventions of fiction as the patterns of life. Needless to say, artistic self-consciousness is not a discovery of the Modernists, for of course a theoretical concern with narrative is present in much earlier literature, especially in the seventeenth and eighteenth centuries, from *Don Quijote* to *Tristram Shandy*. There, however, the effect was often comic and centred above all on the role of the narrator, or was aimed at distancing the reader from any facile identification with the characters. The Modernist rediscovery of self-consciousness is more radical for its being foregrounded against the premises of Realist convention and because it puts the very practice of writing at the centre of the creative enterprise. The great theme, if it can be so called, of the introverted novel, is the theme of the novel itself.

Mark Schorer, in his seminal article "Technique as Discovery," makes the observation that the modern novelist's real significance is "not only that he pays so much attention to his medium, but that, when he pays most, he discovers through it a new subject matter, and a greater one."[2] Paying attention to the medium is what Ortega y Gasset surely had in mind in the early part of *La deshumanización del arte* in a passage which directly inspired the title of this book:

imagínese el lector que estamos mirando un jardín a través del vidrio de una ventana. Nuestros ojos se acomodarán de suerte que el rayo de la visión penetre el vidrio sin detenerse en él, y vaya a prenderse en las flores y frondas. Como la meta de la visión es el jardín y hasta él va largado el rayo visual, no veremos el vidrio, pasará nuestra mirada a su través, sin percibirlo. Cuanto más puro sea el cristal menos lo veremos. Pero luego, haciendo un esfuerzo, podemos desentendernos del jardín y, retrayendo el rayo ocular, detenerlo en el vidrio. Entonces el jardín desaparece a nuestros ojos y de él sólo vemos unas masas de color confusas que parecen pegadas al cristal. Por tanto, ver el jardín y ver el vidrio de la ventana son dos operaciones incompatibles: la una excluye a la otra y requieren acomodaciones oculares diferentes.[3]

Seen in this way, "dehumanisation" is not to be conceived of as a negative term, but it naturally implies a rejection of any unselfconscious reader identification on the level of plot or character in human or emotional terms. At the same time, however, the reader is invited to become involved in the processes of the text's production. Fiction which reflects "the garden" back on to "the window" is providing a commentary on its own generative processes. Ortega y Gasset went on to define the difference between artistic and experienced reality and suggested that nineteenth-century realism was an "arte bizco" in its attempt to equate the two:

La percepción de la realidad vivida y la percepción de la realidad artística son, en principio, incompatibles por requerir una acomodación diferente de nuestro aparato receptor. Un arte que nos proponga esa doble mirada será un arte bizco. El siglo XIX ha bizqueado sobremanera .... estilizar es deformar lo real, desrealizar. Estilización implica deshumanización. Y viceversa, no hay otra manera de deshumanizar que estilizar.[4]

We may find nowadays that this notion of style is a little antiquated, but there is no doubting the validity of Ortega's assertion of the distinctiveness of the enabling means of handling the content, that is, language, and its embodiment in the text. Modernist introversion is a stage in the movement away — in both literature and criticism — from author (Romanticism), then from the social and historical world (Realism) as the authenticating sources of the work. Modernism is text-centred, and we might see the stage of post-Modernism through which we are now passing as that of placing the emphasis upon the reader himself. Reality is not simply mediated in fiction but constructed in language, and the reader has a role in that construction. This awareness of the co-producing role of the reader

131

is already present in the Modernist novel. The simplest reminder of this is the address to the reader, which we have observed in Ayala's novels, and which implicates him in some way in the making of the text. In *Belarmino y Apolonio*, the reader who is "impaciente de acontecimientos" can create his own kind of novel by skipping certain sections dominated by dialogue and ideas. Modernist self-conscious fiction stresses above all the imaginative process, in the reader as well as in the author.

In an earlier chapter we have seen how the use of existing literature in a new work is one manifestation of the self-consciousness which is so characteristic of Modernist fiction. The stimulus for a new work comes from an older one, so that the whole body of literature can be conceived of as being essentially self-contained and inward-looking. *Prometeo* is an example of the ironical literary self-consciousness of Modernism: Odysseus is a Professor of Greek, his wanderings are limited in both time and space, Homeric style is consistently parodied. Such an approach transcends realist practice in pursuit of artistic awareness: the myth is reincarnated in a modern idiom; the ordinary is mythified. A curious literary osmosis takes place. On the other hand, the novel highlights the fractures in its own composition and hints at the formlessness and lack of common culture in modern reality. *Prometeo* points the way towards a deconstruction of writing practice. The position of the artist/novelist is called into question, as are the conditions in which art is created. Thus parodic intent does not necessarily involve ridicule of the older form. Parody is an aspect of defamiliarization: it calls attention to literary codes, invites a literary reading. Thus it involves a recognition of tradition in literature and an exploration of similarity and difference between literary modes. Therefore, parody could arguably be conceived of as the quintessence of overtly self-conscious fiction. Parody offers reinterpretation and liberates the reader from conventionalised expectations. It also liberates him from a curiosity about the plot and distances him from the text so that his response to it can be more imaginative, aesthetic or, in Ortega's terms, "dehumanised." This is not to be construed negatively but simply as the most appropriate response to a literary text. In the case of Pérez de Ayala the most sustained example of this is *Prometeo*, described by one critic as "un pequeño juguete literario,"[5] implying that in it Ayala plays the game of literature. This is a subversion of the Romantic notion of originality for, as Edward Said points out, "Since there is no such thing as an absolutely primal text, each act of composition involves other texts, and so each writing transmits itself, receives other writing, reconstitutes by displacement other writing"[6] One association of the Promethean figure that is frequently overlooked in criticism of this short novel is that of the creative artist. In the story of Marco, is Ayala dramatising the anguish of the writer who conceives his ideal work, anticipates its effect upon his readers and even on the course of the world, prepares it carefully and meticulously, only to produce something pitiful, scorned and doomed to failure? Ayala constantly struggled to come to terms with his art, to overcome the "maldición originaria del novelista," to create the perfect work. He wrote of this ideal in *Principios y finales de la novela*: "Quizá el soñado ideal de todo gran novelista ha sido escribir una sola novela universal, en el otoño de su existencia . . . Pero se escribe antes porque uno no tiene la vida garantizada, y el futuro reside en el regazo de los dioses."[7] We glimpse here that sense of artistic crisis which is so characteristic of Modernism in which the fiction itself impresses by its own elegance, yet depresses by its own inadequacy. Ayala's fictional constructs highlight the paradoxical complexity of the relations between the world and the word. In this respect no novel could be more introverted than *Belarmino y Apolonio,* where the whole process of the novel's making is exposed for the reader to see. The effect is partly humorous, but it has its serious side in that it ostensibly curtails the realistic potential of the text, implicating the reader in the autonomous structures of the fiction itself. And it implies, of course, that the making of fictions is a serious pursuit. Many critics see the dialectic between fiction and reality as a characteristic of the novel genre present in *Don Quijote*, which is not only a realistic novel but a self-reflexive one, not just the story but the very telling of the story are part of the narrative, and this Cervantine tradition was one on which Pérez de Ayala was ready to draw.

It is in *Belarmino y Apolonio* (1921) that Ayala most appears to have the example of Cervantes before his mind. The First Prologue to *Don Quijote*, where Cervantes describes himself sitting before a blank page, deep in thought, and then discusses his book with a friend, is echoed in Chapter II of Ayala's novel, where he discusses some technical problems of his craft with his imaginary character don Amaranto, who appears in a vision. In other words, both authors begin by detaching themselves from their works and by calling the reader's attention to the facts of their composition. In this same novel, Ayala talks of his characters in words strikingly similar to those of Cervantes: "Belarmino y Apolonio han existido y yo los he amado. No digo que hayan existido en carne mortal sobre el haz de la tierra; han existido por mí y para mí." In *Don Quijote* II, Chapter 74, we read: "Para mí solo nació don Quijote, y yo para él." At least one critic has seen Belarmino and Apolonio as re-incarnations of Don Quijote and Sancho[8] and, while this may perhaps be to claim too much, there are clear Cervantine features in Ayala's novel. Even on the simple level of description, for example, we notice that Belarmino has "el rostro enjuto," whereas Don Quijote is "enjuto de rostro." Belarmino's cobbler's stool is called Clavileño. In Chapter 18 of Part II of the *Quijote*, the Caballero del Verde Gabán thinks the knight is to be taken more "por loco que por cuerdo." The interplay between sanity and madness is a feature of *Belarmino y Apolonio*:

133

don Guillén uses the "locura-cordura" antithesis when describing Belarmino: "no sé si era un loco cuerdo o un cuerdo loco." The use of the multiple perspective, regarded as Ayala's most significant achievement in his novel, is already present in Cervantes, as E.C. Riley observes. Most significantly of all, perhaps, is the fact that it is in *Belarmino y Apolonio* that Ayala expresses his greatest praise and admiration for Cervantes:

> Por el estilo del autor se viene en conocimiento de su inteligencia: estilo metafórico, estilo engolado, estilo arcaico, estilo recortado, estilo desnudo, estilo llano, estilo exquisito, estilo colorista, estilo abstracto, etc. etc.; todos ellos, cada uno de por sí, denotan inteligencia limitada y escasez de pensamiento. La totalidad y fusión de todos ellos, predominando cada manera según la sazón del pensamiento: Cervantes, el primer pensador español. (IV:216)

Ayala's admiration for this versatility, this diversity of styles, has led him to parody and pastiche so that his novels at times appear to be rhetorical exercises in imitating other writers or genres. This self-consciousness, the obvious literary quality it imparts to the work, is one way in which Ayala deviates from the conventions of nineteenth-century Realism. It would be wrong, however, to identify Ayala completely with that group of writers in early twentieth-century Spain who totally reject Realism. Ayala's position is more ambivalent and it is in this context that the Cervantine parallel is significant. In a sense, Ayala's novels sustain a dialogue with the previous fictional tradition, and the *Urbano and Simona* novels, despite their apparent preoccupation with the sexual education, reflect many of the author's own ideas and doubts about his own creative enterprise. *Luna de miel, luna de hiel* and *Los trabajos de Urbano y Simona* are, to borrow the phrase J.B. Avalle-Arce applies to the *Persiles*, "la verdadera novela de un novelista."[9] Significantly, *Los trabajos de Persiles y Sigismunda* is Cervantes' most literary creation, both in its borrowings from other works and in its self-analytical presentation of critical problems and precepts. Where Ayala directs himself to the legacy of Realism, Cervantes confronts the Classicism of his own age, built upon Horace's *Ars Poetica* and Aristotle's *Poetics*. Thus Ayala's interest in Cervantes extends far beyond the adaptation of incidents or subject-matter to embrace issues fundamental to the reading and writing of imaginative literature. Cervantes offered Ayala a model of a work which would combine imagination and public acceptability in much the same way as Heliodorus offered a model to Cervantes himself three centuries earlier. In the sixteenth century literary theorists condemned the popular romances of chivalry for their failure to conform to the precepts of Horace and Aristotle. The discovery of Heliodorus' *Ethiopic History* provided a form of prose fiction which satisfied classical literary standards. The work was praised for its exemplary nature, its moral wisdom and erudition, as well as being found acceptable on aesthetic grounds by virtue of its unity of action through the proper integration of its episodes and its successful use of the *in medias res* technique. Moreover, it could be seen to observe the principle of verisimilitude. Readers of the time, observes M. Bataillon, admired its "verosimilitud, verdad psicológica, ingeniosidad de la composición, sustancia filosófica, respeto de la moral."[10] That Cervantes claimed to rival Heliodorus testifies to the importance of these considerations in the *Persiles*, particularly the thematic significance of contemporary literary theory. Pérez de Ayala shows remarkably similar concerns. The modern novel, in its refusal to offer an artificially idealistic portrayal of reality, was subject to no less strong moral objections than its Golden Age predecessor, though these were directed from a slightly different angle. If the romances were criticised for their basic untruthfulness, for their power to excite the passions of the reader or, more mildly, as simply a waste of the reader's time, the Realist novel was attacked as sordidly unedifying in its treatment of contemporary life. Yet once this controversy ceased to dominate theoretical consideration of fiction, Realism itself had become so influential that any departure from it appeared to be the very negation of the novel. The whole question of verisimilitude became an important one as readers rejected the fanciful, the implausible, in favour of accuracy and authenticity. Just as the *Persiles*, then, engages in an ambivalent debate with Aristotelian precept, so too do *Luna de miel, luna de hiel* and *Los trabajos de Urbano y Simona* explore the questions of the proper subject-matter for literature, the nature of the creative act, the pleasures of the fictitious.

The opening pages of the novel are full of literary allusions: Adam and Eve, Daphnis and Chloe, Plato, Calderón, *Il Novellino*, "cuentos de hadas y encantamientos." The relationship between life and literature is a central theme in the novel, and it is don Cástulo who is most immersed in books: "don Cástulo vivía dos vidas paralelas, autónomas y sin mutuo contacto entre sí: una vida real y una vida imaginaria. Los ratos de ocio y solaz los consumía en leer autores eróticos, griegos y latinos" (IV:247). Thus Cástulo is the most appropriate character to provide a literary commentary on all that is taking place. The narrator himself, of course, constantly calls attention to the fantastic nature of this tale. He describes Urbano and Cástulo on their way back to El Collado as "la más rara pareja que vieron los siglos," fitting subjects for the "divina ironía" of Plato himself (IV:279). Cástulo makes it clear that the novel is a reworking of Daphnis and Chloe, but his observations are ambivalent. In a sense, Cástulo is a satire on the intellectual, the man whose vital experience comes only from books. Indeed, he himself qualifies the "erudito" as a "gran mentecato y tonto de capirote." He even refers to the romances of Achilles Tatius and Longus as a "falaz librejo" (he has them bound in one volume), but yet they serve him as his "manual de pedagogía erótica." Cástulo has the capacity to experience all around him as though it were a work of literature and almost seems to be reading the novel Ayala is writing. He experiences the novel of Urbano and Simona, and this experience transforms him. The novel awakens his own emotions, and a parallel is created between the young couple's love and the grotesque love of Cástulo and Conchona. This humorous element partially offsets the pathos of the novel provided by the spectacle of Urbano and Simona struggling with emotions they do not fully understand. The clash of natural instinct and social restraint could be treated with delicacy and tenderness, but Ayala chose to exaggerate this to the point of grotesqueness. The effect of this is to acknowledge the novel's lack of realism without divesting it of its claim to offer a truthful statement on the human condition. This is what gives the novel its universal quality, for the many classical allusions made by don Cástulo are "reveladoras de la poca o ninguna mudanza de hombres y costumbres en muchos siglos" (IV:284). More importantly, though, he heads off accusations of lack of *vraisemblance* by calling attention to the text's artificiality.

Don Cástulo is the most autonomous character in the work and is the instrument whereby the nature of the fiction is discussed. For example, in the second part of *Luna de miel, luna de hiel* he conducts a debate with himself, trying to determine to which genre the novel belongs. He begins to waver from his classical principles: "¿Egloga o tragedia? Nada, que me entrego. El amor es una cosa trágica y grotesca de consuno. Sin duda hay géneros literarios híbridos como hay animales híbridos y personas híbridas" (IV:293-94). A little later he is ready to accept that classicism and romanticism are problematical terms: "cuáles de los clásicos ahora averiguo que eran endemoniadamente románticos" (IV:307). Cástulo's romanticism seems due entirely to his discovery of love and woman and is manifested in his new introspection, grandiloquently expressed as "perpetua adoración ante el Santo Sacramento de Mí mismo" (IV:318). It would appear, in other words, that Cástulo is calling attention to the way in which Ayala allies the pastoral mode with romantic subjectivity. Literature is a way of looking at the world, an interpretation of the writer's reality, which can be so persuasive that the reader may even aspire to conform to the model of reality which literature presents. In Chapter I we saw how Galdós handled this perennial literary theme. The result is usually ridiculous or stereotyped behaviour. The grandeur and isolation of the Romantic hero is absent from Cástulo's portrayal of the role, as he himself is made to recognise: "Quise ser un héroe del romanticismo serio; soy un personaje del romanticismo cómico. Pertenezco, sírvame de consuelo, al orden de lo cómico superior, lo cómico-trágico, que es risible e inspira piedad" (IV:349).

A more radical probing of the whole question of the relationship of life to literature is to be found in an earlier discussion between Cástulo and Urbano. Urbano had begun to widen his experience by direct observation of nature, and this provides Cástulo with an opportunity to discuss the message of Rousseau's *Emile,* which advocates a return to nature, to personal experience. There is considerable ambivalence here for although Cástulo advises Urbano to abandon books, he acknowledges that in his own case they are indispensable: "los libros son mi vida, mi mundo, mi Naturaleza, y no podría vivir sin ellos" (IV:324). Moreover, Urbano himself sees the incongruity of a book being written on the subject of the uselessness of books. Cástulo seems to steer a middle course by suggesting that books are a valuable asset in life but no substitute for it: "que colaboren en tus reflexiones sobre tu vida pasada, pero que no se antepongan a tus experiencias, provocándote la embriaguez de una vida imaginaria que te dejará inútil para la vida verdadera" (IV:324). Urbano turns to books precisely because his real life is unfulfilled, and in Alarcón's *El final de Norma* he is able to live a momentary imaginative existence. His emotional reactions confirm Cástulo's description of reading one's first novel as "un pequeño ataque de locura, una breve enajenación" (IV:326). Later, Urbano is able to relate his own experience to his reading of *Genesis.* In addition to the theme of intellectualism versus vitalism, the myth of Adam and Eve introduces the idea of sin and punishment into the myth of innocent love. In Ayala's modern version the archangel is replaced by the bailiffs, and the new version is a debased and more squalid account than the original: "La nueva representación del drama bíblico no la juzgaba tan digna y decorosa como en el libro del *Génesis"* (IV:358), reflects Urbano, who then protests about the author's artistic handling of the situation, his additions to the text, in particular the unnecessary death of doña Rosita. Thus we have a modern novel which offers a re-interpretation of both a Biblical and Greek myth and simultaneously provides a literary commentary on it. This technique is continued in the second part of the novel, *Los trabajos de Urbano y Simona*, although here plot and incident play a larger role in a kind of paramelodrama of which Conchona's confrontation with the thieving servants towards the end of *Luna de miel, luna de hiel* gives a foretaste. There can be little doubt that Ayala was aware of the strains that his tale would place upon the reader's credulity. His solution is openly to acknowledge the problem through the use of a device which is highly reminiscent of Cervantes', and even Unamuno's, use of the autonomous character. Cástulo, in the coach, sits before a group of people who are representative of ordinary humanity and in his mind goes through the argument which asserts that fictional characters really exist: "Os reís de la tragedia como os reís de la mitología. Los mitos los juzgáis inverosímiles y los calificáis de cuentos de viejas. Lo que no comprendéis, decretáis que no existe . . . Yo, el más inverosímil de todos, soy el que menos existe. Pues sí, a pesar del vulgo, a pesar de vosotros, existo. Aquí me tenéis, contra toda lógica y verosimilitud" (IV:390). E.C. Riley makes the point that Cervantes, when his story erred against some literary principle, especially verisimilitude, would have a character discuss the problem openly: "A favourite means of dodging the issue of credibility is to plant it squarely before one, make his characters discuss it and then, having lulled the inattentive reader into thinking it has been dealt with, to pass on, leaving it exactly as it was."[11] Ayala's intention is similar, but on another level he is inquiring into the nature of literary truth, so that as Cástulo develops his ideas he accepts the logic of the novelistic situation and seeks implausibilities within that logic. Thus the whole situation itself is not particularly troublesome, but what is improbable is Cástulo's own sudden departure from El Collado. Ayala treats the very real concerns of realist writers in cavalier fashion by refusing to take their arguments at all seriously. His only criterion seems to be that the only logic of literature is that generated by the imagination and by the inner coherence of the work itself. A development of this theme is to be found in the first paragraph of the *Plenilunio*:

> Los cuentos de hadas son mitad verdad y mitad mentira. Lo triste de los cuentos de hadas encierra una verdad de la experiencia cotidiana, una verdad vulgar; la parte maravillosa todos sabemos que es mentira, pero es una mentira dulce, más preciosa y saludable y, en resolución, más verdadera que la misma verdad. (IV:481)

This is very reminiscent of J.R.R. Tolkien's remarks about fairytales being consolation for the sorrow of this world. To this extent, it would not be derogatory or pejorative to talk of all fiction as being escapist in the sense that it imaginatively constructs a fictive world different from that which is empirically real, a fictive world that is coherent and ordered. Story telling (and story-reading) seem, in this sense, to be essential human faculties. Ayala's novel has precisely this quality in that it reveals a vision of man redeemed, a vision which goes beyond the surface detail associated with realism to offer a glimpse of underlying reality or truth. The novel is a model of the diversity and purpose of the world. We can see this also in Urbano's reflections on the role of the Creator, which are a variation on the theme of the autonomous character. Taking up the ideas contained in his objections to the new version of *Genesis* towards the end of *Luna de miel, luna de hiel*, he queries the Deity's plans for mankind, especially his invention of love for the propagation of the species. Of course, this relates to Urbano's own very unique experience, but the fact that God is designated "Author" deftly establishes a connection between God and Creation and author and work. Such a parallel is an integral part of Ayala's thinking on the art of literature.

138

The main literary ideal of this part of the novel continues to be the pastoral. When Cástulo is at Conchona's country house, he exclaims: "¡Eglógico! ¡Encantador! Uno se imagina transportado a las edades de la poesía auténtica" (IV:437), and Urbano, separated from Simona, sees them together, after a long and arduous pilgrimage, living the simple rural life. Against civilisation, with its complication of human life, its stifling of natural instinct, is set a return not just to nature, but to nature and culture together. In an important passage, Urbano sees the significance of learning, the necessary and beneficial association of life and culture:

Don Cástulo había sido su maestro y no le había enseñado nada. Es decir, eso creía Urbano hasta ahora: que don Cástulo no le había enseñado nada, sino superfluidades, citas poéticas, frases clásicas, episodios de la edad de Maricastaña, zarandajas. ¡Qué equivocado había estado Urbano! Ahora que iba palpando con manos impacientes el cuerpo musculoso y cerril de la realidad cotidiana y que advertía su dinamismo tumultuoso y sus movimientos feos y crueles . . . ahora era cuando Urbano comprendía el alto magisterio de don Cástulo y sus enseñanzas incomparables, sentimientos delicados, pureza de intenciones, amor a la belleza, desinterés en los pensamientos, culto de la inteligencia, elegancia del espíritu. (IV:470-71)

Urbano's tribute to his mentor releases Cástulo from his comic role and at the same time is a testimony to Ayala's belief in the value and importance of culture and learning in human experience. Amorós has consistently seen the novel as an expression of Ayala's vitalism, a hymn to life. More than this, however, it is a tribute to culture. Natural man is not unequivocally extolled, so-called civilised, or social, man does not fare very well. Ayala's ideal, though he puts it forward with some reluctance and even ambivalence, is cultured man. The novel, in fact, does not invite a Naturalist reading but a cultural one. This is something which we can trace right back to Ayala's first novel.

It is evident that Ayala's concern with formal and theoretical questions is present from the earliest stage in his career, in fact, from *Tinieblas en las cumbres*. This may appear strange in the light of the general view of the work as a kind of *novela lupanaria*. Andrés Amorós makes the claim that it is "la 'más novela' en el sentido clásico de la palabra: describe ambientes, crea personajes llenos de vida, evoca antecedentes, nos da realismo 'de cosas', y 'de almas' junto a ideas, etc."[12] There are, of course, problems inherent in any such definition of a novel, but clearly Amorós means that *Tinieblas en las cumbres* operates within the traditions of the genre and that we should approach it with the same preoccupations and expectations with which we approach any novel. Nevertheless the question surely arises, given the plethora of literary allusion in the novel and its manifest self-referentiality, whether it does not undermine traditional Realist assumptions about fiction and indeed imply a theory of fiction totaliy at variance with them.

A significant aspect of the contemporary literary scene at the time of the appearance of Ayala's first novel is the emergence of a new mode of fiction-writing. As Ayala began his writing career in Madrid in 1902, four experimental novels were published, at least two of which, Pío Baroja's *Camino de perfección* and José Martínez Ruiz's *La voluntad*, appear to have some bearing on the genesis and motivation of *Tinieblas en las cumbres*. The title which Ayala eventually gave to his novel is particularly appropriate in this respect, for it contains both a literal and a metaphorical meaning: the actual eclipse of the sun seen from a mountain-top, and the descent of darkness upon man's idealism and on his faith in his secure position in the world. This is none other than the existential crisis of twentieth-century man which the new novel claims to explore, and it is the kind of novel, more than *modernismo*, which *Tinieblas en las cumbres* sets out to parody. Ayala's skepticism about this form of fiction derives not from any dismissive attitude to the crisis which it purports to portray, but from his own understanding of the nature of literary fictions. Put simply, fiction is not fact. Fiction is second-hand rather than first-hand experience filtered through forms that are cultural in origin. In this sense, Alberto in *La pata de la raposa* is more a victim of literature than of life. *Tinieblas en las cumbres* is born out of the intuition of the fallacy of equating or confusing life with literature.

Tinieblas en las cumbres appeared in its first edition under the pseudonym of Plotino Cuevas. In the early stages of his career, Pérez de Ayala had used several such pseudonyms — Clavígero, don Melitón Pelayo, Pánfilo Terranova — for his "pláticas" and "crónicas," and each had a distinctive voice.[13] Although Ayala claimed that the use of a pseudonym was intended to avoid his family any embarrassment, the actual choice of names must in itself be significant. Plotino has unmistakable neo-Platonic resonances, it evokes the Hellenic world, and consequently Cuevas must bring to mind the allegory of the Cave, about which Ayala wrote under a related pseudonym. This clue must surely condition our reading of the novel. A neo-Platonist will not write a Realist novel of the nineteenth-century variety, for he will hold that true realities are general and not particular, and he will use language to abstract from existences to essences. Such fiction generalises and dissociates us from particular reality. Even the pseudonym, then, serves to underline that the claims of reality as commonly perceived are not paramount in this particular novel. *Tinieblas en las cumbres* accedes only to the claims of the art of fiction, the only reality it evokes is its own reality.

If it is true that Ayala holds this view of fiction, it is easy to see why he should use the forms of fiction in a self-conscious way in order to write a work which is both novel and criticism. *Tinieblas en las cumbres* embodies an implied theory of fiction. The notion that fiction can in any way be referred directly back to life is overtly mocked in Ayala's pseudo-picaresque Prologue, which presents the novel as an exemplary tale designed to "escarmentar en cabeza ajena" (I:235). The picaresque itself, of course, is conventionalised fiction, as Quevedo himself recognises in his own Prologue to the *Buscón*, which is literary rather than moral in inspiration. Quevedo emphasises that his work incorporates those features of the picaresque genre which his readers will recognise instantly and to which they will respond. Ayala's Epilogue/Prologue is yet another of the literary "set-pieces" which make up *Tinieblas en las cumbres* and contribute to its patchwork effect. The main inspiration of the novel is, as I have implied, the Spanish philosophical novel of the early century. It is not possible within the confines of this chapter to examine in detail the affinities between *Tinieblas en las cumbres* and novels like *Camino de perfección* and *La voluntad*, but it is possible to isolate and outline some of the characteristics of the proto-Existentialist novel which find their way into Ayala's work.

The most striking similarity between Ayala's novel and the new philosophical novel in vogue at the time is the predominance of the single, preoccupied protagonist reflecting the concerns of the author himself. Often this character is an artist, and thus a feature of the *Künstlerroman* is a concern with the progress of the artist. The unity of the novel is determined by the unity of the artistic consciousness which is elaborated within it. Indeed, a salient metafictional aspect of Pérez de Ayala's first cycle of novels is the degree to which they begin the process of blurring the distinction between literary and critical texts, the reflection, within the artistic form, of and on the artistic form. One of the best examples is the famous scene in *Troteras y danzaderas* where Alberto reads *Othello* to the prostitute Verónica. Less important than what is actually said here on the nature of tragedy is the fact that such a passage is included in the novel at all. Literary characters reflect on other literary characters, literature looks inward upon itself. Verónica's reactions and Alberto's assessment of them expose some of the processes of reading which are at work. The reader transfers his attention from the real to an imagined world, but regards it as in some way a continuation of the real world. The process is to some degree liberating, and in the order of fiction that is created the reader is able to find the satisfaction of coherence that is absent in the chaos of empirical reality. The creation of narratives is acknowledged as a central and significant human activity. And of course Verónica creates, constructs, her own version of *Othello*.

Alberto is the literary successor of Fernando Ossorio and Antonio Azorín. In *Tinieblas en las cumbres*, although he is not allowed to dominate the narrative until its later stages, he is sharply differentiated from the other characters in the novel by his philosophical and artistic preoccupations and, like Ossorio and Azorín, he suffers the legacy of a clerical education, a sense of crisis in his relations with the world and with other people and an adolescent susceptibility to negative influences from his environment and his reading. It is impossible not to have the earlier novels and their protagonists in mind when reading Ayala's work, for certain themes recur. For example, there is a persistent association between sex and religion in *Camino de perfección*, and in *Tinieblas en las cumbres*, in which the erotic element is very prominent, sexual activity is portrayed using religious and devotional vocabulary. Similarly, there is also a close parallel established between art and religion, which is something characteristically *modernista*. The first section of *Camino de perfección*, in fact, is almost a compendium of the major preoccupations of the period and has as its particular theme the spiritual basis of art. For many writers of the time art appeared as a replacement or substitute for religious faith. Alberto's visit to the church with Rosina is an echo of Ossorio's visits to several churches and particularly of his visit to the cathedral in Tarragona in the company of Dolores. Ossorio wants to experience the divinity through art and also through nature. An important scene in the novel is when he walks in the mountains with Schultze and seeks identification with nature. In fact, this is a commonplace in this kind of novel. In Ganivet's *Los trabajos del infatigable creador Pío Cid*, for example, the protagonist experiences his famous *visión blanca* after ascending to a mountain-top. The basic motif of the ascent in Ayala's novel has therefore immediate literary antecedents.

Of course, at the root of these characters' existential crises is the fear of death. Yuste's remark in *La voluntad* is typical: ". . . todo ha de acabar, disolviéndose en la nada, como el humo . . ."[14] Ossorio himself has a morbid preoccupation with death, but as he evolves psychologically he takes refuge and consolation in a belief in "algo invariable, inmutable, que no se puede cambiar, que no se puede aniquilar."[15] Alberto's belief, confided to his friend Yiddy, is strikingly similar: "creo en algo misterioso, de sutilísima esencia que, infundido en nuestro cuerpo, lo anima y le ha de sobrevivir" (I:195). Although I have talked in turn of *modernismo* and the existential novel of the Generation of 1898, in reality the spiritual and intellectual climate which produced them are the same. A clear example of this is the recourse to art in the face of death. Juan Ramón Jiménez, *modernista* par excellence, was writing in 1899 that "Nada

142

importa .... la misma suerte nos aguarda .... iremos a la nada."[16] Alberto claims that "la idea de la muerte me hizo artista" (p. 258), a phrase which can be related equally well to Unamunian philosophical anguish or to *modernista* aestheticism. *Tinieblas en las cumbres*, then, has to be understood in the context of the contemporary literary modes and preoccupations against which it is foregrounded.

A final feature of 1898 fiction which has a bearing in *Tinieblas en las cumbres*, but more importantly on the whole foundations of novel-writing, is the question of subjectivism. One of the premises of Realist aesthetics is that the world exists prior to and independent of the act of creation and that the novel, through the referential use of language, is capable of representing that world faithfully and accurately. However, the problem is that language deals not directly with reality but with concepts. Moreover, the notion of a reality independent of the consciousness that experiences or creates it has in modern times increasingly been called into question, particularly by the writers we are concerned with. An unassailable subjectivity is at the root of Ossorio's assertion that "el mundo de afuera no existe, tiene la realidad que yo le quiero dar."[17] In *La voluntad*, Yuste affirms that "la conciencia crea el mundo. No hay más realidad que la imagen, ni más vida que la conciencia."[18] If man is confined within the limits of his own subjectivity, if there is no verifiable, common reality, in what sense is communication possible and what purpose is there in writing fiction? Fiction cannot tell us anything about the world; it can only reveal the mind of the maker of the fiction, and that only to the extent it is filtered through the reader's own consciousness. There are reasons, then, why Pérez de Ayala should be skeptical about extravagant claims for the value of art as a means of spiritual regeneration. Therefore, apparent similarities between *Tinieblas en las cumbres* an other novels of the period cannot be taken as implying an identity of outlook. In fact, what other writers promulgated seriously Ayala subjects to a corrosive skepticism. Ayala's Modernist-Existentialist hero is, quite simply, a fictional construct with no verifiable equivalent in the real world. He is, moreover, defamiliarised by his context. It will be necessary to examine Alberto more closely later, but he is not the only element in the novel to be defamiliarised. Throughout the work, Ayala engages in an interplay between higher and lower forms in a way which creates ambiguity in the reader as to the nature of the text he is reading. The earliest critics of the novel either affirmed or denied its affinities with the erotic novel then in vogue, and there can be little doubt that Ayala structured his own text around this popular and recognisable form. Moreover, he gave to each chapter melodramatic titles reminiscent of the *folletin*, and these contrast sharply with the erudite apparatus which accompanies the first part, entitled *Prolegómenos*, and the quotations in Greek, Latin and English on the theme of death, which act as epigraphs to the work. In fact, both these devices are suppressed in the third edition, but the contrast between the erudite and the popular remains. The fact is that from an early stage an ambivalent tone is set as two modes, one higher, one lower, stand in self-conscious opposition to one another. The effect on the reader can only be disconcerting. The ephemeral or trivial is foregrounded against a plethora of literary allusion and therefore the novel defamiliarises on two levels, placing both the classical and the mundane in unaccustomed contexts in a way which may be calculated to call attention to the difficulties inherent in the promulgation and comprehension of literary texts. By virtue of its classical allusions, *Tinieblas en las cumbres* refers back to an age when everything conserved in manuscript, and later print, was judged significant, while it itself exists in a context where only a small proportion of what is printed can be deemed to be significant in the sense of having lasting value. The duality of style and theme in the novel invites consideration of its own significance or insignificance. Indeed, in any reading of the novel both significance and insignificance are constantly subject to redefinition. *Tinieblas en las cumbres* is permeated by literary values, it is sustained by constant reference to the canon of literature by means of echo, quotation, allusion, commentary, pastiche, in short, by openly acknowledged debts to the legacy of the Western bookish tradition. Its very eclecticism proclaims the immortality of great texts. Yet at the same time Ayala allows his text to degenerate. He subjects the same reader who can apparently read Greek in the original and understand the other allusions to the story of inconsequential events in the day in the life of a group of revellers and prostitutes on their way to witness an eclipse of the sun. This deliberate compromising of his own erudition surely signals the death of the kind of humanist education which made possible the apprehension of the dense web of reference and cross-reference, intertextuality, on which the life of the literary text depended. This is one interpretation of Ayala's method. His uneasy marriage of high culture and low life is a reflection of the erosion of the old order by the new. This is largely a socio-cultural phenomenon, but underlying it appears to be a philosophical shift, a decline in belief in the transcendent and in the purposeful interconnectedness of all things. Therefore, the undermining of the Hellenic and Latinate legacy by its infusion into the forms of popular fiction is accompanied by another feature of the novel, its philosophical dimension, which necessarily creates a new kind of text and on which Ayala provides his own commentary. *Tinieblas en las cumbres* contains the germ of an idea, enunciated more clearly in *La pata de la raposa*, that literary tradition, book culture, is for many moderns inhibiting in experiential terms, for it mediates everything for us, preventing a direct and unconditioned response to the world's stimuli. It is perhaps intentional that the novel is motivated by a rare astronomical occurrence and also depicts scenes of bacchanalian unrestraint. In the desire for intense, immediate experience, the

144

mediated experiences of past, and present, generations are discarded. There may be in the eclipse a metaphor for the death of a common culture of the educated, the darkness that threatens to envelop the peaks of literate civilisation.

There are other ways, too, in which *Tinieblas en las cumbres* indicates that it is a book about books, a novel about novels. The whole text is largely self-referential. The literary allusions themselves are the subject of comment within the novel by its presumed author: "si he puesto en ocasiones sobrado caudal de citas inglesas, latinas y hasta griegas, no es porque yo haya sido pedante, sino por cierto inmoderado afán, que siempre sentí, de mofarme un tanto de mis presuntos lectores" (I:235). Authorial interventions in the narrative itself signal the existence of a certain self-consciousness and an assertion of the text as artifice. Ayala mocks the traditional concern with verisimilitude in phrases such as "Puntualizamos estas futilidades o nonadas porque en ello sentimos gran complacencia" (I:177), or when the narrator reminds the reader of the contents of two omelettes (I:121). The existence of the Prologue/Epilogue, the preface of the "Coloquio superfluo," the sentimental flashback, the consciously literary passages (for example, the description of the iron foundry (I:131)), all act as reminders of the presence of the conventions of prose fiction. Moreover, Ayala is, on occasions, at pains to show that certain incidents have a literary rather than a realistic basis. A clear example of this is the incorporation into many novels of that symbol of nineteenth-century progress, the train, "que han observado muy atinadamente casi todos los novelistas, desde el invento de Stephenson hasta nuestros días" (I:116). Ayala lays bare the transformation of reality which all fiction entails. Moreover, the train is a classic vehicle of the fictional journey, a place in a sense cut off from the world of reality, a point made simply enough by the prostitutes, who find it to be something "irreal y de sueño" (I:119). Elsewhere Ayala engages in various forms of pastiche. No sooner has the novel opened than two characters are introduced and portrayed in terms reminiscent of nineteenth-century caricature. The emphasis in the remainder of this section of the novel is on physiological behaviour, in a clear echo of Naturalist preoccupations which are present, too, in the themes of sex, prostitution and, later, alcohol. This is taken to absurd lengths in Cerdá's obsession with a "despucelamiento" which he had effected, he imagines, some hours earlier. The physiological aspects of virginity are then given a theoretical, even philosophical, treatment, when Ayala introduces the first of his footnotes into the text. The ironical intention behind the use of these footnotes may be to give a pseudo-scholarly air to something inherently trivial, and the same device is used later in learned references on the subject of prostitution. Andrés Amorós construes these devices as illustrations or manifestations of Ayala's classicism: "en efecto, para el clasicismo de nuestro autor es fundamental la convicción de que todo se repite. De aquí deriva una visión del mundo como encarnación repetida de los mitos clásicos."[19] However, it appears to me that Ayala's practice has less to do with his vision of the world than with his conception of literature. Ayala is a classicist in the sense that he believes novels are based not on life but on other books. This belief is, of course, profoundly Modernist. For one thing, Modernists conceive of the totality of literature as a complete synchronic system in which the contemporary and the ancient co-exist. Such a conception, moreover, implies the essential autonomy of literature: the body of literature is a system of interrelated texts, and the text itself is a system of interrelated elements. In both cases, the primary reference is inward, not outward. That Ayala espoused and endorsed the notion of intertextuality from an early stage is evident in his previously quoted remarks on originality: "El autor es tanto más original — y no hay paradoja — cuanto más remotas son las resonancias que en él se concentran; como si dijéramos que sus raíces beben la sustancia de las tradiciones literarias primordiales." Such a position is naturally in direct opposition to the Romantic idea of the writer turning personal experience directly into words. Rather, it accepts that all literature is conventionalised. In order to create works of literature, and indeed to understand works of literature, it is necessary to have acquaintance with works of literature, to have assimilated the conventions within which they operate. Pérez de Ayala acknowledges this fact, thereby enhancing the fictive quality of his narrative. His practice is to conform to or to deviate from existing models. This, in his view, is also the practice of all writers, though they may not admit it or be aware of it. In his approach to reality, he is aware less of reality than of the ways in which it has been represented in literature. Books grow out of antecedents. Ayala's footnotes, then, acknowledge the existence of a book-culture, the existence of a corpus of texts as sources of authority. Ayala admits that he is indebted to the past, that he has rewritten what has already been written. The footnotes and the quotations enable Ayala to play a game with the cult of originality. When we use footnotes and quotation marks, or attribute sources, we acknowledge our indebtedness, we refuse to appropriate the ideas, insights, and words, of others. But in so doing we imply that all the rest, which is not signalled in this way, is truly our own, is fully original. For Ayala, nothing is truly original in this sense. For the classicist, and Modernist, literature is one corporate entity which he appropriates and modifies at will. Moreover, it is quite clear that the pattern of narrative, as embodied in plot, is archetypal: it is a literary form justified by the exigencies of the genre and not by anything existing outside the work in everyday, objective reality. Indeed, as the basic form is subject to variations, the gap between literature and life is, if anything, widened. In *Tinieblas en las cumbres*, the whole section entitled "El pasado" is an archetypal story of innocence betrayed, and it is an example of the way in which literature idealises. Provided that this is taken as idealisation there is no problem, but readers can all too easily equate the life offered inside books with the life experienced outside them. The Rosina story is portrayed in terms associated with popular literature which falsifies life by romanticising it and, above all, simplifying it. A sophisticated reader can see the falseness and superficiality of popular forms, but Ayala seems to imply that the same principle applies to all narrative: it stands as an alternative to reality, not as an imitation of it. This section of the narrative contains a description of the life of the circus, which seems to have interested Ayala considerably: it appears more fully in *La pata de la raposa*, and the wider world of entertainment and performance is treated in *Troteras y danzaderas*. One cannot be sure of this, but the circus and other forms of spectacle may appear to Ayala as metaphors for the creative work as he conceives it. The circus forms a world apart, an autonomous sphere of activity based on the cultivation of unusual skills, the acceptance of a set of conventions which have become established, the repetition of a restricted number of acts or variations of them. The world of the circus is like the land of fiction. The author is like the circus performer who, once the performance has ended, returns to the world of ordinary men. Of course, literature is more complex than this, for it made of words, which are what we use to make sense of the world. In fiction, words are substituted for the world, but the substitution lasts only as long as the fiction lasts. The world of fiction exists in the author's head, and for both author and reader it is, quite simply, a world of words.

It has been my contention, then, that while *Tinieblas en las cumbres* has been construed as a philosophical novel, or at least a novel about a philosophical crisis, fundamentally it is concerned with exploring certain assumptions about books. "La jornada," to my mind, is the most significant part of the novel from this point of view. It is the part of the novel which most seems to express contemporary ideologies, most especially through the character of Alberto. Ayala's treatment of Alberto is therefore crucial to our understanding of the work. He appears as a "joven incógnito, de aspecto insignificante y vulgar para quien no reparase en la complejidad de su sonrisa y en el torbellino de fuerzas confusas y luminosas que erraban por detrás del vidrio de su pupila" (I:114). The narrator also refers to glimpses of his "tediosa seriedad" (I:114). Such an attitude, though quite obviously foregrounded against the insouciance of the other characters ("bien humorados y exentos de preocupaciones" [I:115]) seems nevertheless to be treated in a somewhat tongue-in-cheek manner by the narrator, and this is confirmed soon afterwards when he describes Alberto as a "pintor novicio" que "traía entre ceja y ceja no sé qué cosquilleos transcendentales sobre arte y hasta teología y otras zarandajas, todo lo cual disimulaba por cortesía" (I:115-16). Already "cortesía" suggests that his crisis has not made

147

inroads into his bourgeois good manners, and thus suggests an element of pose or affectation. More importantly, the use of "cosquilleos" and "zarandajas" are unmistakable pointers to the narrator's position, and it is difficult to see how D.L. Shaw takes such a serious view of Alberto as a typical 1898 hero.[20] He would appear to be rather a parody of one. He is a parody too of the *modernista*, devoted to Beauty and frustrated by his inability to give it adequate artistic expression. The desire to find and express the spiritual in Nature is articulated, and simultaneously mocked, in Alberto's own words to Travesedo (I:163). Later, in his conversations with Yiddy, he proclaims pompously: "La belleza ejerce sobre mí imperio absoluto" (I:194), revealing himself as the *fin-de-siècle* man seeking in art and beauty a refuge from the world. Alberto is trying to live in the world as an artist. One can only live in the world as a man, and live as an artist only in art.

The theme of the artificiality of art, of literature, is taken up and developed in the "Coloquio superfluo," where Alberto's altered state of consciousness is subjected to the skepticism of Yiddy, who has outgrown a similar experience. The close proximity of nature awakens in Alberto latent feelings of communion with the world, a state of ecstasy in which the individual is fused with the totality of creation. The physical self seems to dissolve into pure consciousness, overcoming the conflict which Yiddy sees represented in his own name, Adam Warble, corporeality versus spirituality (I:184). Giving a character a significant name is, of course, a literary device. In real life we do not expect any particular correlation between a person's name and his character. Yiddy is an emblematic rather than realistic character, intended to illustrate the dangers of lyricism as a counterweight to Alberto's romanticism. Yiddy himself wrote verse "imitando a Shelley" (I:185), further evidence of the self-contained character of the body of literature. Yiddy also makes the point that "misticismo" and "panteísmo" have proved to be "ideas extravagantes" and, more significantly, literary inventions: "tengo para mí que la mayoría de los autores que nos hablan de estas cosas no han pasado por ellas" (I:186). Any idyllic notions are literature-inspired. What Yiddy now dismisses as folly, Alberto embraces in his adolescent idealism as "una de las cumbres más altas, transparentes y gloriosas del espíritu humano" (I:188). Alberto is totally imbued with that spiritual idealism which Donald L. Shaw identifies as a persistent strain in the intellectual life of the early century in Spain.[21] It is this idealism which directs him towards art, both because the art he creates will inspire idealism in others and because art is a means of overcoming death. Art outlives the artist and thereby guarantees him a kind of immortality by enabling him to live in others before and after his own physical death. In a highly significant passage of the dialogue, Alberto explains why he chose not to pursue a writer's career despite his natural initial inclinations in that direction. He seems to have been astute enough to realise that any immortality he might achieve is totally dependent upon the durability of language itself. Thus his initial desire to be a writer is confounded by his awareness of the inadequacy of the medium in which he has to work, language. Here we come very close to the heart of the Modernist crisis. Alberto's remarks on language, culminating in his assertion that "Si el lenguaje humano fuera perfecto e inspirado en la naturaleza, como lo es el arte de la pintura y de la escultura, podríamos realizar maravillosos poemas" (I:194), have been described by Carlos Longhurst as "fatuo naturalismo."[22] They could be construed in this way, but I think that underlying them is a sense of unease about the relations between words and the world, a loss of confidence in the power of language, the very faculty that appears to lie at the centre of man's dominance of the world. Firstly, language, being imperfect, is unequal to the full expression of the artist's personal vision. This is, of course, a literary commonplace, as for example in the Petrarchan sonnet, or in mystical writing, which wrestles with its own efforts to articulate the ineffable. Alberto seems to construe the inadequacy of language as a question both of expression and of comprehension: each man speaks a different language. This idea is further developed in *Belarmino y Apolonio*, one element of which concerns Belarmino's dissatisfaction with language and his unease about the separation of language and experience to the extent that he is lured by the temptations of silence. On the specifically literary level, Alberto seems disillusioned with literature itself and its conventionalised rhetoric. He was, after all, attracted to "las bellas letras" by the study of rhetoric at school. Rhetoric partakes of the problem of all literature: it is conventionalised and divorced from real experience. It can be no accident, moreover, that Alberto's thoughts on art and immortality are enunciated in a context which emphasises decisively the here-and-now. His companions are immersed in the spontaneous sensations of the moment and naturally reject any sacrifice of the present, either for the dead traditions of the past or the promise of future fame. Another difficulty is the modern debasement of language, and it is also no accident that Alberto's and Yiddy's dialogue is punctuated by language used at its most vulgar and debased level (I:190). Literary language is thus under threat both from within and without. Finally, Alberto, in his allusion to "boticarios materialistas" (I:196), implies a threat in the form of the exact sciences which undermines both theological-mythological systems and the metaphorical nature of the language which transcribed them. New nonverbal systems of representing phenomena indicate a need for exactitude and precision rather than suggestiveness. Alberto's turning to painting is an indication of this crisis and anticipates, curiously, the twentieth-century's progressive abandonment of the written word in favour of the visual image. We can see, therefore, that the "Coloquio superfluo," apparently about metaphysical despair, has much to say on the conditions in which art is created and books written. Its importance and introspective nature are appropriately signalled by the author's short preface to it.

The remainder of the novel dwells rather more explicitly on Alberto's spiritual crisis, deepened by the cataclysm of the solar eclipse, but the manner in which he is projected to the reader is so self-consciously literary, so unreal, that his status as an existentialist hero cannot seriously be sustained. His desire for self-annihilation, his ridiculous outpourings in the face of nature: "Espíritu Misterioso, Ciega y Terrible Potencia . . . ." (I:214), his readiness to retreat from the world back to the womb, his cloying self-pity, his oscillation between different poses, all embody Ayala's critique of the spiritual climate of the times. His impulse to flee to Paris, the Mecca of artists and aesthetes, is soon followed by a resolve to immerse himself in physical sensation and then by a quasi-religious desire to return to the innocence of childhood. The narrator makes it plain, as he does in a similar pastiche in the opening of *La pata de la raposa*, that all this is "obra de la embriaguez" (I:225). We find, therefore, that Alberto is the repository of certain *modernista* or *fin-de-siècle* literary attitudes which are treated with a degree of ambivalence or detachment, and on occasions downright scorn, by his creator. At the same time, these contemporary concerns are related to a much wider exploration of the role and position of art, particularly fictional or imaginative literature, in the modern world. This concern, which forms part of the crisis of Modernism, is the principal unifying feature of the novel. We may conclude, then, that the crisis depicted in *Tinieblas en las cumbres* is the crisis of fiction itself. The novel is born out of the multifarious cross-currents of the early twentieth-century literary and cultural scene, in which Ayala was an intelligent and critical participant. In the novel, the excesses of *modernista* aestheticism and existential despair are shown to emanate from and respond to a shared spiritual situation. They, and the climate which produced them, are the primary stimulus for Ayala's probing of certain assumptions about the writing and reading of literature and about the nature of literary fictions. Ayala stresses the fictional character of narrative, reveals the artificial and conventionalised nature of the structures that underlie it, and maintains that literature draws its inspiration not from reality, but from other literature. He emphasises that all books relate to previous books by incorporating into his work a plethora of pastiche, parody, citation, and allusion and implies that all novels are created within a tradition that imparts value to certain kinds of experience and to certain modes of representing it. He interprets true originality not as novelty, but as an acknowledgement of sources, of origins, and highlights the persistence of tradition in an overtly self-conscious way by imitating directly or obliquely classical antecedents. At the same time, the juxtaposition of classical and popular forms, the ironical use of footnotes, the blend of erudition with the crudest naturalism, all point to the death of a high literary culture. For one thing, the referential richness of literary texts is lost on those who lack the humanist education necessary to their full appreciation. In fact, the whole humanist value-system is shown to have been undermined. Notions such as the immortality of great works, and of their creators, are no longer regarded as unassailable. Indeed, the lasting is threatened with engulfment by the ephemeral, and the unique status of the literary text is eroded. *Tinieblas en las cumbres* challenges comfortable definition. Most importantly of all, perhaps, language itself is shown to be in a state of crisis. Its stability and reliability are undermined. It, like literature, can be considered a self-referential, self-sustaining system with no corresponding object in the outside world. The most significant experiences are increasingly held to be those which totally exceed their own verbalisation. Words are suspect, and recourse to them leads inevitably to falsification or cliché. All these notions, not always entirely consistent with one another, combine to make *Tinieblas en las cumbres* a remarkably rich and perceptive, if uneven, novel. The unevenness derives perhaps from the attempt to let the lower mirror the higher as a means of suggesting the fundamental dichotomies existing within both language and literature in the modern world, between what we might term the elitist and the popular. In this respect *Tinieblas en las cumbres* is ambivalent, and in its treatment of this aspect of the Modernist crisis it is tantalisingly Modernist itself in its indeterminacy. Is it a ceremony of mourning for the impending death of literature or a celebration of its increasing marginality, and hence perhaps its enhanced value, in the modern world? As likely as not, it is both, and if it continues to have claims upon our attention it is because it embodies within the willed discontinuities of its own form the disorientation of the "man of letters" in the world of the twentieth century. The theme of the artist is continued in the remainder of the first cycle of novels, especially in *La pata de la raposa*.

In an earlier chapter we have seen how Alberto's reaction to the world was perceived from a psychological point of view. At that point, Alberto's conversion of life into literature was examined from this psychological perspective, but it has of course relevance to the metafictional dimension of Ayala's fictions in that it acts as an image of the artist in the process of creation. Alberto epitomises that obsessive self-consciousness that characterises the narcissistic text: he is incapable of a totally unmediated, or natural, perception of the world, for almost everything is seen in terms of its artistic representation. In like fashion, Pérez de Ayala's novels acknowledge that there can never be a simple reproduction or registering of reality in fiction, merely a construction which is itself culturally determined. Our way of apprehending the world is shaped by language and art. The most celebrated example of this is the scene in *La pata de la raposa* which takes place in the *chigre*: everything is filtered through famous works of art: "El cuadro de la taberna . . . . era Jordaens o Teniers," the landscape is like "esas creaciones de Patinir," a girl's song like "las romanzas de Grieg y Rimsky-Korsakof," another girl appears taken from "las kermeses de Rubens," and her skirt "añil muy vivo . . . . semejante a los añiles de Fra Angélico," and so on (I:259-60). Alberto becomes finally aware of this process and, reflecting upon himself, acknowledges that he, like any literary text, is the amalgam of a set of pre-existing permutations: "La realidad permanece ajena y misteriosa para mí. Entre ella y yo se interponen las imágenes y las sensaciones experimentadas por otros sentidos . . . . ¿Soy un hombre o soy un portafolio de estampas?" (I:262). We could even push this argument further to suggest that what we are seeing is the character calling attention to his own status as a literary construct, defying our attempts and wishes to see him as an autonomous individual. This, in fact, is a frequent process in Pérez de Ayala and relates in a more general way to his appropriation of images and terminology from that genre which up until now has barely concerned us, the drama. In fact, Mariano Baquero Goyanes, the first critic to apply the term "tragicomic" to Pérez de Ayala's novels, was early to notice their theatrical qualities: "Cualquier lector atento descubrirá en las novelas de Ramón Pérez de Ayala una peculiar textura teatral, perceptible en temas, situaciones, diálogos, modalidades descriptivas."[23]

The conventional critical view of this phenomenon has been to attribute it to Ayala's view of life as a tragic drama in which man simply plays his role and often vainly stands out against the power of destiny. Such is the view of Carlos Zamora: "Pues así es que él veía la vida: como un drama trágico en el que tanto los actores que lo representan, como los espectadores que lo presencian, actúan movidos por la fuerza implacable del Destino."[24] Or, on a more specifically social level, theatrical references are related to characterisation: characters make absurd theatrical gestures and adopt dramatic roles which reveal either their romantic self-delusions or their shallowness and lack of feeling. Emeterio Barros, in *Tinieblas en las cumbres*, a prototype for the more fully developed Vespasiano Cebón in *Tigre Juan*, sets out to woo Rosina by adopting a variety of roles, firstly that of the "trovador exaltado de caudalosa vena poética," then the "mancebo entristecido, lacio, inapetente" and finally the "amante terrible y dominador" (I:32-33). This is a calculated pose. In other contexts, the theatrical gesture can make the character appear absurd. A case in point is Felicita Quemada in *Belarmino y Apolonio*. As Anselmo Novillo, the object of her love, lies dying, Felicita is subject to hallucinations, and perfectly everyday sounds are transformed into the sounds of death. Her repetition of "¿Qué ruido es ése?" gives the scene a melodramatic quality and thus undermines any serious pretensions her questioning of her own reality might have: "¿Sueño? ¿Eres tú? ¿Soy de carne? ¿No somos fantasmas?"

(IV:154). In a Realist novel, such a device would be aimed at undermining the character's exaggerated sense of being a romantic victim. Here it appears rather to signal Felicita's existence as a fictional character (her name already implies a caricaturistic intent) and her affinities through the body of literature with earlier romantic heroines, they too being essentially fictional constructs. A more interesting but less obvious case is that of D. Sabas Sicilia in *Troteras y danzaderas*, who is defined in terms of his public *persona* or mask:

> Echábase de ver al punto que era hombre público por la carátula que llevaba puesta, ocultándole la verdadera y móvil expresión del rostro, esa carátula social de las personas que han vivido muchos años ante los ojos de la muchedumbre, carátula que tiene vida propia, pero vida escénica, y tiende a tipificar con visibles rasgos fisionómicos el ideal y singulares aspiraciones del individuo, de manera que facilita la labor del caricaturista, porque la carátula tiene ya bastante de caricatura. (I:520-21)

Over the next ten pages or so, the image of the mask is sustained, apparently to highlight the difference between the authentic self and the false exterior. What is more relevant here, however, is the way in which Pérez de Ayala calls attention to the art of caricature, a literary means of handling character, a means of constructing a particular person for the reader. In literature, and in life, the construct is the only reality there is, and therefore in an almost covert way the mask is used as a self-reflexive literary reference.

Caricature, of course, is a dehumanising technique and therefore is connected with that conscious stylisation to which Ortega y Gasset alluded in the extract cited at the beginning of this chapter. By dehumanising his characters, Ayala removes the possibility of any facile identification with the humanity of the characters and therefore also precludes any simple equivalence of fiction and reality. In this respect some of the scenes in Ayala's novels are reminiscent of the *sainetes* of Carlos Arniches, for example, the opening conversation between Manolo and Teresuca in *La pata de la raposa,* or the scene where Teófilo attempts to enter Rosina's house and is impeded by the "portera" in *Troteras y danzaderas.* Interestingly enough, Ayala wrote two articles on Arniches which are published in *Las máscaras* (on *La señorita de Trevélez* and *¡Qué viene mi marido!*). These helped consolidate Arniches' reputation and also offer a definition of the "tragedia grotesca" which for Ayala is rooted in the notion of "arbitrariedad inverosímil." The two characters who open *Tinieblas en las cumbres,* Jiménez and Cerdá, are animalised and dehumanised. They are "pequeños monstruos inofensivos." Cerdá appears as a "gran maniquí con rígidos y escasos resortes" and architectural terms interspersed with animal references are used to describe him: "obra de mampostería," "obelisco o columna," "cilíndrica," "cupulino," "columna capital," "ladrillo," "porquetas o cucarachas." Jiménez has the "súbitas y graciosas actitudes de joven animal que juega," and there are references also to the "boscaje de las cejas" and the "triángulo de la nariz." The reader is distanced from the characters, and at the same time he is made aware of the creating presence of the author. And this treatment is not confined to early works nor reserved for minor characters. In Ayala's novel *Tigre Juan*, the early descriptions of the main protagonist endow him with animal-like qualities: "ojos de gato montés," "pelambre . . . . como montera pastoril de piel de borrego," and dehumanise him; "fruncía las cejas con metódico ritmo y rapidez, este recio capacete piloso resbalaba, de una pieza, hacia delante y hacia atrás, como lubrificado, sobre la gran bola del cráneo . . . . el pescuezo flaco, rugoso, curtido, avellanado y retráctil . . . . el rostro cuadrado, obtuso . . . . su piel parecía de cobre pulimentado" (IV:553-54). The primacy of the author's vision is paramount, combining disparate areas of language and experience. He reconstructs characters and situations and recombines them through the power of language. A good illustration of this is to be found later in the novel with reference to Vespasiano:

La mirada de Vespasiano era táctil, como si del oscuro agujero de sus pupilas irradiasen elásticos y transparentes tentáculos de molusco, que iban a palpar el objeto con una caricia blanda. Las mujeres sentían que las desnudaba con aquellos brazos, traslúcidos, viscosos y cautos que le salían de los ojos. (IV:679)

His eyes have become tactile by virtue of the author's ability with language, just as a little later Herminia is attracted to him so that her eyes are glued to his lips: "quedaron adheridos, presos, en los labios brillantes y pegajosos de Vespasiano como un ave atolondrada en la liga" (IV:681). In all these cases, and indeed in the opening pages of *Tigre Juan*, where the Plaza del Mercado is described, Ayala constantly makes the reader aware of his own presence and of his own attitude, which is as often as not ambivalent. He adheres, apparently, to most of the conventions of fiction-making but makes clear in numerous ways his awareness that everything — plot, character, setting — are merely ingredients with which the novel is composed. Dehumanisation is not, then, essentially a matter of moral or social satire, as is usually claimed, but yet another metafictional element in an invariably narcissistic narrative to which the generic displacement towards drama frequently holds the key.

Another way in which Pérez de Ayala undermines the claims of his characters to be considered real people is to refer to them openly as "personajes." He does this as early as *Tinieblas en las cumbres*,

154

and in *El curandero de su honra* we find him doing it again, highlighting the dramatic nature of his work:

> Los personajes de la tragicomedia de *Tigre Juan* y *Curandero de su honra* hubieron de atravesar un período de eliminación de las pasiones y reflexión sobre sí mismos .... Los personajes, buscando su propia expresión, y enardeciéndose en exprimir su quintaesencia, se deleitaban en el placer lenitivo de infatigables coloquios. (IV:771)

Or he can make the characters themselves question their own dubious status. In *Troteras y danzaderas* Alberto asks himself about the nature of his role: "¿Soy actor de coturno y persona, dignidad y decoro incorporado a la caudal tragedia humana, o soy fantoche en una farsa lacrimosa y grotesca?" (I:577). Life is viewed as a work of art, and simultaneously the character is aware of his own fictional role. This ambivalence is evidenced in the switch from actor to spectator. Alberto in *La pata de la raposa*, made aware that he is deceived by Meg, undergoes such a change: "De actor de la tragedia, azotado por furias fatales, se había convertido en espectador que recibe deleite en seguir el encadenamiento de los hechos, y con el pathos de los personajes depura sus pasiones" (I:461). On one level this can be interpreted psychologically as the peace that accompanies certainty, but it also points to the separation of the aesthetic and the sentimental, the dehumanisation of art, deliberately foregrounded, overtly self-conscious. In *El curandero de su honra*, doña Mariquita regrets not having been an "actriz partiquina" in the "desenlace feliz de la tragedia amorosa entre Tigre Juan y Herminia" (IV:772). The narrator, incidentally, had already termed Juan's attempted suicide an "anagnorisis." In the same work doña Iluminada aspires not to the role of actor, but to that of author ("la autora de todo") and steps out of the text, as it were, to signal her own literary role: "La adversidad se ceba en todos vosotros, y a mí, la autora de tanta tragedia, egoísta maese Pedro de este aflictivo retablo, monumento de nubes, tan presto levantado como venido al suelo" (IV:740). In this she is like other co-producing authors in Ayala's novels (don Amaranto and even don Guillén in *Belarmino y Apolonio*, for example) and has written a script not only for Juan and Herminia but also for Colás and Carmina. Life is made to follow the order of art. Playful and inventive, Ayala's method points up the fictitious nature of all artistic and cultural constructs.

Sometimes the characters are made to enact the roles of other characters. Clearly Tigre Juan is consciously and parodically modelled on the Calderonian husband, a new don Gutierre, just as Vespasiano Cebón is drawn not from life, but from the Don Juan of Tirso de Molina's *El burlador de Sevilla*. Deliberate echoes of other plays enhance the literary qualities of the novels. *Othello* is the basis of the celebrated discussion of the nature of tragedy to be found in the second section of *Troteras y danzaderas* entitled "Verónica y Desdémona." In this same novel an imaginary play is performed — Teófilo Pajares' *A cielo abierto* (a parody of a typically *modernista* work) — just as Apolonio's *El cerco de Orduña* is used in *Belarmino y Apolonio*. Both characters are dramatist-figures. The gravedigger scene from *Hamlet* provides an important motif in *La pata de la raposa*, and in the latter half of the *Urbano and Simona* novels motifs and situations from the "comedia de capa y espada" recur. In addition to all these borrowings, there are occasions in the novels when the dialogue between the characters is set out in play-format again highlighting the conventionalised nature of literary production. The effect of this is not to make the scene more dramatic and to increase immediacy and verisimilitude. Quite on the contrary, everything is derealised as the nature of the artistic transposition is made apparent.

Pérez de Ayala's conscious parodying is therefore an acknowledgement that all literature is a kind of parody of life. The Realist writers subverted the often absurd situations of Romantic convention, not realising that they themselves were creating in their own way stereotyped images which, although perhaps more sophisticated than those of their Romantic predecessors, were nonetheless of a similar order of conventionality and fictionality. Pérez de Ayala's novels are both parody and self-parody. Some of his plots are so banal and trite that they cannot be taken seriously on that level alone; the notorious happy endings of his major novels where all the conflicts are finally resolved are the products of literature, not of life. They constitute a disruption of any sense of continuity between literature and life. Just as the Rosina story in *Tinieblas en las cumbres* is an overt parody of the "novela erótica," so too the love story of Pedro and Angustias in *Belarmino y Apolonio* partakes of all the ingredients of the traditional love story with some ironic inversions: the dishonoured woman does not become a nun, but the man becomes a priest; their ultimate reunion is described in terms of the language of the Breviary. At all levels in these novels we are aware of the mediation, we try to apprehend both the window and the garden. Pérez de Ayala's novels, then, are in their practice entirely consistent with the main thrust of Modernist introversion. Self-reflexive, self-questioning, self-parodying, their covert narcissism subtly subverts Realist practice. So ambivalent, however, is Ayala's manipulation of his material that many critics regarded him, initially at least, as a continuer of the Realist tradition, though with marked intellectual leanings. Others pointed to his deficiencies as a novelist, seeing in his work banal plots and situations, implausible characters, the whole being merely a pretext for the expounding of the writer's own ideas. Other studies have been more sympathetic, but none has placed Pérez de Ayala where he truly belongs, in the vanguard of twentieth-century metafiction. At first sight it appears that Pérez de Ayala's principal target is Realist aesthetics, which it is, but only because it is here that all of the central assumptions which he questions are taken for granted. He repudiates any notion of authorial objectivity by openly manipulating narrative distance in a way that calls attention to the presence of the creating mind and at the same time opens up a dialogue with the reader, denying him the passivity which Realist practice seemed to afford. His presence frequently seems to undermine his own text: the logic of the narrative is broken by some extended intellectual speculation or halted by diverting the reader's attention towards some learned footnotes; plot and character are often foregrounded for what they are, ingredients in a fictional fabrication; opposites and antinomies are overtly set up, antitheses openly resolved; the reality of characters and objects in the world are denied any stability as the narrator's perspective switches to create a sense of a shifting reality; the constructing processes of perception are constantly shown at work; temporal and spatial references are greatly diminished in scope and importance. The fictional work seems to be accorded a somewhat ambivalent status, neither total form nor total content, neither a means nor an end. The presence of the author dissociates the work from the world, but at the same time the emphasis on the creator reduces the autonomy of the work. Book and world appear ostensibly discrete entities but paradoxically, when all is said and done, the work finally emerges as the only world there is. This self-sustaining nature of the work, its paradoxical existence as a world of its own, depends upon its own structural and linguistic resources. Its significance and justification reside in its existence as a fictional heterocosm.

NOTES

[1]Virginia Woolf, *To the Lighthouse* (Harmondsworth: Penguin, 1964) 219. Originally published in 1927.

[2]Mark Schorer, "Technique as Discovery," *Hudson Review* (1948). Reprinted in *Twentieth-Century Literary Criticism*, ed. David Lodge (London: Longman, 1972).

[3]José Ortega y Gasset, *La deshumanización del arte, Obras completas* (Madrid: Revista de Occidente, 1957) Vol. II:357-58.

[4]Ortega y Gasset 367.

[5]Maruxa Salgues de Cargill 52.

[6]Edward Said, *Beginnings: Intention and Method* (Baltimore: Johns Hopkins University Press, 1975) 218.

[7]*Principios y finales de la novela* 15.

[8]Maruxa Salgues de Cargill, "Mito de Don Quijote y Sancho en *Belarmino y Apolonio*," *Insula* 274 (Sept. 1969):16.

[9]J.B. Avalle-Arce, Introduction to his critical edition of *Los trabajos de Persiles y Segismunda* (Madrid: Castalia, 1969) 27.

[10]M. Bataillon, *Erasmo y España* (México: Fondo de Cultura Económica, 1950) Vol. II:224-25.

[11]E.C. Riley, *Cervantes' Theory of the Novel* (Oxford: Oxford University Press, 1962).

[12]*La novela intelectual* 124.

[13]See Angeles Prado, "Seudónimos tempranos de Pérez de Ayala," *Insula* 404-405 (July-August, 1980):1, 18 and 19.

[14]José Martínez Ruiz, *La voluntad*, ed. E. Inman Fox (Madrid: Castalia, 1969) 97.

[15]Pío Baroja, *Camino de perfección* (Madrid: Caro Raggio, 1974) 259.

[16]*Vida Nueva*, 50 (25th May 1899). Quoted by Richard A. Cardwell in "Juan Ramón Jiménez ¿noventaiochista?," *Cuadernos Hispanoamericanos* 376-78 (1981):340.

[17]*Camino de perfección* 133.

[18]*La voluntad* 74.

[19]Introduction to his Critical Edition of *Tinieblas en las cumbres* (Madrid: Castalia, 1971) 27.

[20]D.L. Shaw, *The Generation of 1898 in Spain* (London: Benn, 1975) 188-89.

[21]D.L. Shaw, "*Modernismo*, Idealism and the Intellectual Crisis in Spain, 1895-1910," *Renaissance and Modern Studies* 25 (1981):24-39.

[22]Carlos Longhurst, "Sobre la originalidad de *Tinieblas en las cumbres*," *Insula* 404-405 (July-August 1980):5.

[23]Mariano Baquero Goyanes, "La novela como tragicomedia: Pérez de Ayala y Ortega y Gasset," in *Perspectivismo y contraste* (Madrid: Gredos, 1963) 161.

[24]Carlos Zamora, "La concepción trágica de la vida en la obra novelesca de Ramón Pérez de Ayala," *Hispanófila* 42 (1971):21.

CHAPTER SIX
THE FICTIONAL HETEROCOSM:
LANGUAGE AND STRUCTURE IN PEREZ DE AYALA

Traditional Realism enjoyed such hegemony in the nineteenth century that its influence has extended right throughout the twentieth century, both in the form of the many novels which continue to be written more or less in the realist mode and, more importantly, in its shaping of the perspectives that characterise much novel criticism. Even though the forms of fiction have proliferated multifariously, the theories which surrounded criticism of fiction, have, until relatively recently, remained fossilised in allegiance to nineteenth-century fictional practices. It is well to bear this in mind, for even the most deviant novels are defined by their deviance from the norm of Realism. Pirandello reacted against what he called "stupidissima verosimiglianza."[1] Unamuno asserted the primacy of inner over outer reality: "la realidad es la íntima. La realidad no la constituyen las bambalinas, ni las decoraciones, ni el traje, ni el paisaje, ni el mobilario, ni las acotaciones . . . ."[2], aligning himself with other "subjective realists" of the early century like Virginia Woolf ("Must life be like this?")[3] or Proust, whose narrator asserts that "la littérature qui se contente de 'décrire les choses' . . . . est celle qui, tout en s'appelant réaliste, est la plus éloignée de la réalité."[4] Although these Modernist writers were, consciously or unconsciously, foregrounding their work against that of their Realist predecessors, they were not, as Linda Hutcheon admirably demonstrates, entirely divorced from a central narrative tradition, that represented by Cervantes himself, whose *Don Quijote* is essentially a book about books. Hutcheon traces this tendency back even further and makes the point that even Aristotle, in the *Poetics*, stressed the importance of artistic ordering in addition to imitation:

> What exponents of "traditional realism" ignored, when they turned to classical mimetic theory for support, was that the instinct to imitate is complemented, in the *Poetics*, by an equally strong impulse toward ordering. Aesthetic imitation involves the completed and harmonised integration of parts into an organic whole, even if such parts should involve the irrational or the impossible. Mimesis is never limited to naive copying at the level of product alone.[5]

It is the purpose of this chapter to show how Pérez de Ayala's novels undertake this literary structuring through language to create apparently autonomous and coherent "heterocosms," or fictive worlds, in an overtly self-conscious way. This process is common to Modernist writers, and it corresponds to changes in the ways of knowing, changes in the conception of literature and changes in the relationship between the two. This is a fact of profound importance for the novel, because of all the genres it has most assiduously resisted attempts to limit its referential potential. It has done this partly by its size, which renders it less amenable to assimilation by readers, and analysis by critics, as a single system. A reader confronted with a large piece of prose begins by referring the language of the text to his experience, to the empirical world, much as he does with non-imaginative discourse. However, reading progressively orders the linguistic elements within the text, so that the reader perceives, or perhaps even creates, a separate world, a literary cosmos, the self-sufficient fictional heterocosm. We might even feel that an acknowledgement of this fact is present in the work of those critics who practiced a kind of rhetorical analysis of texts, tracing patterns of detail and symbol in avowedly mimetic narratives in order to demonstrate the functionality of apparently insignificant detail in relation to thematic significance. It is precisely the existence of such aesthetic patterning that for critics like Roman Jakobson constitutes the essence of literariness. What happens in much Modernist fiction is that the process of creating an ordered world is regarded to be significant in itself, however much that might diverge from the notion of imitating an objectively existing order. While for some this may be a form of escape, for others it can represent a genuine liberation.

There can be little doubt that an art-form so conceived will differ radically from traditional mimesis, and this is one of the ways in which Modernism involves a degree of historical discontinuity. Modernist fiction, as we have seen, is essentially self-conscious and anti-representational in its endeavour to transcend the real (as commonly or culturally perceived) and create an autonomous order of art, an art which creates rather than imitates, which probes the depths of the artist's own consciousness and his creative potentialities, and which builds artistic structures outside the traditional categories of space and time. Arguably, this represents simply a flight into form, into games of sophisticated ingenuity, towards the very outer limits of the genre itself. In a sense, this is true, but Ayala and other Modernist writers, who appear to sever completely the link between art and life, eventually realign the two in a new synthesis. In fact, their enterprise is more a matter of extending the traditional novelistic paradoxes of the interaction of fiction and reality which are manifest even in the novel's most referential phase, that of nineteenth-century Realism. So while Modernist fiction shows itself to be skeptical or ironical in its transactions with empirical reality and often presents itself as alienated from "life," it often implies a redefinition, not only of art, but of reality itself. In short, it refuses to endorse the traditional notion of reality, that consensus of belief upon which the novel has been based, but engages fully with questions of relativity, fragmentation, the subconscious, the dislocation of language, the subversion of time and causality. If this implies a break with the past, it also implies an absorption of it into the modern experience as part of the Modernist desire for totality, embracing reason and unreason, past and present, the objective and the subjective. It is this which imparts to Modernism its transitional quality as it plays with the paradoxes and contradictions of its own situation. Pérez de Ayala embodies fully the Janus-like nature of Modernism characterised both by an awareness of multiplicity and a desire for integration, a sense of chaos and a quest for pattern. Such a view must push the novel along the axis of poetry or metaphor, for if time, for example, is no longer construed as a sequence or history as a process of causal evolution, then a novel cannot merely recount or rely upon the concept of plot. The Modernist novel creates an alternative order and, paradoxically, in so doing reasserts its own vital function, that of using man's imaginative capacity to make sense of his own experience. Modernist fiction not only recognises the chaos and complexity of the modern situation but devises formal strategies for coming to terms with that chaos and complexity. We can construe this as the coherence of art providing the meaning absent in everyday experience, and it can be viewed negatively or positively. In a negative view, art is simply a fanciful illusion, a momentary escape into an unreal world. But in a positive view, the question of what is real and what is unreal is felt to be a relative one, and for the Modernist the reversal of the usual relation of art imitating life to the notion of life imitating art is a profoundly significant one. Reality is not fixed, but created, and we create it by means of mental structures which are cultural in origin. If we change the structures, for example, by changing the paradigms of our fictions, we can change reality, or create a different one. Truly revolutionary literature is not that which contains politically subversive content but that which exhibits the greatest radicalisation of form. It is for this reason that in early Modernism the formal properties of the text are deliberately foregrounded and that the status of the text as text is self-consciously signalled. In this way, the text of a novel works against its own inherent linearity, its story-telling dimension, to assert its totality and coherence as an artifact. It is not surprising, therefore, that several critics have identified synchronicity as the essential element of Modernist style. This manifests itself in several ways and, while not categorising them as such, I have referred to two of them in earlier chapters: the compacting of past and present through the use of the literature of the past in the new work as one, and a concern with the atemporal aspects of temporal experience as the other. In this chapter I shall be more concerned with the structural implications of the text as a synchronic system and the use of language to create a network of interrelated elements.

From his earliest works, Pérez de Ayala deviated from the classic pattern of narrative. In fact, only *Belarmino y Apolonio* adheres to the traditional division into chapters and it, of course, is the most experimental of all his novels. The novels of the first cycle use structure to call attention to their literary nature as, for example, in the case of the picaresque prologue/epilogue to *Tinieblas en las cumbres*, or the patterning of *La pata de la raposa* around the movement of the day. *Troteras y danzaderas* is divided into five parts, each with a dualistic title. *Luna de miel, luna de hiel* and *Los trabajos de Urbano y Simona* are divided into four parts corresponding to the phases of the moon. Even *Tigre Juan* and *El curandero de su honra*, perhaps Ayala's most conventionally told novel, possesses features which distinguish it significantly from traditional narrative. Apart from the device of the double column, to which I shall turn presently, the most striking structural feature is the division into two parts, each with its own title, as in Ayala's previous novel. In place of the usual division of the narrative into chapters, Ayala adopts a structure designated by musical terminology: *Adagio* and *Presto* in *Tigre Juan, Presto, Adagio* and *Coda* in *El curandero de su honra*, in an effort to convey the effect of a symphonic whole in which themes are carefully orchestrated and counterpointed. This principle of organisation creates an alternative structure, free from the exigencies of plot, based on alterations of tone and mood, changes in tempo, effects of antithesis and contrast, the creation of symmetries and parallels, the repetition with variations of key themes. Almost simultaneously with Pérez de Ayala's experiment, André Gide was contemplating a parallel venture: "Ce que je voudrais faire, comprenez-moi, c'est quelque chose qui serait comme l'*Art de la fugue*. Et je ne vois pas pourquoi ce qui fut possible en musique serait impossible en littérature."[6] This is true for many of the Modernists, and one need only think of the "petite phrase de Vinteuil" in Proust's great work. The early theorist of the novel, E.M. Forster, also speculated on the possibility of employing musical analogies in fiction:

> Music, though it does not employ human beings, though it is governed by intricate laws, nevertheless does offer in its final expression a type of beauty which fiction might achieve in its own way. Expansion. That is the idea the novelist must cling to. No completion. No rounding off but opening out. When the symphony is over we feel that the notes and times composing it have been liberated, they have found in the rhythm of the whole their individual freedom. Cannot the novel be like that?[7]

Of course, in the case of Pérez de Ayala, the creation of patterns in ways analogous to musical composition reflects an aesthetic and philosophical position. Two-part novels, dualistic titles, the pairing of characters, the building-up of effects of contrast, opposition and duplication, all reinforce a vision of reality as a co-existence of discordant parts forming an ultimate order and harmony apprehended only by art. By imposing order upon the work, by making meaningless experience conform to a superior pattern or design, he provides the reader with an illusion of universal concord. The drawing together of the various strands of the novel in the *Coda* and *Parergon* is an analogue of the wider integration within the whole of creation, itself expressed in the poem with which the *Coda* ends. Here are inter- woven images of light and darkness, fire and water, joy and sorrow, to express the mystery and fullness of life. The interplay of dualities and antitheses is the most salient feature of the novel's structure and indeed is the aesthetic equivalent of another complementary relation- ship which we examined in Chapter IV, that of the conscious and the unconscious, itself a psychological analogy of universal harmony which encompasses apparent contradictions in a sort of "acorde dis- cordante." So on one level the musical dimension corresponds to a peculiar kind of "cosmovisión," and on another it reflects contem- porary experimentation with the boundaries of fiction itself. In fact, the most perfect summary of some of the effects achieved by Pérez de Ayala is the celebrated passage contained in *Point Counterpoint*, published in 1928, only two years after *Tigre Juan* and *El curandero de su honra*:

> The musicalization of fiction. Not in the symbolist way, by subordinating sense to sound .... But on a large scale, in the construction. Meditate on Beethoven. The changes of mood, the abrupt transitions .... More interesting still, the modulations, not merely from one key to another, but from mood to mood. A theme is stated, then developed, pushed out of shape, imperceptibly deformed, until, though still recognizably the same, it has become quite different .... get this into a novel. How? The abrupt transitions are easy enough. All you need is a sufficiency of characters and parallel, contrapuntal plots. While Jones is murdering a wife, Smith is wheeling the perambulator in the park. You alter- nate the themes. More interestingly, the modulations and variations are more difficult. A novelist modulates by redup- licating situation and character. He shows several people falling in love, or dying, or praying in different ways — dissimilars solving the same problem. Or, vice versa, similar people confronted with similar problems. In this way you can modulate through all the aspects of your theme, you can write variations in any number of moods.[8]

There are many examples of these "modulations and variations" in Pérez de Ayala's fiction, though naturally we must be aware of the metaphorical basis of this terminology. *Prometeo* develops its major themes in an overtly structural fashion — in the counterpointing of the prose text and the initial poems (a feature of all three "novelas poemáticas"), in the orchestrated change of tone and perspective (the opening is mock-heroic, consciously literary; the ending is

163

coldly objective, a studied detachment which is consciously unliterary). In other words, the same reality is viewed in contrasting ways just as, incidentally, the *Parergon* of *El curandero de su honra* offers a discursive perspective on material that had been dramatised in the narrative. In *Luz de domingo* the ballad form underscores the substance of the main narrative, but of the three "novelas poemáticas," it is *La caída de los Limones* which most clearly reveals the hand of the creator who holds together all the themes in a kind of symphonic arrangement which enables the discords of reality to be harmonised within the work as "un juego de bellas fuerzas naturales." The novel's structure is an exercise in contrast which in its play of perspectives anticipates *Belarmino y Apolonio*. The beginning of the narrative is delayed until Chapter III, where an omniscient author replaces the narrator-witness of Chapters I and II. The time, setting and indeed the style are quite different as well. Chapters I and II were set in the banal world of a Madrid *pensión* and the style is appropriately prosaic, whereas in Chapter III the remoteness of Guadalfranco is emphasised by the archaic and defamiliarised language. There is an obvious foregrounding effect. Chapter IV introduces the perspective of the fairy-tale, so characteristic of Pérez de Ayala, and it is clear that what matters in this narrative is not really the story, nor the psychological motivation of the characters, nor the social implications of the crime on which it is based, but the play of perspectives itself. In short, what is involved is the creation of a fictional heterocosm into which the reader is drawn. The process is well described by Ortega y Gasset:

> Hace falta que el autor sepa atraernos al ámbito cerrado que es su novela y luego cortarnos toda retirada, mantenernos en perfecto aislamiento del espacio real que hemos dejado .... Es menester que el autor construya un recinto hermético, sin agujero ni rendija por los cuales, desde dentro de la novela, entreveamos el horizonte de la realidad.[9]

This effect is partly achieved by, to use Aldous Huxley's words again, "duplicating situations and characters." Thus Belarmino and Apolonio are complementary mirror images. In the same novel the love of Pedro and Augustias is refracted in the grotesque romance of Anselmo Novillo and Felicita Quemada, just as Urbano and Simona's idyllic love is paralleled in that of Don Cástulo and Conchona. Similar aesthetic patterns can be discerned on the level of plot, as F.W. Weber observes in relation to this same novel:

> The plot may split into diverging trajectories; the young Urbano's sudden revulsion towards sexual love occurs just as his mother, on the verge of old age, for the first time feels desire for her husband, a desire grotesquely underscored by

her precipitate physical decline which is, in turn, matched by the equally sudden and horrible aging of don Leoncio's mistress; concurrent reversals are paired in an improbable and farcical equilibrium.[10]

Weber, of course, implies that this is done for comic effect. Undoubtedly some of the effect is comic, but there is little doubt that it responds to an awareness of the process of construction itself.

All of Ayala's novels are experimental to some degree, but no technique of his has aroused as much interest as the double column which is found in *El curandero de su honra*. This technique is apparently an attempt to substitute for chronological linearity a synchronic perspective, a preoccupation of Ayala's that has already been commented upon in relation to Chapter Two of *Belarmino y Apolonio,* where Don Amaranto and the narrator discuss the inadequacy of the traditional resources of narrative to produce effects of simultaneity. This chapter compares the spatial form of painting with the temporal form of narration and is therefore related to the Modernist desire to replace the discursive and successive order of traditional narrative with something akin to a spatial pattern, an alternative order outside the implacable logic of time. Of course no novel can escape time completely, neither in the sense of the time it takes to read the novel nor in the sense of the fictional time of the narrated events themselves, so that when we speak of the spatialisation of narrative form this can only be a metaphor for the peculiar organisation of a Modernist work where the reference is primarily inward, not outward. Moreover, when the temporal flow of a narrative is interrupted, the attention of the reader is directed at the play of relationships within the work itself. The conventional form of narration is destroyed and unity is maintained through a process or principle of constant cross-reference. Rather than follow the progress of a story, the reader has to discern a pattern, and this is a participatory requirement of the reader. Hence the paradoxical effect of distantiation and involvement produced by texts of this kind. On the one hand, the signalling of the formal devices of the narrative undermines any potential engagement at a humanly emotional level with the characters and events of the narrative, but the very devices which achieve this effect are precisely those which engage the reader most fully with the creative potential of the text.

We can therefore consider the double column of *El curandero de su honra* in the context of these temporal experiments. The events are juxtaposed not on the basis of sequentiality or causality, but of similarity and simultaneity, and the method adopted by Ayala is a perfect illustration of the way in which the elements of a Modernist novel are organised in such a way as to demand, in vain, instantaneous comprehension. Of course, Ayala's experiment is barely possible within the limits of the double column; it would be impossible to sustain over a whole work. However, this would be perhaps to overestimate the ambitiousness of his project and perhaps too, as we shall see, to underestimate its ironic dimension. For the present, the only way to read the double column would appear to be to constantly to reread them, for they are intimately related on a linguistic level.

Critics have reacted in different ways to the device. For Leon Livingstone, as an attempt to render synchronicity it is "a brilliant failure."[11] On the other hand, Frances Wyers Weber, in accepting the author's assertion that "Entre una y otra vida y a través de la distancia era fatal que existiesen mutua correspondencia, misteriosas resonancias, secreta telepatía e influjo recíproco," which can only be apprehended from "una perspectiva ideal de la imaginación," sees the device as "an attempt to show, through a series of cross-column and vertical word-plays, the relations, oppositions, counterpoints and coincidences between the two lives"[12] and is able to analyse them in detail. Andrés Amorós believes that an analysis "con lupa" would be necessary to reveal these cross-references.[13] Weber, I think, tries to give too realist an orientation to Ayala's method by dwelling on the human dimension of the separated lovers. This level is present, but what surely happens is that the reader reads one column, and then reads the other in a way which is affected by his first reading. Words, phrases and ideas bounce back and forth across the page, undermining the inherent consecutiveness of language. The reader perceives the elements of the narrative as juxtaposed in the space of the text rather than developing in some extratextual time.

The first significant word to appear in both columns is "perder." Juan uses the word in one sense meaning simply to lose, "la posibilidad de perder a Herminia," whereas Herminia is thinking of ruin, perdition, "Caída, perdida estoy para siempre." Her willful perdition ("voluntad") through following Vespasiano is taken up in Juan's "querer es poder," whereupon the two meanings of "querer" come into play and are linked to "libertad." Juan relates the concept of freedom to free-will ("albedrío"), while Vespasiano is thinking in terms of free love, which harks back to "perdición." Just as Vespasiano gives an openly sexual meaning to "querer," Juan also thinks of the other meaning of "perder.'" His fears of Herminia's lover's "blandos halagos" and "frases deleitosas" are confirmed in the second column by Vespasiano's very words, "tesoro mío," "te quiero apasionadamente," "te deseo con angustia." The spectre of the deceived husband and the dreadful demands of the honour code now enter Juan's mind, but his thoughts are interrupted by a humorous intercalated tale of the peasant beating his wife. This farcical interlude is, as we have seen earlier, a comic variation on the honour theme. The reduction in tension which this sudden switch of perspective achieves is highly characteristic of Ayala's technique, complicating the reader's responses, preventing him from identifying too closely with any grandiose concept of honour, and undermining Juan's tragic potential.

Herminia's pregnancy is revealed discreetly in both columns, through Iluminada's gentle hints to Juan, who only slowly realises the truth, and then through Herminia's nausea on the train. The couple is united in parenthood. A new life is about to come into the world as an old life, that of don Sincerato, is about to depart it, thereby creating further symmetry. The high point of this part of the novel is the activity of St. John's Night and is centred on the concepts of blindness and enlightenment. The motif of blindness adumbrated by Juan earlier: "ciégame, Señor, los ojos del alma y los del cuerpo" (IV:712) is now taken up in the image of light dispelling darkness which, as we have seen, is an important feature of Calderón's play. In succeeding pages the blindness-enlightenment contrast is worked out and given visual representation in the rites of Midsummer. The bonfires blaze in both columns, and both characters experience a moment of illumination, or epiphany, when they become aware of the true nature and meaning of their love. Weber comments that the narrator welds the parallel columns "into a dense web of inseparable components. Actions, descriptions, and word-plays fit so neatly together that the reader takes a phrase from one column, an image from the other, a scene here, a speech there, and braids the threads into a single chain."[14] Out of the "ceguera-claridad" motif, a new theme grows, "engaño," and the word is explored in all its possible meanings. Colás and Carmina are practising a deception on the people of Mañas (which itself means cunning), while in the opposite column Juan is thinking of Engracia and his own self-deception. He is now hallucinated, his senses deceive him, and Engracia's ghost appears to tell him: "No te engañé. Te engañaste. Te engañaste porque no supiste amarme." "Amor" figures prominently in both columns: St. John's Night is the feast of lovers and while the others, Carmen and Lino, Carmina and Colás, are united, Juan and Herminia are aware of their solitude. Juan says "¡Qué solo me he quedado!" and almost directly opposite in the second column we read: "Herminia se sentía tan sola." Reflecting on love, Colás develops the "engaño" motif: "La vida está entretejida de sutiles engaños. No hay sino una gran verdad." But this truth, love, is also an illusion, so that the plethora of associations which the word evokes leads to continuous punning and paradox. Juan has undergone a process of "desengaño," he has seen the light of truth and is ready to receive the life-giving illusion of love. "Ilusión" also means happiness. The two principal characters are brought to the same point by a series of intuitive discoveries: "El diálogo procedía por intuiciones profundas, que sólo se producen en las crisis de tensión emocional" (IV:736). The parallel course of their experience is revealed in the echoes and cross-references provided by the device of the double column. All that remains now is that they be reunited, and this reunion constitutes the final scene of the *Adagio*. Ayala uses the double column again when they are face to face. The parallelism is much more obvious now, for the passage is much shorter and identical sentences are used in both columns, while the principle of reverberating echoes is maintained. The pairing of opposites, "honor"/"deshonra" and "vergüenza"/"desvergüenza," is used to show Juan's transformation and progression on to a new level of understanding.

While it is naturally tempting to give a thematic explanation of this, there is little doubt that much of the force of these pages resides in the actual disposition of the words on the page. The reader is required to perceive the narrative as a complex of elements juxtaposed within the same temporal space. An inevitable consequence of this process is that to a certain extent the referential value of language is subordinated to the manifestations of the words themselves as they appear before the eyes of the reader. The text reads inward as much as outward, and the reader's attention is focussed more on the reality of representation than on the representation of reality. This applies on a much more general level to all of Ayala's fiction: the elegant and polished texture of his prose encourages us to savour the language as language without too much reference to its meaning. Instead of seeing through words, we see words themselves. In fact, Ayala's last novel is a veritable linguistic patchwork. Thus he moves from the peasant speech of Nachín de Nacha with its reproduction of Asturian dialect (*tolo, gueyo, tabarica, afuxi*, etc.), to the language of philosophical debate, to the creation of effects of synaesthesia in which sensory functions are interchanged, to the rendering of abstract concepts in concrete terms, all of which reveal his concern with the expressive possibilities of creative language, which is part of his exploration of the relationship between the fictional world and the real world. By using words and concepts as structuring elements in his narrative, Ayala highlights the role of language in shaping human behaviour. At times Ayala's manipulation of language is so extreme that it can become the principle upon which a whole scene is constructed. When this occurs, the novel again asserts its own reality as a verbal structure. *Tigre Juan* and *El curandero de su honra* may appear to use reality as a starting point, but it is reality in words, and ultimately language generates its own logic which carries the work along and sustains it through its least realistic phases. Through the power of language, one word leads by association to another, and the novel is justified not by its fidelity to any model of empirical reality but by the inner consistency of its parts. This can be illustrated in several ways.

A particularly good example of the use of language is to be found towards the end of the *Adagio* in *Tigre Juan*. A letter from

Isabel resurrects Juan's past, and from this point onwards the narrative is built around the various meanings of the word "Apocalipsis." Juan relives the critical moments of his past life. In other words, this is an example of synchronicity. Because of past associations with guilt and repentance, it is also like a "Juicio Final," a raising of the dead to life. In fact, the other characters are refracted through Juan's deforming vision so that they appear to enact some weird dance of death. Then this bodily resurrection is made manifest in the reincarnation of Engracia in the person of Herminia, and Juan realises the truth in a moment of genuine revelation. So language is the structuring principle: a single word generates the complex web of associations with which the *Adagio* ends.

In the *Presto*, too, words are shown to have a special power. In particular, the dialogue between Iluminada and Herminia contains a play on the word "querer" which, with its associations of wanting and loving, relates to other words and ideas like free will, marriage, duty. The conversation is raised onto a more elevated plane in a way which anticipates *El curandero de su honra*. Indeed, these same words reverberate through the double column itself. To Iluminada's assertion that she wants for Herminia what she would only want for herself, Herminia replies:

> Querer para otros lo mismo que para sí es ir contra el querer de los demás. Así quieren las personas mayores, que como ya no pueden querer porque no pueden conseguir, sólo quieren obligar a los otros a que quieran sin querer. Pero los jóvenes no queremos así, porque queremos de verdad. ¡Queremos! ¡Queremos! Eso es todo. Queremos para nosotros. No podemos querer sin querer ni dejar de querer queriendo. (IV:659)

A similar display of word play occurs soon afterwards when the concepts of truth and illusion, illusion and happiness are contrasted. Herminia says: "a la verdad que me lastima, prefiero la mentira que me halaga, y con ella me abrazo, porque el gusto que la mentira me da no es mentira . . . . sino que es verdad, verdad, la única verdad amable" (IV:661). The *Presto* has given the novel a new orientation; argument and discussion have yielded to a more oracular use of language. Their words, with their hidden meanings and multiple connotations, echo through the text and build up a dense texture of cross-reference which holds the text together as a self-sufficient artifact.

Another method, which is very characteristic of Modernist fiction, for calling the reader's attention to the text's quality as an artifact is to introduce a central symbol around which the elements of the narrative are systematically arranged. A good example of this is the lighthouse in Virginia Woolf's *To the Lighthouse* which, always present in the narrative, integrates the different perspectives of the characters. There is nothing quite comparable to this in the work of Pérez de Ayala, but the motif of blood, for example, which recurs in *Tigre Juan* and *El curandero de su honra,* fulfills an analogous function. It is, of course, present in Juan's occupation, that of "curandero," it comes to be a symbol of his guilt, of the crime of killing his first wife. It is also present in the real blood when he cuts his hand by accident, in the bleeding feet of Herminia and in the deliberate echoes of Calderón's *El médico de su honra*, in the purging of his own bad blood and finally in the blood which he transmits to his son (along with the blood of Herminia).

There is also in the text a contrast between light and darkness, related to the theme of illumination and revelation. This is present in the double column but it is alluded to as well in the name and the description of Doña Iluminada, who is characterised in terms of light and dark. A parallel is sustained with Juan's evolution from ignorance to comprehension, and of course the same antithesis is present in Calderón's work. It is implied also in the creation of don Sincerato's college for the blind and deaf-mutes, which acts as a kind of symbol of man's inability to come to terms with the world through the use of the senses. This idea is given its most eloquent expression in the silent poem which deals with the paradoxes of existence: "Lo que se oye no escuches. No fíes de lo que miras. / Lo que no oyes, entiende. / Lo que no ves, adivina. / La verdad es como el aire, / transparente y cristalina: / no la ve el hombre, mas siente / si le falta. La mentira / tiene voz. En el silencio / largo, la verdad anida." (IV:688-89). Light and darkness, too, are prominent elements in the evocation of St. John's Night, when the bonfires illuminate the scene. These bonfires, moreover, play an important part in the Asturian rituals of St. John's Night, fire representing the male element, water the female. Juan had been identified with fire throughout the novel, and the water of the stream which cools his fiery imagination prefigures his baptism with the morning dew, traditionally held to have curative powers and hence related to the theme of purgation and to the blood symbol. Thus it is clear that the text transcends any notion of strict mimesis, for it is clear that Ayala imparts to it a markedly artistic texture in which design takes precedence over plot, in which form is more important than verisimilitude. Naturally, Realist writers were concerned with form, with the mode of narration, but this concern was rarely so intense or problematical that it had to be contained within the imaginative work itself. The fictional heterocosm of literary Modernism is self-supporting, and its primary reference is not outward, but inward.

The Modernist novel sets out to confront the infinite complexity of reality, the plurality of perspectives which are opened up once the subjectivity of every individual viewpoint is recognised. This situation is explained nowhere better than in the first chapter of *Belarmino y Apolonio*, the *locus classicus* of perspectivism, in which don Amaranto de Fraile points to the disintegration of reality as the defining characteristic of our age and expresses regret for that past when man had access to that "conocimiento íntegro" which is no longer possible in the modern world. As we have observed earlier, to recognise that the world is different for each one of us poses a problem for Pérez de Ayala, who seeks a form which does justice to the complexity of life and at the same time maintains coherence and artistic unity. Herein resides Modernism's greatest challenge and greatest achievement. Ayala's novels fragment reality, but at the same time they are attempts to realise the somewhat ambitious aim of the author, an aim which he shares with André Gide, for example, to write "la novela integral, que se propone abarcar la realidad entera," to create a literary form which will express the immense complexity of experience, which can present reality as fragmented and as whole at the same time. Ayala had written that the problem of art is to see "lo uno en lo múltiple y la continuidad en el cambio." Thus the idea of the integral or integrating fiction is something which Ayala shares with other Modernist writers. Ayala conceives of the novel as a kind of superior synthesis of art and reality and consequently accords to the creative imagination a vitally important role. When he writes that "Por el conocimiento estético vamos tomando posesión del mundo exterior y de nuestro mundo interior, mediante nuevas formas," he identifies himself clearly with the guiding ethos of Modernism: art provides the coherence lacking in everyday reality. An aesthetics thus conceived will destroy the forms of the traditional novel: indeed, it will reverse its priorities. Reality does not exist to be imitated but is created by the artistic process (and indeed by other mental processes). In *Belarmino y Apolonio*, Ayala writes that "conocer es crear," the act of creating becomes an act of knowing, the theme of any novel resides in its own form. This is a totally perspectivist point of view, an idea which was in any case present in Schopenhauer: "The world is but my representation." More important, from our point of view, is the legacy of Saussure, whose principles of linguistics have had profound implications for the direction of literary Modernism. Thus Saussure's notion that "c'est le point de vue que crée l'objet" is fundamental to the way in which Modernist writers confront their material. Faced with apparent chaos, they adopt the perspectivist position which creates an ordered universe in which everything falls into place. In short, there is a recognition of the potential variety of ways in which the universe might be apprehended but asserts the particular order created by the rigorous adoption of a perspective. Jonathan Culler talks of "literary versions of the Modernist claim that unity and wholeness need not be lost but can be preserved if one adopts a perspective through which the heterogeneous elements can fall into place, as elements of a system."[15] Ayala himself affirms in

Belarmino y Apolonio that "hay tantas verdades irreductibles como puntos de vista," but while recognising the multiplicity and variety of the universe he maintains that totality and unity can be preserved if one adopts a stable perspective. It is interesting to compare this with the observation made in Virginia Woolf's *To the Lighthouse*. James Ramsey, now grown up, approaches the lighthouse and compares the vision he has of it now with that which he had when he was a child: "So that was the Lighthouse, was it? No, the other was also the Lighthouse. For nothing was simply one thing."[16] If one multiplies the perspectives, the truth is not simply the sum of the different perspectives but the relationship which is established between them. There is a shift from a conception of the world as a set of essences to a conception of the world as a system of relations. We have seen how this operates on a linguistic level in *Tigre Juan* and *El curandero de su honra* and how it is related to the notion of synchronicity, the escape from time, from temporal succession, which has been naturally inseparable from narrative itself. This is something which preoccupied Ayala for a considerable part of his novelistic career. I have, of course, referred to the Prologue of *Belarmino y Apolonio,* and I shall look more closely at the structure of that novel in the light of what I have been saying. However, it is worth pointing out that there are moments in Ayala's novels where he aims to neutralise time, or at least lift the action of the novel outside the normal temporal dimension. In *Tigre Juan* and *El curandero de su honra*, for example, while Ayala does not interfere with the accepted logic of occurrences in the physical world, his treatment of time is not straightforward. Towards the end of the *Adagio* of the second part Colás poses questions about how things change in the material world and yet remain the same and thus implicitly queries any one-dimensional concept of time, implying a temporal order beyond ordinary experience. There are moments in the narrative which seem to stand outside time. On St. John's Night "Tigre Juan .... contemplaba ahora, *sub specie aeterni*, la realidad como un sueño evanescente .... percibía que, involucrados unos en otros los elementos, el mundo se desintegraba y fluía ...." (IV:734). When Juan and Herminina come face to face for the first time after their separation, time seems to stand still: "El tiempo había detenido también su andadura; si pisaba, era como si no pisase" (IV:747-48). The significance of the encounter is heightened by freezing it in time, so that although Ayala does not question our chronological experience of time, he does not regard it as the only temporal dimension. Moments of intense emotion seem to involve an intersection of ordinary time with eternity and through them different orders of reality are linked. This makes for a different kind of understanding. Jonathan Culler's remarks on the advantages of synchronic description are applicable here: "The principle of the independence and priority of synchronic description has two important implications. First of all, it suggests that causal explanation is not the only or most significant kind of understanding. Secondly, it indicates that the process of under- standing may in many cases be assisted if one brackets and abstracts away from temporal development."[17] Culler is of course referring to the revolution of Saussurean linguistics, but what he says applies fully to the Modernist perceptions inherent in Ayala's vision, especially when he goes on to talk of these changes in perception as representing "the triumph of the formal imagination." When Juan's and Herminia's lives follow different but parallel paths, this pattern can only be apprehended from the superior vantage-point offered by art, "una perspectiva ideal de la imaginación." Thus Ayala's use of the freezing device in this narrative, although it is akin to the Romantic moment of illumination or epiphany, transcends this in an endeavour to make the whole work function, as it were, synchroni- cally. Thus the novel works against its own desire to tell a story. Gertrude Stein, commenting on this phenomenon, writes that "there is at present not a sense of anything being successively happening, moving is in every direction beginning and ending is not really excit- ing, anything is anything, anything is happening .... And this has come to be a natural thing in a perfectly natural way that the narrative of today is not a narrative of succession as all the writing for a good many hundreds of years has been."[18] Of course, no narrative can totally eliminate sequence, if only in the sense of the sequence in which the elements of the narrative are apprehended by the reader, but Ayala strives to create an alternative order outside the implacable logic of time. As is well known, *Belarmino y Apolonio* rejects the traditional presentation of events along a linear axis and imposes upon events a pattern outside normal chronology. This is not to say that we cannot reconstruct a normal chronology, for if we focus on Pedro's narrative, the different parts of the novel fit together per- fectly. The priest's narration provides a framework of chronological references, but we should remember that it is only a framework and not the very substance of the novel, for if we focus upon the narrator we can see that the elements of the narrative are juxtaposed for their relational value. We are made aware of the potential variety of inter- pretations that we can give to existence: to adopt a perspective in relation to which everything is seen inevitably involves a modification of what is seen. The novel suggests that there is no stable reality and that things are defined by virtue of their relationship with other things. *Belarmino y Apolonio* asserts itself as a structure of relationships.

In the novel Lirio asserts that the human imagination constructs the world that we perceive, and the novel sets out to exemplify his conviction by disintegrating into several points of view. In fact, the story is told from three separate perspectives: that of the omniscient author (Chapters III, V and VIII), that of the narrator-witness (Prologue, Chapters I, II, IV, VII, and the Epilogue) and that of one of the characters, don Guillén, who gives his own account, in Chapters IV and VII, to the narrator-witness. The difference between the omniscient author and the narrator-witness is not great except that the former does not participate in the action, nor indeed does he even refer to himself as "yo." In many respects he is a legacy of the classic nineteenth-century narratorial voice, apparently invisible, creating the impression that what unfolds happens entirely independently of his presence. The narrator-witness, on the other hand, presents himself as part of the action, and therefore the split in the narrative voice creates two orders of fictional reality. In fact, with the exception of Chapter II, where the Rúa Ruera is described jointly by Lirio and Lario via the narrator's account, the narrative split corresponds to the spatial and temporal divisions of the narrative, the narrator being linked to the fictional-real world of Madrid and the omniscient author to the more obviously fictional world of Pilares. This naturally blurs the boundaries between the real and imaginary worlds but more importantly foregrounds the actual construction of the written text. Already in the Prologue, the narrator calls attention to his creating-constructing role: "Pero hoy me siento en humor de salvar del olvido un drama semipatético, semiburlesco, de cuyos interesantes elementos una parte me la ofreció el acaso, otra la fui acopiando en años de investigación y perserverante rebusca. Por eso lo considero casi como una obra original mía." (IV:21). This reference to artistic freedom highlights the classic tension between mimesis and imagination present in any narrative, and it finds its echo at the end of the novel when the narrator asserts in the Epilogue: "Belarmino y Apolonio han existido , y yo les he amado. No digo que hayan existido en carne mortal sobre el haz de la tierra; han existido por mí y para mí" (IV:219). Apart from the obvious Cervantine precedent on which we commented in the preceding chapter, what is important is the way in which Ayala moves the reader from pseudo-naturalist documentation to an assertion of the artist's imaginative vision and the ideal status of fictional artifacts.

The third narrative voice, that of don Guillén, offers apparently the subjective version of his relationship with Augustias, but paradoxically it comes across as the least involved of the three and raises incidentally the whole question of the making of a narrative, for this is what he is required to do: convert his life into a narrative. Narrative and character are in this case virtually coterminous. Don Guillén functions also in another way. A fundamental aspect of the structure of *Belarmino y Apolonio* is the fact that there are two time-scales operating within the text and corresponding to different spatial dimensions. The action in Madrid (which falls to the narrator) spans six days, from Tuesday of Holy Week to Easter Sunday; the action in Pilares (mostly the preserve of the omniscient author) extends over a period of years which ends some years before the events in Madrid occur. Don Guillén's narrative partakes of both temporal spans, which converge in the last two chapters, apparently contemporaneous with one another.

What we have seen, then, is the most obvious manifestation of structure which betrays an awareness of the text both as product and as process, the simultaneous treatment of the material and the reflection on that treatment. All the theoretical support which accompanies the novel points to the need to construct coherent worlds and to acknowledge their fictionality. Language and structure are inseparable insofar as story-telling is an imaginative, ordered construction in language. This is one of the contradictions embedded in *Belarmino y Apolonio*. On the one hand there stands the tendency to treat language as communication and therefore as a means, but against this stands a tendency to treat language as the material for constructing an artifact and therefore as an end. The meaning of the text is its form, for the reader is invited to participate in and give meaning to the construction of imaginary worlds of words. *Belarmino y Apolonio* draws its whole *raison d'être* from the application of structural principles — essentially binary ones — which configure virtually every element in the work. Moreover, at every point it exhibits a sense of internal crisis about its own tactics of presentation. We have seen in an earlier chapter how, in the first instance, this manifests itself in the elaboration of a theory of narrative. Thus, having posed a technical problem, the novel sets out to solve it as far as the limitations of the medium allow. In other words, the pattern of the narrative dramatises the difficulty of establishing the material and giving it a significant artistic order. The process of telling the story becomes a central part of the story. This is a complete inversion of traditional mimesis, for the novel no longer justifies itself as an imitation but as a process. All the traditional elements of narrative, for example, plot, setting, characters, are problematised to the degree that they are foregrounded in the act of narration rather than being disguised within the representation. The narrative is exposed for what it is, a verbal construct. It is not therefore surprising that the self-consciousness of the work extends to language itself, the real raw material of fiction. The most striking feature of *Belarmino y Apolonio*, however, is its very distinctive narrative structure, which overtly dramatises the process by which the *fabula* becomes *sujet*, by which the story in its most objective form, as it "really" could have happened, is converted into its enactment in the text with all the literary ordering which this inevitably entails. Literary ordering constitutes the identity of a text, makes us respond to it the way we do. Pérez de Ayala is among the earliest of the Modernists to recognise that a novel is not to be judged by virtue of a comparison with some model of empirical reality, for the level of a text's operation depends above all on the handling of the material. *Belarmino y Apolonio* is "about" the author's mediation of his subject-matter. Whereas Realist narrative tends to obscure the fact that the patterns of the text derive from the

175

conventions of literature and create the illusion that they are somehow the pattern of life itself, in much Modernist writing artistic order is shown for what it is, one order of many that may be imposed upon the face of reality. If, for the Realists, the "logic of events" and the "logic of coherence," to use Jonathan Culler's terms,[19] could be forced into a perfect marriage, for many Modernists they could not. Henry James' dissatisfaction with the "those loose baggy monsters" of the nineteenth century, to take an obvious example, resides in his search for some kind of organic unity: "A novel is a living thing, all one and continuous, like any other organism, and in proportion as it lives will it be found that in each of the parts there is something of the other parts."[20] But as James, and Pérez de Ayala, recognise, there is an infinite variety of human responses to the world, the world is different for each observer. It is not for nothing that Ayala's *Belarmino y Apolonio*, concerned with the theory of fiction, should explore it in tandem with an exploration of perspective, and that that exploration should begin with a consideration of modern science.

A persistent theme in *Belarmino y Apolonio* is a rejection of the materialism of the nineteenth century, whether this takes the form of the exploitative commercialism of the bourgeoisie alluded to in Don Amaranto's opening remarks (IV:20) and realised in the victory of Martínez's mass-production techniques over Belarmino and Apolonio, representing the victory of business over poetry and philosophy, or whether it refers to the mechanical model of the world accepted by nineteenth-century science. Don Guillén, in fact, in his disquisition on the Breviary, gives a very modern view of the forces of the universe:

> La materia en equilibrio, en inercia, es realidad a medias. La materia en transformación, en descomposición, es realidad íntegra, porque está creando vida y nuevas energías. Y la energía es el elemento espiritual del universo. (IV:169)

It is not difficult to relate this view to that of certain philosophers of science around 1900 observing the new world of the twentieth century, which does away with the old idea of order and replaces it with the notion of relativity in which energy finds its proper place. Alfred North Whitehead, for example, challenges the notion of "independent existence:" "There is no such mode of existence; every entity is to be understood in terms of the way it is interwoven with the rest of the universe." Security, as Pérez de Ayala also acknowledges, has vanished, at least in the sense that nothing can be itself by virtue of itself alone: "The event is what it is by reason of the unification within itself of a multiplicity of relationships."[21] Such a view must undermine any narrowly mimetic view of art and must call into question any simple acceptance of a direct affinity between words and things. Language is not a mirror of some eternal fixed

176

essences in the world but is rather a system of structures which lies parallel to it. This is the beginning of the structuralist revolution, the Saussurean recognition that language is a system of relations, that signs communicate by virtue of the differences between them. Identity is not something independent, but relational. In a wider sense, the particular order that one imposes upon reality is relative to one's point of view. If one adopts a perspective, then everything can be made to fall into place as elements of a system. To return, therefore, to our question of unity in a work of fiction, the use of perspectivism becomes an important strategy. If, as F.H. Bradley says, modern man has "to take reality as many, and to take it as one, and avoid contradiction,"[22] a novelist like Pérez de Ayala copes with the complexity and plurality of the world by containing it within a perspective-dominated system which is the work of fiction itself. Any work of fiction thus conceived will not handle the usual categories of character, plot, and so on in terms of their plausibility in a conventional sense but as part of the total realisation of the fiction itself. They will exist within the system of relations created by the work. Character provides the clearest illustration of this.

A central Modernist perception is that character is not given but is the product or construct of a series of social relations. Personal identity is therefore a movable or relative entity and not the manifestation of some unique core of individuality. Common sense persuades us to accept the objective existence of the individual as something distinct and unique, but the fact is that our sense of this individual is created conceptually through language. Persons are socially constructed through language, and indeed this is precisely what happens in the literary text. In *Belarmino y Apolonio* the first "character" we fully encounter is Don Guillén. He appears to be presented in the unilateral way that we have come to expect through the classic techniques of nineteenth-century Realism: he is introduced, then the narrator deduces what he can from his external appearance and manner, in particular from what he reveals of himself through dialogue. However, don Guillén's characterisation is deliberately ambivalent: he is given a variety of names which those around him can choose at will: "Me llamo Pedro, Lope, Francisco, Guillén, Eurípides; a elegir ...." (IV:22). Each can construct the character in his own way according to his taste, disposition or prejudices: character is seen as a process of construction. Don Guillén has no "essential" character, as the narrator concludes: "¿Qué era aquel hombre? ¿Un hedonista? ¿Un incrédulo? .... ¿Un desengañado, ¿Un atormentado?" (IV:31). The position alumbrated here permeates the whole text and extends to Belarmino and Apolonio themselves. Of his father, Guillén says: "mi padre .... era autor dramático y zapatero, o zapatero y autor dramático, según el orden de prelación que usted prefiera" (IV:23), and Angustias suggests the similarly shifting perceptions which surround her father: "Mi padre era zapatero y otra

177

cosa, que él decia filósofo bilateral .... los profesores de la Universidad venían a oírle .... Mi madre, que tenía mal carácter, decía que mi padre era un zángano, y que los que venían a oírle le tomaban el pelo. Pero mi padre es un santo" (IV:26). Thus, returning to don Guillén, he is defined as a matrix of possibilities. For the reader, his character is not fixed but is a process, a process, moreover, involving contradiction—in his names, in his inner and outer selves, in his construction of his own past. All of this is constructed through language, so that even the introduction of Guillén is related to the later questions of language posed by the text. The introduction of Pedro, too, must be seen in the context of the Prologue which again brings up the question of the relationship between philosophy and literature. For Plato, whose presence lurks in many parts of *Belarmino y Apolonio*, poets feign, simulate and substitute fictions for truth. Much of the narrative gently plays with this age-old quarrel between the two and appears to propose both poetry (drama) and philosophy as a means of access to knowledge through emotional involvement and detached contemplation. However, if for Amaranto drama means involvement and philosophy means detachment, for Escobar, whose Epilogue mirrors Amaranto's Prologue, just the reverse is the case. The existence and equal solidity in reason and experience of these two viewpoints is evidence of the plurality of the constructed world. Thus both at the level of the broad structure of the novel and at the level of each individual character element, the same process of construction is revealed. Our world is both created and known through language. At every stage in its creation the novel looks inward at the processes by which it makes itself known. Where this first becomes clear is in our recognition that Guillén exists as part of a work of literature and that what we know of his character is textually formed, initially through the regularity of recurrent traits. Therefore it is highly significant that when Guillén is introduced he is given a plethora of names. A name is the most fundamental literary context of character; it has the effect of naturalising the individual in terms of our normal expectations, and its recurrence helps stabilise and fix the "character" within the narrative; it provides coherence. Ayala deliberately subverts this and therefore destabilises. Not surprisingly, when the narrative gets properly under way, a single name (don Guillén) predominates. But the initial textual subversion is a reminder of the conventional expectations we have of fictional characters. What is equally interesting is the way in which the potentiality of Guillén's character is left, as it were, in suspension at the end of Chapter I. For him to become more of a character we need more of the text which will support his character. In this respect, the ending of the chapter harks back to the beginning. Guillén acquires character only by entering the novel: the narrator explicitly states that he would be insignificant if he had not been "en la mesa redonda de una casa de huéspedes" (novel?).

178

Outside the circumstances created by the text Guillén has no existence.

When we turn to look at Belarmino and Apolonio we can see that a fundamental aspect of their characterisation is the opposition between them, so perfect as to be symmetrical. This symmetry in characterisation is highlighted by virtue of the fact that it is analogous to the symmetry which characterises the book's total structure. It is in this way foregrounded so that we may see it for what it is. This is something more than a clash of personalities, say, or a simple comparison for the purposes of contrast. The difference is something essential to the characterisation, for through it Belarmino and Apolonio mutually define one another. They become what they are because and through one another and cannot in any sense be conceived of as autonomous, independent individuals with a given human nature but are created (known) through their very differentiation. By formulating the question of characterisation in this way, Ayala points up the fact that character in fiction is formed. There is no longer any sense that characters in fiction reflect real persons outside. Character is produced by very specific means. This might not be the case in reality, but it certainly is the case in literature. However, as language is the forming agent it may well be the case that character in reality (whatever that may be) is similarly constructed. This is not the inescapable conclusion of *Belarmino y Apolonio*, however, for it seems that Ayala's great novel is less concerned with the ideological implications of this vision for man and society than with using the medium of fiction to expose and investigate the processes by which fiction is created and generates meaning.

Not surprisingly, in view of these concerns, *Belarmino y Apolonio* confronts the question of language itself through the figure of Belarmino, the shoemaker-philosopher, the most elaborated of a series of characters who have interested themselves in language in many of Ayala's novels. Escobar, in fact, functions as a kind of disciple of Belarmino and interprets for us his language and its aims. In his Epilogue, he points to the essential dilemma of language: it is both common and individual. For Escobar, each person is locked in this own world of language:

> Cada hombre que es una cosa de veras, habla un idioma distinto que no entiende el que no es esa cosa, porque tienen alma distinta. El chalán habla su idioma, el contrabandista el suyo, el suyo también el político, y el artista, y el ferretero, y el soldado, y el dentista. El mundo es como una gran lonja, llena de sordos que aspiran a verificar sus transacciones; todos gritan; hay un horrendo rebullicio; pero como no se oyen los unos a los otros, no se concluye ningún trato. (IV:128)

179

This is phenomenon which we find occurring constantly in the novel in the face of Belarmino's wilfully obscure dialect. Indeed, such is the case when we first encounter him in the Círculo Republicano in Pilares, where his language is the source of his alienation from most of those around him. Of course, Belarmino's language initially defies comprehension, but behind the comedy of his presentation there are serious points being made about the nature of language and its relationship to thought. Belarmino's language is clearly built upon association and is metaphoric in inspiration, connecting things which are perceived to be similar. For any cultured person language works in this way, is replete with associations, with semantic density. However, in Belarmino's case a parallel process is at work. Some of the words he uses are unknown to him, and therefore the associations he creates are his own, they are entirely private, and can, by virtue of this freedom, partake of a plurality of significations. For Belarmino this recreation of meaning becomes a profound art of knowing. Belarmino shows himself to be aware of the conventionality of the linguistic sign: "La mesa—decía—se llama mesa porque nos da la gana; lo mismo podía llamarse silla" (IV:78). What matters is that the differences between the signs enable communication to take place. Belarmino simply destroys the conventional attribution of names and substitutes new ones. The principle is the same, for he sets up a new system which is entirely coherent within itself. As he reads the dictionary he is "ajenado de la realidad externa" as the dictionary itself becomes the word. Hence the equation of "diccionario" and "cosmos"—the world is the word. Therefore Belarmino remakes language and in so doing remakes the world.

> El diccionario, en su opinión, era epítome del universo, prontuario sucinto de todas las cosas terrenales y celestiales, clave con que descrifrar los más insospechados enigmas. La cuestión era penetrar esa clave secreta, desarrollar ese prontuario, abarcar de una ojeada ese epítome. En el diccionario está todo, porque están todas las palabras; luego están todas las cosas, porque la cosa y la palabra es uno mismo; nacen las cosas cuando nacen las palabras; sin palabras no hay cosas, o si las hay, es como si no las hubiese, porque la cosa no existe por sí ni para otras cosas—por ejemplo, una mesa no sabe que existe, ni la mesa existe para una silla, porque la silla no sabe de la existencia de la mesa—, sino que existe solamente para un *Inteleto* que la conoce, y en cuanto que la conoce, le da un nombre, le pone una palabra. Conocer es crear, y crear conocer.   (IV:97-98)

It is clear that this theory repudiates the idea of a natural language which was adumbrated in *Tinieblas en las cumbres*. Words have no natural meaning or no natural affinity with the objects they designate. The statement "la cosa y la palabra es uno mismo" implies that it is only the concept we grasp, that language creates reality but does not represent it. The novel is an exploration of the relationship between words and things, between language and the world. Belarmino recognises himself as a prisoner of language in that it enslaves man to a particular perception. By changing the language, by renovating it, man acquires a new perception, and therefore Belarmino redefines the words he finds in the dictionary in order to defeat the routine procedures of language use which condemn him to a lack of real engagement with the world, to a deadening of response, to an absence of genuine knowledge. Belarmino seeks liberation from the prison-house of language and posits a close connection between language and thought. Of course, Belarmino is a "philosopher," and it is accepted that philosophers have their own specialised and frequently extremely difficult discourse, as El Estudiantón points out to Belarmino's detractors (IV:127). Behind his observation is the idea that new thoughts require new forms of expression, but this eminently conventional view implies that thought is in some way anterior to its articulation. Naturally, Belarmino's quest appears to have the same motivation — he seeks a language to express the ineffable. However, also in his thoughts on language, he appears to recognise that thought is inseparable from its expression, from its point of articulation. Indeed, Belarmino constantly dialogues with his *Inteleto*, and this dialogue is creative. The use of language is a process of discovery, and thought is formed as it is enunciated. Language and thought interpenetrate; man and language are interdependent. In an essay on poetry, published ultimately in *Las máscaras*, Pérez de Ayala talks about the private nature of language: "cada hombre es un prisionero de sí propio; un pequeño cosmos sellado, inaccesible para los demás." In order to liberate this "hombre interior prisionero de sí propio," new words are required, but this is not possible, so that one must "adoptar las palabras usuales, pero con una acepción desusada, original: imantar cada palabra vetusta con el magnetismo de la emoción subjetiva hasta hacer de ella un centro de asociaciones inéditas y múltiples." In this way, one supposes, language creates rather than describes. Pérez de Ayala shares with other Modernist writers a sense of the inadequacy of language. Those who accept unthinkingly the normal meanings of words accept unconsciously a ready-made world, a world already interpreted by others. If man exists in language, then any change in language will lead to a change in man. Belarmino distances himself from ordinary language in search of authentic life, in pursuit of active creation. To do so he seeks to rescue the word from its status as a mere sign. The basis of his language is therefore essentially metaphorical and his ultimate — heroic and quixotic — aim is to find "una sola palabra" which contains all the truth, all of reality. This would presumably be the ultimate categorisation of all human thought, and there might exist one word which contained such a totality within it. This mystical notion, of course, implies the possibility of a natural language which could be recovered, in which sound and sense might exist in perfect harmony. This is the language referred to earlier in the quotation from *Tinieblas en las cumbres*, and now in *Belarmino y Apolonio* the crazy shoe-maker strives to express the ineffable and is faced with the inadequacy of language. His final stance is in fact one of silence, which is explained in translation by Escobar:

> Una vez era un hombre que, por pensar y sentir tanto, hablaba escaso y premioso. No hablaba, porque comprendía tantas cosas en cada cosa singular, que no acertaba a expresarse. Los otros le llamaban tonto. Este hombre, cuando supo expresar todas las cosas que comprendía en una sola cosa, hablaba más que nadie. Los otros le llamban charlatán. Pero este hombre, cuando, en lugar de ver tantas cosas en una sola cosa, en todas las cosas distintas no vio ya sino una y la misma cosa, porque había penetrado en el sentido y en la verdad de todo; al llegar a esto, este hombre ya no volvió a hablar ni una palabra. Y los demás le llamaban loco.   (IV:163-64)

Interestingly enough, this silence anticipates that of his creator, Pérez de Ayala himself, who in 1926 abandoned novel-writing completely. This is not the place to rehearse the possible reasons for this, but it is appropriate to mention here Livingstone's view that relates Ayala's silence to the question of language itself.[23] Language is contradictory in that it is both the instrument of and an impediment to communication. We find this in many authors. Augusto Pérez, in *Niebla*, protests that "El hombre en cuanto habla miente, y en cuanto se habla a sí mismo, es decir, en cuanto piensa sabiendo que piensa, miente .... La palabra, este producto social , se ha hecho para mentir .... Lo que es producto social es la mentira."[24] The same conflict between personal authenticity and social pose is to be found in Luis Martín-Santos' *Tiempo de silencio*. For the writer of fiction, however, the dilemma is intensified, for his work can be seen as simply linguistic virtuosity rather than an exploration of himself or of reality. The classic twentieth-century artistic response to this dilemma has been to show art for what it is: art. Fiction is foregrounded as fiction, never as fact. In the case of *Belarmino y Apolonio*, however, the whole question of simulation is openly explored through the contradictory natures of the two protagonists. In fact, as we have seen, Pérez de Ayala inverts our normal expectations in that the dramatist, who appears to live intensely, is a mere simulator, whereas the philosopher, apparently serene, is actively and emotionally involved in that which he contemplates. The contrast between the two men is maintained on a linguistic level. Apolonio is theatrical, effusive, eloquent; Belarmino repudiates "el habla común" and searches for a language which will restore unity to the world by making it represent the interconnectedness of all things. Thus he prefers words which have a plurality of associations, seeks to "ensanchar la palabra," and thereby aligns himself with those modern writers who mistrust language or are dissatisfied with it. Pre-occupation with language within the text is a constant reminder that the text is not reality but discourse. This is the introverted novel, the novel, conscious of itself. It is conscious of its own status as a linguistic object, in essence not unlike John Banville's *Doctor Copernicus*, in which the character is equally aware of the power of silence: "instead of approaching the word, the crucial word, (his work) was careering headlong into a loquacious silence. He had believed it was possible to say the truth; now he saw that all that could be said was the saying. His book was not about the world, but about itself."[25] In Pérez de Ayala we find the paradox of the writer who revels in language and who terminates in silence. This is not, of course, any sterile silence. In his last novel we find the amusing but significant case of don Sincerato Gamborena, whose "coro mudo y cabalístico" proclaims: "En el silencio / largo, la verdad anida."

But the matter cannot be left at that. Belarmino's linguistic trajectory inevitably involves the destruction of language. Silence eliminates the possibility of any communication, and this is recognised by Belarmino himself when he buys a magpie to maintain his contact with ordinary language so that he may continue to communicate with his daughter. It is recognised, too, in the need for translations of his words and in the lexicon provided by Escobar at the end, just as in *Tigre Juan* Sincerato has to translate "los silenciosos movimientos en palabras." In other words, to give words a private meaning quite irrespective of their accepted meaning is to abolish the communicative dimension of language completely. Belarmino's language can, as some critics have sensed, be interpreted as parodic (of philosophical or poetic language), but surely it functions as a dimension of the self-referentiality of the text itself, a reminder that the world of perception is language-shaped, that everything is inscribed in discourse. *Belarmino y Apolonio* therefore contributes to the characteristically Modernist engagement with the text in making the reader aware of its status as a culturally and conventionally determined product by emphasising its formalistic and linguistic nature, by exploring the ways in which it creates meaning and invites interpretation. In other words, it reminds us of the particularly literary context in which its discourse exists and lays bare the conventions by depriving them of their traditional motivation. As far as language is concerned, M.K. Read, in an interesting article, sees *Belarmino y Apolonio* as Ayala's attempt to dramatise opposing attitudes to language — the positivist and the idealist — which are fundamental to the Western tradition.[26] The novel shows the inadequacies of both attitudes and argues the need for a synthesis of the two. We have already seen Amaranto's strictures on the philosophical basis of Positivism, developed further in the dialogue between Lirio and Lario. The Idealist emphasises man's creativity through language: this is what it becomes for Belarmino, a personal creation and a personal exploration, a new language meaning a new vision. But at the same time such a personal quest leads inevitably to a breakdown of communication with others, and therefore Belarmino shows clearly the essential conflict in language use between its conventional status and creative potential. Moreover, *Belarmino y Apolonio* continues to grapple with a concern that was present in Ayala's work from *Tinieblas en las cumbres*: the problem of education and culture, the element of tradition in language which makes it function in a particular way. Belarmino's "revolution" is twofold: it is a form of liberation but also a negation of culture on which language and indeed the life of the literary text depends. There is, then, an ambivalence on the part of the reader as to how he should react to it. On the one hand, it reflects the crisis of language characteristic of literary modernism. On the other, it is essentially abstract and apparently limited, and the fact that its author is a crazy shoemaker undermines to some extent its claims to seriousness. Thus in its metaphorical nature it is obscure, but is this a productive obscurity? We could see Belarmino as someone who has abandoned language in pursuit of pure thought (and ultimately silence) and his counterpart Apolonio as someone who has abandoned thought for pure language (his "delirios poéticos"). That there is this ambivalence, however, is a further dimension of the self-consciousness of the novel, its probing of its own resources. In literature, the only resource is language, and language is a social and historical product which cannot be separated from its past or disrupted beyond a certain point. The aim of the innovatory Modernist writer can only be to strain language to certain point of tension, but to dislocate it completely leads inevitably towards non-communication, non-meaning and perforce silence. Contradictions of this kind are the mainsprings of Modernist art, and they are part of the reason why Modernist novels try to resist the imposition upon them of a single, authoritative meaning, why their irony encompasses their own status as fictions. This is where the textual self-preoccupation we have examined ultimately leads: to the creation of an aesthetic mode which is born of the need to create coherent worlds and which nevertheless is imbued with a skepticism about art's ability to provide order beyond the simple consolations of form. Thus the creation of fictions is complemented by the acknowledgement of their fictionality. Language and structure are the essentials of the Modernist fictional heterocosm. In this respect, Modernist fiction is no different from Realist fiction: the difference lies in the fact that these are not at the service of the novelist's moral or social concern but are themselves his most obsessive preoccupations.

NOTES

[1]Luigi Pirandello, *Il fu Mattia Pascal* (Milan: Mondadori, 1965) 256. Originally published in 1921.

[2]Miguel de Unamuno, Prologue to *Tres novelas ejemplares, Obras completas* (Madrid: Afrodisio Aguado, 1958) Vol. IX:418.

[3]Virginia Woolf, "Modern Fiction," *Collected Essays* 108.

[4]Marcel Proust, *A la Recherche du temps perdu* 8 (Paris: Gallimard, 1964) 243.

[5]Linda Hutcheon, *Narcissistic Narrative. The Metafictional Paradox* (London and New York: Methuen, 1984) 41.

[6]André Gide, *Les Faux-Monnayeurs* (Paris: Gallimard, 1958) 1084.

[7]E.M. Forster, *Aspects of the Novel* (Harmondsworth: Penguin, 1970) 170.

[8]Aldous Huxley, *Point Counterpoint* (Harmondsworth: Penguin, 1955) 297-98.

[9]José Ortega y Gasset, *Ideas sobre la novela, Obras completas*, III (Madrid: Revista de Occidente, 1957) Vol. III: 410-11.

[10]F.W. Weber, *The Literary Perspectivism of Ramón Pérez de Ayala* 47.

[11]Leon Livingstone, "Interior Duplication and the Problem of Form in the Modern Spanish Novel," *Publications of the Modern Language Association of America* LXIII (1958):405.

[12]Weber 82.

[13]*La novela intelectual* 365.

[14]Weber 84-85.

[15]Jonathan Culler, "Linguistics" in "Modernism: A Symposium," *The New Review* 10 (January, 1975):16.

[16]V. Woolf, *To the Lighthouse* 211.

[17]Culler 16.

[18]Quoted by Jonathan Culler in "Modernism: A Symposium" 17.

[19]Jonathan Culler, "Some American Contributions to the Study of Narrative." Quoted by D. Lodge in *Working with Structuralism* 153.

[20]Henry James, "The Art of Fiction," in *The House of Fiction* (London: Rupert Hart-Davis, 1957) 34.

[21]A.N. Whitehead, *Science and the Modern World* (Cambridge: Cambridge University Press, 1929).

[22]Quoted by Jonathan Culler in "Modernism: A Symposium" 16.

185

[23]Leon Livingstone, "Lenguaje y silencio en *Belarmino y Apolonio*," *Simposio Internacional Ramón Pérez de Ayala* (Gijón: University of New Mexico, 1981) 72-90.

[24]Miguel de Unamuno, *Niebla* (Madrid: Espasa-Calpe, 1968) 96.

[25]John Banville, *Dr. Copernicus* (New York: Norton, 1976) 116.

[26]M.K. Read, "*Belarmino y Apolonio* and the Modern Linguistic Tradition," *Bulletin of Hispanic Studies* LV (1978):329-35.

CONCLUSION

Literary history and criticism are not exact sciences, and their lack of precision and exactitude is seen nowhere more clearly than in the intense debates provoked by the classification of works according to genre or literary movements. This study of the fiction of Ramón Pérez de Ayala does not claim to be literary history, but a central assumption underlying it has been that our received version of early twentieth-century Spanish fiction has been less than adequate. The rigid demarcation between Generation of 1898 and *modernismo*, the very notion of the 98 as a defining term for the fiction of the period, are of only very limited value in accounting for the significance of a writer such as Pérez de Ayala and of virtually no value at all in enabling us to understand the nature and development of narrative itself. It is, moreover, difficult not to see the novel in historical or chronological terms, by which I do not mean that it is essentially a product of history, but rather that it is manifestly an actively evolving form. In this respect it probably differs in kind from other genres in the sense that a poem, for example, can be isolated and analysed on its own terms without reference to its position on a supposed poetic evolutionary scale. The New Critics, of course, and those who followed them, had a tendency to study novels in this way but, despite their considerable contribution to increasing our awareness of novels as essentially verbal structures, they do not seem fully to take into account the way in which the novel, uniquely among literary genres, has been inseparable from man's imaginative involvement with the world he inhabits. Each development has represented a degree of progress in that involvement which is, arguably, absent from other forms of literary discourse. While it is certainly surprising from our present perspective to see Pérez de Ayala's novels being criticised for being highly formal and artificial, such criticism is only a proof or acknowledgement of the very close correlation between realism and the novel form. The nineteenth century is, for many, the heyday of the novel, the century in which it made its greatest advances, in both technique and subject-matter. As Ian Watt has shown, the realist novel is closely bound up with the fortunes of the middle classes and in its rejection of traditional values accorded unprecedented importance to individual experience and individual expression. Thus it was always open to the new, to the novel, and was characterised by artistic freedom.[1] The Modernist novel, in turn, is an evolution from literary Realism, and for this reason the opening chapter of this book attempted to define Modernism in terms of the dynamics of its relation to the Realist tradition. It is appropriate now, as a kind of conclusion, to look forward in a general way and ask what seeds of evolution are contained in Modernism: what kind of Modernism do the novels of Ramón Pérez de Ayala embody and what are the broader implications of his work, produced in those three vital decades for modern fiction, from 1900 and 1930, for the novel itself.

Harry Levin, writing some twenty years ago about the work of the French Realists, observed that the novelist "must feel a peculiar tension between the words, conventions, ideas, that the masters of his craft have handed on to him, and the facts, impressions and experiences that life continues to offer."[2] Seen in this way, the novel is not totally free, but is culturally conditioned. Even if a writer has "new" experiences, the form bequeathed to him inevitably exerts an influence over the shape that experience will take. Inscribed within the Modernist novel in particular is an inherent tension between the tradition of the novel, basically Realist, and an impetus for innovation. At the same time, however, we can say that the legacy of form itself is a stimulus for change, that the novel evolves not primarily by imbibing new experience, but by modifying or reacting to the forms that "the masters . . . . have handed on." Innovation is not a matter of experience, but of form. On another level, though, there is in Modernism a tension between form and experience in the sense that whereas fiction is more making than communication, it is difficult to deny its relations with a reality that lies outside it. In other words, Realism, though undeniably a system of conventions, tended, we might say, towards life, towards experience, the empirically real, while Modernism, though undeniably bearing a relationship to experience, tends towards art, towards convention, the aesthetically significant. These are broad tendencies, the propensities of each mode, and the two co-exist in a kind of creative antagonism. The break which Modernism constitutes merely involves a modification of the relationship between the two, between literature and reality. One way of describing this is to say that the balance between "matching" and "making" is altered: Realism foregrounds "matching," that is, the devices which highlight the mimetic nature of the text are to the fore (the creative process and the creative product are distinct), whereas Modernism foregrounds "making" in that it is characteristically concerned with its own genesis, methods of composition and so on (the creative process and the created product become indistinguishable). To the extent that the Modernists have explored in their work the possible permutations of art and life, one is inclined to wonder whether there is anything new for the novel to do while remaining a novel. Of course, to state such a question — are the limits of the novel reached in Modernism? — is to repeat for post-Modernism what was said in objection to the experiments of the Modernists. In the case of Pérez de Ayala, one need only quote the author's own recollection of the reaction of the writer and journalist Luis López Ballesteros to the recently published *Troteras y danzaderas*. He said, according to Pérez de Ayala: "su libro me gusta y me interesa mucho; pero confiese usted que no es una novela" (IV:909). This observation offers a useful pointer towards a way of conceiving the writing of Pérez de

Ayala and that of many contemporary European writers: they wrote works which are manifestly novels, but ones which contribute to the process whereby genre itself dissolves into discourse. Pérez de Ayala's novels are to some extent destructive of genre, as we have seen in his blurring of the limits of fiction and autobiography (in a manner akin to Joyce and Proust) and indeed between the novel and other kinds of writing: we need think only of his fusion of the novelistic and the dramatic, and of the terms "novela poemática" and "novela-ensayo." For much modern writing, characterised by generic plurality and stylistic multiplicity, we need to rethink our terminology, invent new categories, if we are to retain the clarity and validity of our critical perceptions. The relationship of much modern writing to our concept of the novel is undoubtedly problematical, and it is perhaps for this reason that we feel that in the work of the Modernists the limits of the novel have been reached.

There is another sense, too, in which we might see the Modernist novel in some measure as the end of a road. José Ortega y Gasset, whose astute and influential writings on modern art have already provided us with one set of images to describe the modern novel, offers another as he detects in the work of the moderns a kind of terminal quality expressed in the image of the quarry to convey the idea of the novel as a genre which has been fully exploited and is now near to exhaustion:

> Es un error representarse la novela — y me refiero sobre todo a la moderna — como un orbe infinito, del cual pueden extraerse siempre nuevas formas. Mejor fuera imaginarla como una cantera de vientre enorme, pero finito. Existe en la novela un número definido de temas posibles. Los obreros de la hora prima encontraron con facilidad nuevos bloques, nuevas figuras, nuevos temas. Los obreros de hoy se encuentran, en cambio, con que sólo quedan pequeñas y profundas venas de piedra.[3]

Interestingly enough, as far as thematic material is concerned, Pérez de Ayala seems to concur. None of his novels is characterised by an original theme, and all of them appear to be totally devoid of actuality. It is this, paradoxically, which makes of him such a radical writer. If his novels do appear to show any social concern (relations between the sexes, for example), such concern is inevitably refracted through some literary antecedent so that the refraction rather than the theme is the primary focus of interest. He totally abandons the social perspective of nineteenth-century Realism, aware, firstly, that society and history do not give a true account of reality and, secondly, that fundamental to the aesthetics of fiction is the relationship between literature and reality. The clearest example of this is *Belarmino y Apolonio,* which explores through its very structure the

189

literary application of the theories of relativity and perspectivism while at the same time providing a commentary on its own processes of composition. In this novel, and in others, Pérez de Ayala deliberately shuns the extremes of realism and aestheticism and strikes a balance between adhering to some of the conventions and accepted modes of literary representation and deviating sufficiently from them to dramatise the problems of the practice of writing. In this way, he foregrounds writing as a heavily conventionalised activity, as opposed to its being a direct and unproblematical imitation of experience. Indeed, in his assertion that "crear es conocer," he implies that the modes of knowing create experience itself.

A principal attribute of works such as *Belarmino y Apolonio* is the tension that exists within them between the familiar and the unfamiliar, so that the reader is made aware of the act of reading itself. In the terminology of Ortega y Gasset, the perceiver is aware of the window as well as of the garden. *Belarmino y Apolonio* subverts traditional ways of writing and traditional modes of thought—it is not surprising that one of its preoccupations is the changes that constantly take place in scientific knowledge—and suggests that what we know is simply a function of the way we know. Thus Modernist writers often make extravagant claims for the validity of an "aesthetic" reality, the reality of the imagination, timeless and absolute, as embodied in the novel, "the one bright book of life," as D.H. Lawrence describes it. The novel for Lawrence is the supreme book, as this confident assertion implies: "Books are not life. They are only tremulations on the ether. But the novel as a tremulation can make the whole man alive tremble. Which is more than poetry, philosophy, science or any other book-tremulation can do."[4] Pérez de Ayala conceives of the novel as creating a new sense of unity and integration, imposing form on what is merely contingent. Naturally, this almost visionary enterprise is highly characteristic of Modernist writing, but the desire to impose order upon brute experience is not entirely divorced from, say, the traditional novel's containment of reality within the confines of a plot. As Bernard Bergonzi states: "The novel is concerned, above all, with carving shapes out of history, with imposing a beginning, a middle and an end on the flux of experience."[5] The Modernist differs from the Realist in his open acknowledgement of and his calling attention to the novel's shaping potential.

The nineteenth-century novel did not reflect upon the nature of its own enterprise, nor was it subject to any degree of uncertainty about what it was doing. Few Realist novels concern themselves with novel-writing itself, just as all Realist novels exhibit an impersonal mode of narration in which the author completely effaces himself. By contrast, in Modernist novels the presence of the author is constantly felt, but not necessarily as an original, individual voice. On the contrary, a novelist like Pérez de Ayala consciously treads in the foot-steps of earlier writers and acknowledges that his fictions are not born of his unique, individual experience by writing his work in rela-tion to other literature. He challenges the notion of originality, uses myths, fables and existing works to impart form to his new creation, imitates not life, but literature. *Prometeo*, for example, is a reworking of the myths of Prometheus and Ulysses, and part of the pleasure the reader derives from the work is his satisfaction in perceiving the emergence of a pattern, the completion of a form. In this poematic novel, and in *Luz de domingo* and *La caída de los Limones*, life and literature are made constantly to interact, though in different ways. In one, the mythical world appears to clash with the real world; in another, the fictional world acts as an emblem of the character's fic-tionalising of his own reality; in another, the world of literature emerges as an ideal, a momentary escape, the imposition of the illu-sory upon the real. In the Urbano and Simona novels, the use of liter-ary sources, particularly of the tradition of prose romance, both classical and Golden Age, sustains the work's consideration of the processes of narrative, for these earlier works themselves contained a considerable amount of literary-critical reflection. Theory and practice merge as the author, like his predecessors, discriminates between historical and poetic truth in a way that would have been inconceivable for a nineteenth-century Realist. In these works, and in *Tigre Juan* and *El curandero de su honra* (incidentally, probably his most apparently mimetic narrative), Pérez de Ayala bypasses the Realist tradition to link up with older forms of narrative in which the aesthetic was not subordinate to the verisimilar. Moreover, by refer-ring to and incorporating other works, he suggests that the "mean-ing" of a novel is not unique or independent but is defined by its relationship to the larger system of literature, of which it is a partial expression. Two consequences stem from this. Reality is not medi-ated directly but is evoked through its most famous representations in literature and, more significantly, the device relates very directly to that fundamental principle of Modernist aesthetics, synchronicity, the manifestations of which are numerous. The text itself is a system of interrelated elements, of which the relationship of the new work to existing works is one. The search for synchronicity also involves a departure from the successive order of narrative towards attempts at simultaneous narration and at registering the atemporal aspects of psychological experience. In the Modernist portrayal of conscious-ness we find an achronological tendency, and past experiences are refracted through the present. In the case of Tigre Juan, whose state of consciousness is portrayed with great psychological intensity, his emotions are experienced as a wave of tempestuous and chaotic feelings which burst into consciousness. Here again the notion of synchronicity is relevant: past and present are integral parts of the same experience, an assimilation of sensations, associations and fragmentary memories inherent in the present but always in contact with a perception of the past. The presentation of consciousness is kept distinct from the restraints of normal chronology. One recalls the words of the psychologist William James who, comparing consciousness to a stream, says that "the knowledge of some other part of the stream, past or future, is always mixed up with the present thing."[6]

Pérez de Ayala's concern with consciousness shows a significant development over the course of his literary career. The early novels exhibit an interest in many of the psychological-philosophical ideas prevalent at the turn of the century. Their quasi-autobiographical protagonist, Alberto Díaz de Guzmán, appears as the alienated individual of the twentieth century who, although he experiences difficulties in his interpersonal relationships, is more preoccupied with much wider questions of purpose and finality, in a manner which anticipates the Jungian dimension of Ayala's later work. Alberto's crisis leads firstly to a loss of faith in all absolutes and then to a desire to reconstruct everything afresh and restore it to its original value. Thus Pérez de Ayala's novels exemplify the integrating tendency of Modernism, which seeks to reimpose a unitary vision in the face of the fragmentation and disorder of modern reality. In the early novels, Ayala had not formulated a theory of art which could be reconciled with a genuine experience of life: art and life were to some degree seen as antitheses, polarities which remained unresolved. By the time he comes to write *Belarmino y Apolonio*, the possibility of art's having an integrating function has assumed greater importance. The characters form complementary doubles, and the novel itself strives to integrate its various perspectives into a single, coherent whole. Unity is perceived as a system of relations in which the disorders of reality are contained. It is precisely in their desire to achieve and retain coherence that the Modernists differ from the postmodernists. T.S. Eliot's dictum is typical: "A poet's mind is constantly amalgamating disparate experience."[7] This is a characteristically *fin-de-siècle* attitude implying a markedly aesthetic view of the mind: artistic consciousness is superior to what is merely life. Whereas in his early novels Ayala appears to adopt an ambivalent stance with regard to this position, in his later novels he positively embraces the notion of the function of art in coming to terms with experience. *Tigre Juan* and *El curandero de su honra* offer the supreme illustration of this. Together they form a complex work in which many disparate elements are held together by an underlying set of psychological ideas. The split in Juan's personality is healed by symbolic means, and his final aim as an individual becomes the full realisation of his total personality. In the novel, Ayala postulates a close connection between the integration of the personality and the art of fiction itself. Fiction has the function of bringing man's inner world of imagination into a more harmonious relationship with the whole of creation. Through Juan the theme of human love is explored in psychological terms as a quest for integrity within the individual personality through the development of a mature relationship with another person. When this state has been attained, the individual experiences a sense of fulfillment and inner harmony which is commonly accepted as a characteristic of aesthetic experience.[8] Fiction, for Ayala, does not loosen man's grip upon reality, but actually serves to strengthen it. It provides the means of linking consciousness and reality.

Another way in which Ayala conforms to the integrating tendency of Modernism is seen in the interest he shows in polarities and in the theme of the reconciliation of opposites. Belarmino and Apolonio are complementary halves of the same person; in Tigre Juan the introvert and the extrovert co-exist. The idea is prevalent in literary Modernism. The two sexes are combined in the figure of Tiresias in T.S. Eliot's *The Waste Land*. In Virginia Woolf's *The Waves*, there is a character who cannot distinguish between pleasure and pain, "such is the incomprehensible combination, such is the complexity of things."[9] Confronted with fragmentation and disconnectedness, the Modernist seeks to control them by shaping confusion and disorder into a balanced play of opposites, like Virginia Woolf's Sasha Latham who contemplates a garden both bathed in "a cloud of gold" or reduced to "prosaic daylight" and can ask "which view is the true one?"[10] Things and phenomena which are evidently distinct are simultaneously the same, forming, in the words of Gottfried Benn, "an integrated ambivalence."[11] The Modernist ambition is to create a literary form which will express the immense complexity of experience, which will present reality as simultaneously fragmented and whole.

This faith in the validity and potentiality of art is, however, accompanied by a degree of skepticism and divergence between the theory and practice of fiction. Synchronicity again provides a useful illustration. Modernist writing strives to overcome the essential dichotomy between past and future by attempting to convert successiveness into simultaneity. Pérez de Ayala is an early participant in the revolt against chronology which is continued in the work of, say, Michel Butor (*L'Emploi du temps*) or Juan Goytisolo (*Makbara*). The formal organisation of the Modernist work is more spatial than temporal, even though it is ultimately impossible for the novelist to escape time completely, either in the sense of the time taken to read the novel or in the sense of the fictitious time of the narrated events. But when the temporal flow of a novel is halted, or altered, the reader's attention is directed towards the play of relations within the work itself. Instead of following the course of a story, the reader is required to discern a pattern. Writers try to achieve in their work something of the effect of a Cubist painting or of a musical composition in which themes are taken up with variations and cross-references. However, the fact that there have been so many examples of this kind of experiment suggests that the problem is really insoluble, and here we glimpse something of the contradictions inherent in Modernism itself. To some degree, the novelty to which it aspires is checked by the essential conservatism of the form of the novel and indeed of language itself. It is not surprising, therefore, that the Modernist's claims for art give rise to an art which itself evaluates the validity of those very claims.

Just as the Modernist novel looks inward towards the workings of consciousness, so too does it look inward at its own resources and processes as a linguistic fiction. One way in which it does this is by overt parody, which calls attention to the varieties and conventions of artistic modes, thereby inviting, in the case of the novel, a cultural rather than a naturalist reading. Such a conception of fiction is present from Ayala's earliest novel, *Tinieblas en las cumbres*. This novel is capable of being, and usually is, read as an exemplification of the spiritual or philosophical crisis of the Generation of 1898, or even as the exposition of some typically *modernista* or *fin-de-siècle* literary attitudes. However, a more suggestive reading is to see it as an exploration of the artistic crisis of Modernism itself in which a writer, imbued with humanist values, prefigures the crisis of humanism which occurs later in the century, pointing up the unreliability of language and eroding the unique status of the literary text itself. Pérez de Ayala, then, embodies that irony which pervades the spirit of Modernism. His exposition of ideas in his novels may give an impression of him as being lucid and clear, but in fact he is not. Each of his novels is characterised by a kind of indeterminacy born of a fundamental ambivalence of tone. The boundaries between the serious and the comic are blurred. All his experiments with the form of fiction seem curiously double-edged for, while Pérez de Ayala was very alive to the cultural climate of his time, to new artistic and literary currents, his attitude is a paradoxical blend of fascination and detachment. Thus the musical section-titles of his last novel may not be entirely serious and the same can be said of his return to myth, his use of perspective, his conscious dehumanisation. All respond to the new Modernism, but each seems curiously self-conscious. Thus the celebrated double column may be self-referentially parodic in relation to the Modernist desire for synchronicity. After all, it reminds us — as do all peculiar arrangements of words on the printed page — of the typographical nature of the medium. However much novelists struggle in pursuit of the new, the actual shape of the book itself is a conservative and stabilising force. So too is language. Modernist texts foreground the linguistic medium in an endeavour to ensure that the reality of the representation takes precedence over the representation of reality. Language itself becomes a central area of concern. In his creation of Belarmino, Ayala highlights the dilemma of language: it is both common and individual. Each man is locked within the confines of his own language, yet language, the patrimony of all, is the instrument of communication. Belarmino, in remaking his language, remakes the world but isolates himself from the world of common perception. If the Realist novel aims to narrow the gap between words and reality, the Modernist novel is forever aware of the tension between the world of shared meaning and common experience and the multiplicity of the language of fiction. The Modernist exhibits both a fascination with language and a profound mistrust of it, a sense that it is both liberating and enslaving. Just as Belarmino's apparent liberation of language also seems to lead to its destruction, so too is the whole of the Modernist enterprise founded on the precarious apprehension of both the renewal and the death of fiction, on a concern with both beginnings and ends, which the title of Ayala's collection of essays, *Principios y finales de la novela*, so neatly encapsulates. It would appear that contradiction is the very quintessence of Modernism and that the root of this contradiction resides in the complex of relationships between the word and the world, which the Modernist novel so relentlessly probes. In this, Pérez de Ayala stands alongside Joyce, Proust, Gide, Unamuno, and eventually Borges, in their concern with the nature and significance of the fictional illusion. An art so self-absorbed can produce many variations, but it is difficult to see how it might develop, and it may be that we see the novels of Pérez de Ayala and his contemporaries, poised between the realist and aesthetic poles and fiction, as the limit of what the novel might achieve, and that we value them so highly because, in constructing their fictional worlds, they maintained such an admirable balance between the picture and the frame, the window and the garden.

NOTES

[1] Ian Watt, *The Rise of the Novel* (Harmondsworth: Penguin, 1972).

[2] Harry Levin, *The Gates of Horn* (New York: Oxford University Press, 1967) 137.

[3] José Ortega Y Gasset, *Ideas sobre la novela* in *Obras completas* III (Madrid: Revista de Occidente, 1957) III:388-89.

[4] D.H. Lawrence, *Selected Literary Criticism* (London: Heinemann, 1955) 105.

[5] B. Bergonzi, *The Situation of the Novel* (London: Macmillan, 1970) 13.

[6] William James, "The Stream of Consciousness," in *The Modern Tradition*, ed. Ellmann and Feidelson, 315-23.

[7] T.S. Eliot, "The Metaphysical Poets," in *The Modern Tradition* 95.

[8] See, for example, Anthony Storr, *The Dynamics of Creation* (Harmondsworth: Penguin, 1976).

[9]V. Woolf, *The Waves* (London: Granada, 1977) 103.

[10]V. Woolf, "A Summing Up," in *A Haunted House and Other Short Stories* (London: Hogarth Press, 1953) 140.

[11]Gottfried Benn, *Gesammelte Werke*. Quoted by James MacFarlane in "The Mind of Modernism," in *Modernism* (Harmondsworth: Penguin, 1976) 86.

SELECT BIBLIOGRAPHY

Most of Pérez de Ayala's writings have been collected into the *Obras completas* 4 vols. (Madrid: Aguilar, 1964-69). For the convenience of the reader, references are to this edition and are incorporated in the text in the form of volume followed by page reference. More recently, Andrés Amorós has produced a series of scholarly editions, and these are listed below. Where these give a more correct reading, reference is made to them in a footnote. There are two bibliographies of Pérez de Ayala criticism: Pelayo H. Fernández, "Ramón Pérez de Ayala: bibliografía crítica," *Hispanófila* 55 (September, 1975):1-31, and Marigold Best, *Ramón Pérez de Ayala. An Annotated Bibliography of Criticism* (London: Grant and Cutler, 1980).

1. **Works by Ramón Pérez de Ayala**

   (i)   FICTION (in order of first publication)

   Tinieblas en las cumbres. Madrid: Castalia, 1971.

   A.M.D.G. Madrid: Cátedra, 1983.

   La pata de la raposa. Barcelona: Labor, 1970.

   Troteras y danzaderas. Madrid: Castalia, 1972.

   Tres novelas poemáticas de la vida española:
   Prometeo, Luz de domingo, La caída de los Limones.
   Obras completas. Madrid: Aguilar, 1965. II:589-723.

   Belarmino y Apolonio. Madrid: Cátedra, 1976.

   Luna de miel, luna de hiel. Los trabajos de Urbano y Simona. Madrid: Alianza, 1969.

   Tigre Juan. El curandero de su honra. Madrid: Castalia, 1980.

   (ii) ESSAYS (in order of first publication in collections)

   Las máscaras, Obras completas. Madrid: Aguilar, 1966. III:11-660.

   Divagaciones literarias, Obras completas. Madrid: Aguilar, 1969. IV:801-1042.

   Principios y finales de la novela. Madrid: Taurus, 1958.

   El país del futuro. Mis viajes a los Estados Unidos, 1913-14, 1919-20. Madrid: Biblioteca Nueva, 1959.

   Más divagaciones literarias, Obras completas. Madrid: Aguilar, 1969. IV:1043-1269.

   Amistades y recuerdos. Barcelona: Aedos, 1961.

   Fábulas y ciudades. Barcelona: Destino, 1961.

197

Tabla rasa. Madrid: Ed. Bullón, 1963.

Pequeños ensayos. Madrid: Biblioteca Nueva, 1963.

Tributo a Inglaterra. Madrid: Aguilar, 1963.

Ante Azorín. Madrid: Biblioteca Nueva, 1964.

Nuestro Séneca y otros ensayos. Barcelona: Edhasa, 1966.

Viaje entretenido al país del ocio. Reflexiones sobre la cultura griega. Madrid: Guadarrama, 1975.

Las terceras de ABC. Madrid: Prensa Española, 1976.

Apostillas y Divagaciones. Madrid: Cultura Hispánica, 1976.

Crónicas londinenses. Murcia: Universidad de Murcia, 1985.

2. Critical Studies on Ramón Pérez de Ayala

(i) BOOKS

Agustín, Francisco. *Ramón Pérez de Ayala. Su vida y obras.* Madrid: G. Hernández y Galo Sáez, 1927.

Amorós, Andrés. *La novela intelectual de Ramón Pérez de Ayala.* Madrid: Gredos, 1972.

— — —. *Vida y Literatura en <u>Troteras y danzaderas</u>.* Madrid: Castalia, 1973.

Bobes, María del Carmen. *Gramática textual de <u>Belarmino y Apolonio</u>.* Madrid: Planeta, 1977.

Coletes Blanco, Agustín. *Gran Bretaña y los Estados Unidos en la vida de Ramón Pérez de Ayala.* Oviedo: Instituto de Estudios Asturianos, 1984.

Concha, Víctor G. de la. *Los senderos poéticos de Ramón Pérez de Ayala.* Oviedo: Archivum, 1970.

Derndarksy, Roswitha. *Ramón Pérez de Ayala: zur Thematik und Kunstgestalt seiner Romane.* Frankfurt: V. Klostermann, 1970.

Feeny, Thomas. *The Paternal Orientation of Ramón Pérez de Ayala.* Valencia/Chapel Hill: Albatros/Hispanófila, 1985.

Fernández, Pelayo H. *Ramón Pérez de Ayala: tres novelas analizadas.* Gijón: Yepes, 1972.

— — —. *Estudios sobre Ramón Pérez de Ayala.* Oviedo: Instituto de Estudios Asturianos, 1978.

Fernández, Casiano E. *En torno a la obra narrativa de Ramón Pérez de Ayala.* Oviedo: Instituto de Estudios Asturianos, 1982.

Fernández Avelló, Manuel. *Pérez de Ayala y la niebla.* Oviedo: Instituto de Estudios Asturianos, 1970.

198

– – –. *El anticlericalismo de Pérez de Ayala*. Oviedo: Private edition, 1975.

– – –. *Recuerdos asturianos de Ramón Pérez de Ayala*. Oviedo: Biblioteca Popular Asturiana, 1980.

González Calvo, José. *La prosa de Ramón Pérez de Ayala*. Salamanca: University of Salamanca, 1979.

González Martín, Vicente. *Ensayos de literatura comparada italo-española. La cultura italiana en Vicente Blasco Ibáñez y en Ramón Pérez de Ayala*. Salamanca: University of Salamanca, 1979.

Lozano Marco, Miguel Angel. *Del relato modernista a la novela poemática: la narrativa breve de Ramón Pérez de Ayala*. Alicante: University of Alicante, 1983.

Macklin, J.J. *Ramón Pérez de Ayala: Tigre Juan and El curandero de su honra*. London: Grant & Cutler, 1980.

Matas, Julio. *Contra el honor: las novelas normativas de Ramón Pérez de Ayala*. Madrid: Seminarios y ediciones, 1974.

O'Brien, MacGregor. *El ideal clásico de Ramón Pérez de Ayala en sus ensayos en La Prensa de Buenos Aires*. Oviedo: Instituto de Estudios Asturianos, 1981.

Pérez Ferrero, Miguel. *Ramón Pérez de Ayala*. Madrid: Publicaciones de la Fundación Juan March, 1973.

Rand, M.C. *Ramón Pérez de Ayala*. New York: Twayne, 1971.

Reinink, Kasper Willem. *Algunos aspectos literarios y lingüísticos de la obra de don Ramón Pérez de Ayala*. The Hague: University of Utrecht, 1959.

Rivas Andrés, Victoriano. *La novela más popular de Ramón Pérez de Ayala. Anatomía de A.M.D.G.* Gijón: Private edition, 1983.

Salgues de Cargill, Maruxa. *Los mitos clásicos y modernos en la novela de Pérez de Ayala*. Jaén: Instituto de Estudios Giennenses, 1971.

Solís, Jesús Andrés. *Vida de Ramón Pérez de Ayala*. Candás: Private edition, 1979.

Suárez Solís, Sara. *Análisis de Belarmino y Apolonio*. Oviedo: Instituto de Estudios Asturianos, 1974.

Urrutia, Norma. *De Troteras a Tigre Juan. Dos grandes temas de Ramón Pérez de Ayala*. Madrid: Insula, 1960.

Weber, Frances Wyers. *The Literary Perspectivism of Ramón Pérez de Ayala*. Chapel Hill: University of North Carolina Press, 1966.

(ii) ARTICLES

Adams, N.B., and Stoudemire, S.A. "Introduction" to *Selections from Pérez de Ayala*. New York: W.W. Norton, 1934. ix-xxxv.

Baquero Goyanes, Mariano. "La novela como tragicomedia: Pérez de Ayala y Ortega y Gasset," *Perspectivismo y contraste*. Madrid: Gredos, 1963. 161-70.

— — —. "Perspectivismo y contraste en Ramón Pérez de Ayala," *Perspectivismo y contraste*. Madrid: Gredos, 1963. 171-244.

Beck, Mary Ann. "La realidad artística en las tragedias grotescas de Ramón Pérez de Ayala." *Hispania* XLVI (1963):480-89.

Bobes, María del Carmen. "Notas al *Belarmino y Apolonio* de Pérez de Ayala." *Boletín del Instituto de Estudios Asturianos* XXXIV (1958):305-20.

Brown, G.G. "Pérez de Ayala." *A Literary History of Spain. The Twentieth Century*. London: Benn, 1972. 37-45.

Campbell, Brenton. "The Esthetic Theories of Ramón Pérez de Ayala." *Hispania* 50 (1967):447-53.

— — —. "Free Will and Determinism in the Theory of Tragedy: Pérez de Ayala and Ortega." *Hispanic Review* XXXVII (1969):345-82.

Clavería, Carlos. "Apostillas al lenguaje de Belarmino." *Cinco estudios de la literatura española moderna*. Salamanca: Colegio Trilingüe de la Universidad, 1945. 71-91.

— — —. "Apostillas adicionales a *Belarmino y Apolonio*." *Hispanic Review* XVI (1948):340-45.

Cordua de Torretti, Carla. "Belarmino: hablar y pensar." *La Torre* XXXII (1960):43-60.

Dobrian, W.A. "Development and Evolution in Pérez de Ayala's *Tigre Juan*." *Literature and Society*. ed. Bernice Slote. Lincoln: University of Nebraska Press, 1964. 187-201.

Fabian, Donald L. "Action and Idea in *Amor y pedagogía* and *Prometeo*." *Hispania* LXI (1958):30-34.

— — —. "The progress of the artist: A Major Theme in the Early Novels of Pérez de Ayala." *Hispanic Review* XXVI (1958):108-16.

— — —. "Pérez de Ayala and the Generation of 1898." *Hispania* XLI (1958):154-59.

— — —. "Bases de la novelística de Ramón Pérez de Ayala." *Hispania* XLVI (1963):57-60.

Font, M.T. "La sociedad del futuro en Pérez de Ayala, Huxley y Orwell." *Revista de Estudios Hispánicos* 4 (1970):67-83.

200

Franz, T. "Galdós and Ayala: Another Look at Master and Pupil." *Revista de Estudios Hispánicos* 14 (1980):31-38.

García Arias, J.L. "Norma lingüística en *La pata de la raposa*." *Archivum* XXV (1975): 17-75.

García Rodríguez, J.M. "Dos temas de iniciación en el amor: *Luna de miel, luna de hiel*." *Cuadernos dominicanos de cultura* (Santo Domingo) IV (1947):34-48.

Gatti, J.F. "Una interpolación engañosa de Pérez de Ayala." *Filología* (Buenos Aires) XV (1971):281-83.

Gillespie, Ruth. "Ramón Pérez de Ayala: precursor literario de la revolución." *Hispania* (Stanford, California) XV (1932):215-224.

González Calvo, J.M. "Elementos expresivos en la prosa de Ramón Pérez de Ayala." *Archivum* XXV (1975):497-512.

Hafter, Monroe Z. "Galdós' Influence on Pérez de Ayala." *Galdós Studies II*. ed. R.J. Weber. London: Tamesis, 1974. 13-28.

Hartsook, John H. "Literary Tradition as Form in Pérez de Ayala." *Romance Notes* VI (1964):21-25.

Holdsworth, Carole A. "Ideas religiosas en las novelas maduras de Ramón Pérez de Ayala." *Revista de Estudios Hispánicos* 6 (1972):265-81.

Ionesco, Andrei. "Sobre el clasicismo de Pérez de Ayala." *Actas del Quinto Congreso Internacional de Hispanistas*. Bordeaux, 1977. II:481-88.

Johnson, Ernest A. "Sobre *Prometeo* de Pérez de Ayala." *Insula*. 100-101 (1954):13, 15.

— — — . "The Humanities and the *Prometeo* of Ramón Pérez de Ayala." *Hispania* XXXVIII (Sept. 1955):276-82.

Lamb, Norman J. "The Art of *Belarmino y Apolonio*." *Bulletin of Hispanic Studies* XVII (1940):127-38.

Leighton, Charles. "La parodia en *Belarmino y Apolonio*." *Hispanófila* 6 (1959):53-55.

— — — . "The Structure of *Belarmino y Apolonio*." *Bulletin of Hispanic Studies* XXXVII (1960):237-43.

Levy, Bernard. "Pérez de Ayala's *Belarmino y Apolonio*." *The Spanish Review* III (1936):74-81.

Livingstone, Leon. "The Theme of the 'Paradoxe sur le comédien' in the novels of Pérez de Ayala." *Hispanic Review* XXII (1954):208-23.

Longhurst, Carlos. "Sobre la originalidad de *Tinieblas en las cumbres*." *Insula* 404-405 (1980):5.

Lozano Alonso, Maria B. "El tiempo en *Belarmino y Apolonio*." *Boletín de la Real Academia Española* 51 (1971):413-58.

— — —. "Reflexiones críticas de Ramón Pérez de Ayala." *Actas del Quinto Congreso Internacional de Hispanistas*. Bordeaux: 1977. II:611-22.

Macklin, J.J. "Literature and Experience: The Problem of Distance in Pérez de Ayala's *La pata de la raposa*." *Bulletin of Hispanic Studies* LV (1978):129-41.

— — —. "Myth and Meaning in Pérez de Ayala's *Prometeo*." *Belfast Spanish and Portuguese Papers*. Ed. P.S.N. Russell-Gebbett. Belfast, 1979. 79-94.

— — —. "Myth and Mimesis: The Artistic Integrity of Pérez de Ayala's *Tigre Juan* and *El curandero de su honra*." *Hispanic Review* 48 (1980):15-36.

— — —. "Romance and Realism: Pérez de Ayala's Urbano and Simona Novels." *Neophilologus* (1980):208-26.

— — —. "Pérez de Ayala y la novela modernista europea." *Cuadernos Hispanoamericanos* 367-368 (1981):21-36.

— — —. "Tradición literaria en *Luz de domingo*." *Insula* 404-405 (1980):6.

— — —. "*Un alto en la vida errante*: un texto olvidado de Ramón Pérez de Ayala y Antonio de Hoyos." *Boletín del Instituto de Estudios Asturianos* 101 (1980):525-35.

— — —. "Ramón Pérez de Ayala y *La Revista Ibérica*: 1902." *Boletín del Instituto de Estudios Asturianos* 107 (1982):683-89.

— — — —. "*Tinieblas en las cumbres* and the Crisis of Modernist Fiction." *Anales de la literatura española contemporánea* 8 (1983):13-30.

Matus, Eugenio. "El símbolo del segundo nacimiento en la narrativa de Ramón Pérez de Ayala." *Estudios Filológicos* 5 (1969):148-69.

Millner, C. "Ontological Inversion in the Novels of Pérez de Ayala." *Mester* 5 (1975):109-11.

Myers, E. "Tradition and Modernity in Ramón Pérez de Ayala's Views on Literary Criticism." *Crítica Hispánica* 2 (1980):157-66.

Newberry, W. "Three Examples of the Midsummer Theme in Modern Spanish Literature: *Gloria, La dama del alba* and *El curandero de su honra*." *Kentucky Romance Quarterly* 21 (1974):239-59.

— — —. "Ramón Pérez de Ayala's Concept of the *Doppelgänger* in *Belarmino y Apolonio*." *Symposium* XXXIV (1980):256-67.

Noble, B. "The Descriptive Genius of Pérez de Ayala in *La caída de los Limones*." *Hispania* XL (1957):171-75.

Rangel, V. "Las novelas poemáticas de Ramón Pérez de Ayala: una interpretación estilística de *Luz de domingo.*" *Explicación de Textos Literarios* 7 (1979):197-205.

Read, M.K. "*Belarmino y Apolonio* and the Modern Linguistic Tradition." *Bulletin of Hispanic Studies* LV (1978):329-35.

Roca Martínez, José Luis. "*Troteras y danzaderas* y *El mal metafísico*: dos novelas de clave." *Boletín del Instituto de Estudios Asturianos* 95 (1978):483-510.

Romeu, R. "Les divers aspects de l'humour dans le roman espagnol moderne III: L'humour transcendental d'un intellectuel." *Bulletin Hispanique* IX (1947):47-83.

Salgues Cargill, Maruxa. "Mito de Don Quijote y Sancho en *Belarmino y Apolonio.*" *Insula* 274 (Sept. 1969):16.

Salgues Cargill, Maruxa and Palley, Julian. "Myth and Anti-Myth in *Tigre Juan.*" *Revista de Estudios Hispánicos* 7 (1973):399-416.

Sallenave, Pierre. "La estética y el esencial ensayismo de Ramón Pérez de Ayala." *Cuadernos Hispanoamericanos* 234 (1969):601-15

— — —. "Ramón Pérez de Ayala, teórico de la literatura." *Cuadernos Hispanoamericanos* 244 (1970):178-90.

Shaw, Donald L. "On the Ideology of Pérez de Ayala." *Modern Language Quarterly* XXII (1961):158-66.

— — —. "Ramón Pérez de Ayala." In *The Generation of 1898 in Spain*. London: Benn, 1975. 187-94.

Sturken, H. Tracy. "Nota sobre *La pata de la raposa.*" *Nueva Revista de Filología Hispánica* XI (1957):198-200.

Sullivan, Constance A. "La modificación del protagonista en las sucesivas ediciones de *La pata de la raposa* de Pérez de Ayala." *Hispanófila* 45 (1972):73-81.

Zamora, Carlos. "La concepción trágica de la vida en la obra novelesca de Ramón Pérez de Ayala." *Hispanófila* 42 (1971):21-34.

— — —. "*Homo impotens* and the vanity of human striving: two related themes in the novels of Ramón Pérez de Ayala." *Revista de Estudios Hispánicos* 5 (1971):413-26.

— — —. "La angustia existencial del héroe-artista de Ramón Pérez de Ayala: la caducidad de la vida." *Boletín del Instituto de Estudios Asturianos* 28 (1974):781-94.

— — —. "La negación de la praxis auto-creadora en la novelística de Ramón Pérez de Ayala." *Boletín del Instituto de Estudios Asturianos* 92 (1977):587-99.

(iii)   CENTENNIAL ESSAYS

Insula 404-05 (July-August 1980).

Homenaje a Ramón Pérez de Ayala. Oviedo: University of Oviedo, 1980.

Cuadernos Hispanoamericanos CXXI. 367-368 (Jan.-Feb. 1981).

Simposio Internacional Ramón Pérez de Ayala. Gijón: University of New Mexico, 1981.

Pérez de Ayala visto en su centenario 1880-1980. Oviedo: Instituto de Estudios Asturianos, 1981.

3. General

Adams, Robert Martin. *After Joyce.* New York: Oxford University Press, 1977.

Allott, Miriam. *Novelists on the Novel.* London: Routledge and Kegan Paul, 1959.

Auerbach, Erich. *Mimesis.* Princeton: Princeton University Press, 1953.

Bell, Michael (ed.). *The Context of English Literature 1900-1930.* London: Methuen, 1980.

Belsey, Catherine. *Critical Practice.* London and New York: Methuen, 1980.

Bradbury, Malcolm and MacFarlane, James. *Modernism 1890-1930.* Harmondsworth: Penguin, 1976.

Bradbury, Malcolm. *Possibilities. Essays on the State of the Novel.* London: Oxford University Press, 1973.

Bradbury, Malcolm (ed.). *The Novel Today.* Glasgow: Fontana, 1979.

Culler, Jonathan. *Structuralist Poetics, Structuralism, Linguistics, and the Study of Literature.* London: Routledge and Kegan Paul, 1975.

— — —. *Saussure.* Glasgow: Fontana, 1976.

Daiches, David. *The Novel and the Modern World.* Chicago: University of Chicago Press, 1960.

Eagleton, Terry. *Literary Theory.* Oxford: Blackwell, 1983.

Ellmann, Richard and Feidelson, Charles (eds.). *The Modern Tradition.* London: Oxford University Press, 1965.

Faulkner, Peter. *Modernism.* London: Methuen, 1977.

Finney, Brian (ed.). "Modernism: A Symposium." *The New Review* 10 (January 1975):12-29.

Frank, Joseph. *The Widening Gyre: Crisis and Mastery in Modern Literature.* New Brunswick: Rutgers University Press, 1963.

Friedman, Alan J. *The Turn of the Novel.* New York: Oxford University Press, 1966.

Gavin, Harry R. (ed.). *Romanticism, Modernism, Post Modernism.* Lewisburg: Bucknell University Press, 1980.

Heath, Stephen. *The Nouveau Roman: a study in the practice of writing.* London: Elek, 1972.

Hemmings, F.W.J. (ed.). *The Age of Realism.* Harmondsworth: Penguin, 1974.

Howe, Irving. *Decline of the New.* New York: Harcourt, Brace and World, 1970.

Hutcheon, Linda. *Narcissistic Narrative. The Metafictional Paradox.* London and New York: Methuen, 1984.

Jameson, Frederic. *The Prison-House of Language: a critical account of structuralism and Russian formalism.* Princeton: Princeton University Press, 1972.

Josipovici, Gabriel. *The Lessons of Modernism.* London: Macmillan, 1977.

— — —. *The World and the Book.* London: Macmillan, 1971.

Kellogg, Robert and Scholes, Robert. *The Nature of Narrative.* New York: Oxford University Press, 1966.

Kermode, Frank. *Continuities.* London: Routledge and Kegan Paul, 1968.

— — —. *The Sense of an Ending.* New York and London: Oxford University Press, 1967.

— — —. *The Genesis of Secrecy: on the Interpretation of Narrative.* London: Harvard University Press, 1979.

Levin, Harry. *Refractions: Essays in Comparative Literature.* New York: Oxford University Press, 1966.

— — —. *The Gates of Horn.* New York: Oxford University Press, 1963.

Lodge, David. *Language of Fiction.* London: Routledge and Kegan Paul, 1966.

— — —. *The Novelist at the Crossroads.* London: Routledge and Kegan Paul, 1971.

— — —. "Modernism, Anti-modernism and Postmodernism." *The New Review* 4. 38 (May 1977):39-44.

— — —. *The Modes of Modern Writing: Metaphor, Metonymy and the Typology of Modern Literature.* London: Edward Arnold, 1977.

— — —. *Working with Structuralism.* London: Routledge and Kegan Paul, 1981.

Lukács, Georg. *The Meaning of Contemporary Realism*. London: Merlin Press, 1963.

— — —. *Studies in European Realism*. London: Merlin Press, 1963.

May, Keith M. *Out of the Maelstrom. Psychology and the Novel in the Twentieth Century*. London: Paul Elek, 1977.

Muecke, D.C. *The Compass of Irony*. London: Methuen, 1969.

Said, Edward W. *The World, the Text and the Critic*. London: Faber and Faber, 1984.

Scholes, Robert. *The Fabulators*. London: Oxford University Press, 1967.

Spender, Stephen. *The Struggle of the Modern*. London: Hamilton, 1963.

Stern, Joseph Peter. *On Realism*. London: Routledge and Kegan Paul, 1973.

Storr, Anthony. *Jung*. Glasgow: Fontana, 1973.

Wilde, Alan. *Horizons of Assent. Modernism, Postmodernism and the Ironic Imagination*. Baltimore: John Hopkins Unviersity Press, 1981.

Williams, D.A. (ed.). *The Monster in the Mirror: Studies in Nineteenth-Century Realism*. Hull and Oxford: Oxford University Press, 1978.

Wilson, Edmund. *Axel's Castle. A Study in the Imaginative Literature of 1870-1930*. Glasgow: Fontana, 1959.